ETHICS AND MORALITY IN SPORT AND PHYSICAL EDUCATION: AN EXPERIENTIAL APPROACH

by

EARLE F. ZEIGLER
Ph.D., LL.D., FAAPE
Professor of Physical Education
The University of Western Ontario
London, Canada

ISBN 0-87563-247-5

Published by
STIPES PUBLISHING COMPANY
10-12 Chester Street
Champaign, Illinois 61820

DEDICATION

To

Dick Fox

(philosopher, former wrestler, and friend)

--who provided some most helpful
guidance along the way

ii

PREFACE

The fundamental purpose of this text is to provide an introduction to the study of ethics and morality insofar as this topic can and should apply to the field of sport and physical education. This book is based on the premise that our profession in North America is past due for the introduction of a required course into its professional curriculum whereby young men and women professional students will understand how to develop and apply a sound ethical approach in their personal and professional lives.

Any reasonably intelligent person in society today understands that, even though a recognizable semblance of victory has been won over what is often a harsh physical environment, people have not yet been able to remove much of the insecurity evident in our efforts to live together constructively and peacefully in the world. Although many philosophers have searched persistently throughout history for a normative ethical system on which people could and should base their conduct, there is still no single, non-controversial foundation in which the entire structure of ethics can be built.

This experiential approach to the learning of ethics and morality in sport and physical education has been designed to meet the needs of a new generation of professional practitioners in the field--be they teachers, coaches, managers, or supervisors at any level in public, semi-public or semi-private, or private agencies. These are people who will be practicing professionally in the art and science of human motor performance as it may be employed in sport, dance, play, and/or exercise. At the moment, the term "sport and physical education" has been accepted as a holding-pattern name for the field.

Any new book being recommended as a text for use by thousands of young people needs solid justification. I believe strongly that such a case can be made for the approach being recommended here. In the first place, I have tried it out and it worked very well basically. Experience indicated where certain modifications seem advisable, and these changes have been incorporated in the present volume.

Secondly, no effort is made to strongly indoctrinate the reader to accept finally any of the approaches to ethical decision-making that are available in the Western world today. (One approach of a normative nature is recommended for initial experimentation with the various debates and case topics included because it is quite consistent with the values and norms of North American society. However, it should be made clear to all that each person must work this out for himself or herself in the final analysis.) This seems only fair in an area where sensitive understanding is needed to treat a subject that is undoubtedly a highly controversial one. Thus, the reader is provided with an overview of the various approaches available (both in the early chapters and in the readings).

An examination of the teaching/learning sequence spelled out carefully (see Appendix A for sample outline) on a day-by-day, week-by-week basis will reveal an approach grounded in what are recognized as some of the best teaching techniques available for a course of this type involving controversial issues present in an evolving democracy. Assuming that the typical course meets three times a week for fifty-minute sessions, the first three weeks may be used to orient the student to the course by laying the necessary groundwork (all of which is provided in this volume, although the instructor may wish to supplement it by the use of other material).

For example, it is recommended that the first session in the first week be used for a discussion of the entire course outline (Appendix A). Next the student may be offered an explanation of a unique philosophic, self-evaluation checklist (see Appendix B) that he or she is then asked to complete privately. Following this, a series of seven lecture/discussion sessions are held to round out the second and third weeks of orientation. Each of these lectures (see Parts I and II) can be supplemented by assigned readings to get the student ready for the several experiential techniques that begin in the fourth week of the course (i.e., formal debates and case discussions). These supplementary readings (see Part III, Chapter 8 and Part IV, Chapter 10) are necessary for use in connection with the lecture/discussion sessions of Week #3. They include a detailed presentation of the debating procedures to be followed, as well as a complete presentation designed to fully orient the student to the case method of instruction (from both the standpoint of the student and the instructor). The lectures, discussions, and readings introduced during the first three weeks are, therefore, designed to get the student ready for the main part of the course experience.

At this point the regular course pattern emerges with lectures on Mondays, debates on Wednesdays, and case discussions on Fridays (or whatever the session and course timetable may call for). During the first session each week, the instructor presents as a lecture one of the leading approaches to ethical decision-making in the Western world. (It is recommended that these lectures be developed from the "major ethical routes" presented briefly in Chapter 3. On Wednesdays (presumably the second class meeting each week), formal debates are held on controversial ethical issues by two teams pitted against each other, the assumption being that team members will employ an ethical approach of their choice. On Fridays each week (the third class session), the instructor leads a case discussion on one of a series of interesting cases based on actual (true-to-life) ethical problems faced earlier by colleagues in the profession. Obviously, if any approach can bring this topic to life for aspiring young professionals, this should be it!

Although there are two other books on this subject available (as this is being written), this text represents the first attempt to teach this subject both from the standpoint of the participating athlete and from that of the professional teacher, coach, or administrator. Fully one half of the course experience is given over to the consideration of professional ethics for the person who is entering the field as a career specialization.

The time appears to be truly ripe for this sort of course experience on the part of today's young people. Although an ethics course per se was not included earlier in this century as part of professional training, there was the ever-present principles course that espoused high ideals and standards for our young people aspiring to be physical educator/coaches. Somehow with the body-of-knowledge, disciplinary thrust of the 1960s, there emerged a period of considerable denigration of the "good, old" principles course resulting in its demise in most colleges and universities. It was supplanted by one of several approaches to the doing of philosophy, each presumably more sophisticated than the other. Where this has left us is now open to serious question.

This overall disciplinary thrust that began in the early 1960s had its important aspects, of course, because any self-respecting profession must have a substantive body of knowledge upon which to build. However, we must be careful not to forget our basic, fundamental social task as a profession either --the professional practice of leading people of all ages into purposeful human movement or motor performance in sport, dance, play, and exercise. Thus, in the 1980s we should seek Aristotelian "middle ground" by striving for a balance among the various aspects of our professional programs, and especially between the so-called sub-disciplinary and sub-professional components of the field.

In this text I am arguing for a steadily improving crop of young professionals undergirded by sound theory based on a high level of research and scholarly endeavor. However, all of this will be in vain if we do not turn out high-calibre young people with <u>high ethical standards</u>. Accordingly, we are faced with the urgent need to make certain that such ethical sensitivity will be attained by our future colleagues. Keeping in mind that this is indeed a troublesome period in which ethical standards are being challenged mightily and the spectre of "unGodly relativism" seems to face us at every turn. Thus, I must conclude that a course experience of this type is absolutely necessary for all of our professional trainees. We can't guarantee, of course, that our successors will think exactly as we thought in the past (Heaven forbid!), because that's just not the way things work in North American democracy. Nevertheless, we should do our very best to provide a type of experience wherein prospective professionals will at least think these presently challenging and controversial issues through in a more explicit manner than would have occurred otherwise. Everything considered, I believe that the provision of such a planned experience for them represents no mean accomplishment.

Finally, I want to emphasize that I have made every effort to use non-sexist language in this text, a truly difficult task where the approach has been one-sided for so long. Further, I want to express my appreciation to those people who provided me with some of their personal case problems at some point along the way. To the best of my knowledge, fictitious names and places have been employed. This is a fascinating area, and I trust that this course experience will be helpful to all who employ it.

I express my continuing appreciation for the relationship that I have enjoyed at Stipes Publishing Company (this is my tenth publication with them). Thank you (Editor & Partner) Bob Watts, and thank you Ms. Marie Mayer for preparing the publication at the Champaign office. Thank you also Bert (my wife) for preparing the index.

Earle F. Zeigler

ETHICS AND MORALITY IN SPORT AND PHYSICAL EDUCATION: AN EXPERIENTIAL APPROACH

CONTENTS

PART I
INTRODUCTION

CHAPTER 1
INTRODUCTION TO ETHICAL PROBLEMS TODAY

Throughout their existence human animals have struggled for survival in a harsh physical environment. A recognizable of victory has been won over difficult surroundings, but somehow we have not been able to remove the insecurity evident in our efforts to live together constructively and peacefully in a world with sharply increasing population. In considering humankind's basic problems, Burtt believed that:

> The greatest danger to his future lies in the disturbing emotions and destructive passions that he has not yet overcome; the greatest promise lies in his capacity for a sensitive understanding of himself and his human fellows, and his power to enter the inclusive universe in which the creative aspirations of all can move freely toward their fulfillment (1965, p. 311).

If our "distorting emotions and destructive passions" do indeed represent the greatest danger for the future, the application of a sound ethical approach--whichever one is chosen--to personal and professional living can be of inestimable assistance to people who are truly seeking a "sensitive understanding" of themselves and their fellows.

In the late 1970s there was evidence that others saw the need for study about ethics from a variety of sources. For example, in 1978 The New York Times reported that "nowadays students in many disciplines are enrolling in new ethics courses in a variety of undergraduate departments and professional . . part of the impetus for new programs stems from the social consciousness of the 1960s" (Feb. 26, 1978). Whether this enrollment in ethics courses can be shown to have a relationship with the earlier social consciousness felt by some at that time is an interesting question. Nevertheless it is true that there have been many indications that people's interest in ethics is increasing. Some examples of this heightened interest, based on some examples selected from the 1975 to 1978 period, are (1) Geoffrey Hazard's article on "Capitalist Ethics" (1978, pp. 50-51); (2) Henry Fairlie's book entitled The Seven Deadly Sins Today (1978); (3) James Chace's piece inquiring as to "How 'Moral' Can We Get?" (1977); (4) Michael Blumenthal's statement that societal changes have occasioned "questionable and illegal corporate activities" (1977); (5) The New York Times' article inquiring whether the growing dishonesty in sports is just a reflection of the American society (1976); (6) Derek Bok's request, as President of Harvard University, that courses in applied ethics be taught (1976); (7) Amitai Etzioni's assertion that the "hottest new item" in Post-Watergate curriculum is "moral education" (1976); Gene Maeroff's review stressing that "West Point Cheaters Have a Lot of Company" (1976); (9) Russell Baker's spoof implying that "good sports went out with bamboo vaulting poles" (1976); (10) Rainer Martens' belief that kid sports may currently be a "den of iniquity" (1976); (11) Ann Dennis's article explaining that the Canadian Sociology and Anthropology Association is considering the adoption of a code of ethics (1975); (12) The Saturday Review special report entitled "Watergating on Main Street" that assessed the ethics of congressmen, lawyers, businessmen, accountants, journalists, physicians, and educators (1975); and (13) Fred Hechinger's query as to "Whatever Became of Sin?" (1974)--to name a most unreliable sampling of the many articles and other statement that sursurfaced during that period of only eighteen months.

Building on this steadily increasing interest in the ethics and morality of our lives, it was an increasing experience to consider the best approach to the topic in the volume at hand. Finally in Part I it was decided to introduce the matter of ethical problems briefly in Chapter 1, and then in the remaining four chapters of this first section to use the following approach:

Chapter 2--The "Good" and the "Bad" in Historical Perspective

Chapter 3--Major Ethical Routes Extant in the Western World Today

Chapter 4--Ethical Outlook--An Implicit/Explicit Experiential Approach

Chapter 5--From Personal to Professional Ethics

Ethics Yesterday and Today

There are many outstanding philosophic texts that treat ethics and morality in great detail, and there is obviously neither nor space to review the problem in this opening essay. (Please see Chapter 2 for a most brief outline history of this branch of philosophy.) The reader should be reminded that typically in ethics the terms "right" and "wrong" apply only to acts, whereas "good" and "bad" refer to (1) the effects of acts;

(2) the motives from which the act was done; (3) the intention of the person carrying out the deed; and (4) the person who is the agent of a particular act. Thus, we might say correctly that "although Smith is a good person, he acted wrongly--with good motives and intentions--when he struck Jones and broke his jaw. The consequences were bad, even though Jones had made some threatening gestures at Smith's smaller brother" (adapted from Hospers, 1953, p. 451).

Interestingly, as is the case with so many words and terms that we use nowadays, the term "ethics" is employed typically in three different ways. Each of these ways has a relation to the other, and all three ways will be used throughout this book. First, it is used to classify a general pattern or "way of life" (e.g., Christian ethics). Second, it refers to a listing of rules of conduct, or what is often called a moral code (e.g., the ethics of a minister, priest, or rabbi). Lastly, it has come to be used when describing inquiry about ways of life or rules of conduct (e.g., that subdivision of philosophy now known as metaethics).

History substantiates that ethics is a description of "irregular progress toward complete clarification of each type of ethical judgment" (Encyclopedia of Philosophy, III, 1967, p. 82). How does one judge exactly, or even generally, how much "irregular progress" has been made since the development of Greek ethics starting with (say) Socrates in the 5th century B.C.? One may argue that the changing political, economic, and other social forces of that time requires the introduction of a new way of conduct--just as today there appears to be an urgent need for altered standards of conduct during this transitional period.

Of course, it would be an obvious exaggeration today to say that there are as many views of ethics and/or moral philosophy as there are philosophers. Conversely, however, there is no single, non-controversial foundation stone upon which to build the entire structure of ethics. This is not to say that there are not some aspects of this branch of philosophy upon which there have been fairly wide agreement. As Nowell-Smith has explained, in the past moral philosophers offered general guidance as to what to do, what to seek, and how to treat others--injunctions that we could well keep in mind in the consideration of sport ethics (1954).

As a rule of philosophers have not tried to preach to their adherents in the same way that theologians have felt constrained to do, although many have offered practical advice that

included pronouncements on what was good and bad, or right
and wrong. Further, many have persistently searched for a
true moral code--a normative ethical system upon which people
could and should base their conduct. The advent of philosophical analysis as a distinct approach during this century in the
Western world has thrust the contemporary analytic philosopher
right into the middle of the struggle between the ethical objec-
tivist and the ethical subjectivist. However, at the very time
when the world is in such a turmoil with "hot" wars, "cold"
wars, terrorists--at the very time when people of all ages want
to know about "what to do, what to seek, and how to treat
others"--the large majority of philosophical scholars are almost
completely silent, avoiding the rational justification of any type
of moral system, and analyzing the meaning and function of
moral concepts and statements on a limited basis.

Others have offered prescriptive and normative advice
freely down through the years. However, because some of us
are evidently afraid to be challenged as illogical or hortatory
by our own colleagues, the field of ethics in life generally--in
politics, in business and economics, in science, in medicine, in
education, and even in sport--is left to people who have given
the topic much less thought than we have. Theologians, dramatists, novelists, poets, medical doctors, politicians (!), educational administrators, business leaders--in no special order of
importance--offer a variety of opinions, ranging from suggestions to dogma, about what is good and bad, right and wrong,
about all aspects of life. Most notable among these categories
recently are scientists, politicians, and comedians, who may
have earned justifiable fame--or even notoriety.

I don't wish to carry this point too far, so I will simply
state that this present situation, in which there has developed
such a sharp distinction between the relatively few moral philosophers concerned with normative ethics and the much greater number involved with analytic (or critical or theoretic) philosophy, should in my opinion be rectified to a considerable
extent as soon as possible. The matter of values in our social
system and culture is far too vital to leave almost completely to
those who can be classified largely as laymen.

Further, there are many of us who are specializing in
what have been called "departmental philosophies." Here I am
referring to such specialties as medical ethics, business ethics,
educational ethics, legal ethics, sport ethics, or what have you.
We need to understand what the relationship between normative
ethics and metaethics should be. There are extremists, of
course, but a more reasonable approach to follow would seem to

be one in which a moral philosopher or ethical theorist--whether he or she be employed in the mother discipline or in a department of educational philosophy--can engage in metaethical analysis if desired, or can become involved in a scholarly approach to normative analysis without fear or reprisal in one way or another by colleagues of the opposite persuasion. All should be working toward the elimination of irrational ethical beliefs while attempting to discover the soundest possible ethical system (s?) for our evolving society.

It should be recognized that the task of normative inquiry can be most difficult, especially when complex issues and specific conclusions tend to stray into the realm of metaethics. It is quite simple to distinguish between the normative ethical statement--"Harsh teaching methods have no place in education" --and the following metaethical statement: "A teacher knows through intuition whether his/her beliefs about teaching ethics are fundamentally true." Further, when a normative ethical theory (such as hedonism) includes a statement such as "Religious teaching is good because it brings pleasure," the non-hedonist could well challenge this statement solely on the meaning of the terms "good" and "pleasure." The obvious difficulty of justifying a normative ethical theory brings to the fore questions about metaethical relativism and subjectivism, questions which when pursued carefully point up the present severity of the "subjectivist threat."

Basically and fundamentally, then, justification of an ethical theory, or even an incomplete set of ethical statements about education, religion, sport, or any other aspect of life revolves around the ability of the theorist to state correctly, elucidate sufficiently, and defend adequately his or her moral or ethical claims and arguments. For example, is a moral judgment objective or subjective? Does a moral judgment differ from a factual judgment? Is an ethical statement about right conduct in medicine, law, or education publicly warrantable-- that is, is there some publicly acceptable procedure for verification that reasonable people would be willing to accept? Finally, should ethical claims be objectively verifiable, and should they be universalizable? This would make them practical for use in everyday life.

Some Points of Clarification

As we move forward in our consideration of what might be regarded as basic introductory information about ethics and morality, there are several further points of clarification that perhaps should be made. For example, we should keep in mind

the distinction between statements of fact as opposed to statements of value. In the first instance, I might argue that
"health is desired" (a fact, in this instance), whereas I might
also state that "health is desirable" for everyone (actually a
statement of value on my part).

We need to keep in mind also that there are two fields of
value theory in philosophy--ethics and aesthetics. As explained earlier, in ethics we are involved with matters of good and
bad, right and wrong, duty and obligation, and moral responsibility. In aesthetics, however, value is viewed somewhat differently. There we take into consideration matters or doctrines
of taste or beauty, meaning, and truth--all typically considered
in an art context.

From another standpoint, we need to keep in mind that,
although the word "good" is central to the subject of ethics,
most of the times we use it we are actually not expressing
moral judgments (e.g., "good apple," "good road," "good game
of tennis"). Thus, if we say, "this is a good X," usually we
mean that X fulfills, to a higher or greater degree than most
X's, the criterion (or criteria) for which this particular X is
designed or intended.

However, it is when we use the word "good" in moral
discussions that a variety of problems arise. For example, we
might state that Jones exhibits "good character" when he plays
tennis, or that Smith shows his "good intentions" when he help
helped Thompson up after knocking him down in football. Thus,
the main moral words used in ethics are "good," "bad," "right,"
and "wrong," but the controversy develops when we use one
or more of them in specific contexts.

Still further, we need to keep in mind that ethics today
is typically divided into two main categories: (1) normative
ethics, in which there is an attempt to discover a rational and
possibly acceptable view that may be defended concerning those
things that are good in this world (i.e., worth aiming at) and
what kinds of acts are right (and why this is so); and (2) metaethics, now regarded as field of inquiry that considers the
meaning of words regarded as ethical and moral, as well as the
actual interrelations of such meanings. As the are of metaethics has developed in recent decades, three principal metaethical theories have emerged as follows:

1. Ethical naturalism (sometimes called definism), a
    position in which it is argued that ethical sen-
    tences can be translated into non-ethical ones

without losing their meaning (usually a difficult accomplishment).
2. Ethical non-naturalism, a position in which it is argued that at least some ethical sentences cannot be translated into any other kinds of sentences (this constitutes an autonomous class).
3. Ethical non-cognitivism, a position in which it is argued that ethical sentences do not express any propositions at all.

The Ethical Problem in Sport and Physical Education

With these introductory statements and ideas behind us, we are in a better position to consider the essence of the ethical problem in sport and physical education. Here I am prepared to argue that this cannot be correctly delineated unless there is also some analysis and understanding of the values and norms of the social system and culture. What is most important for our understanding at this point is that the various sub-systems of society together compose a hierarchy of control and conditioning (e.g., in Parsonian "action theory," these sub-systems are those of culture, social system, personality, and behavioral organism). Moreover, just as there are four sub-systems within the total action system as defined by Parsons and others, there appear to be four levels within the particular sub-system known as "social system" (as indicated immediately above). These levels, proceedings from "highest" to "lowest," are (1) values, (2) norms, (3) the structure of collectivities, and (4) the structure of roles. Typically the higher levels are more general than the lower ones, with the latter giving specific guidance to those segments or units of the particular system to which they apply. These "units" or "segments" are either collectivities or individuals in their capacity as role occupants.

Keeping in mind, therefore, that there is a hierarchy of control and conditioning operating here in both downward and upward directions, typically the greatest pressure for conformity is exerted downward by the values and norms operative within a social system at a given time. In the United States the most important social values are (1) the rule of law, (2) (2) the socio-structural facilitation of individual achievement, and (3) the equality of opportunity. Similar to values, but which should be distinguished from them, are the norms of a social system. Norms are the shared, sanctioned rules that govern the second level of the social structure. The average person finds it difficult to separate in his or her mind the concepts of 'value' and 'norm.' Some examples of norms in the United States are (1) the institution of private property; (2) private enterprise; (3) the monogamous, conjugal family; and (4) the separation of church and state (Johnson, 1969, pp. 46-47; see also Zeigler and Spaeth, 1975, pp. 407-411).

In addition to the discussion immediately above, and recalling that there are a number of cultures and social systems in the world, we can now understand how a great many problems involving values and norms can spring up when the topics of sport, dance, play, and exercise are considered. For example, the amateur ideal of Baron de Coubertin has long since been shattered in Olympic competition, and perennially we witness displays of unbridled nationalism when top professional hockey players "engage in combat" with Russian "amateurs" for supremacy in a sport that has become marred by undue violence on this continent.

Further, if dance may be classified as human movement with a purpose, it is obvious that all is not well here either. Certainly this form of aesthetic expression has not yet found its rightful place within our culture either within the school or outside. One does not need to travel far to hear that the freedom and license of various dance forms undermines the moral fibre of youth. Or take the area of play in our culture. The term "play" is undoubtedly one of the most ambiguous in the English language, the average unabridged dictionary offering approximately 68 definitions for the reader's consumption. Also, too much play in one's life in the eyes of most implies shiftlessness and lack of purpose and direction.

As for the subject of exercise, some say it is excellent as well as vital for good health. Others say it is beneficial in moderation. A third group warns, however, that too much of it is bad, that it is not essential and doesn't belong in the school curriculum anyhow. Is it any wonder that the average person exhibits confusion on the topic; that there is a strong tendency to follow the line of least resistance; and that most people are inclined to do what "comes naturally" to unconditioned bodies--"lie down until the feeling goes away."

It should be completely obvious that such diversity of opinion and belief could exist only in a social system within a culture characterized by pluralistic philosophies both within the philosophic mainstream or in the various departmental philosophies (e.g., educational philosophy). Such a condition is not necessarily bad, of course, and it undoubtedly requires a political state in which a considerable amount of participatory democracy exists. And the paradoxical opinion is often expressed that North America functions in a materialistic fashion basically despite being characterized typically as possessing an over-arching, almost inherent philosophic idealism. Thus, many people today are absolutely convinced that all of the old standards and morals have been completely negated, and that we are all "going to Hell in a handbasket!" Accordingly, only a return to earlier halcyon days can prevent impending disaster. They decry what they believe are the prevailing "situation ethics," because they sense an uncharted course ahead on a rocky road leading to the mythical year 2000.

Oddly enough, at the very time when people seem to need guidance, many have turned away from organized religion and a large percentage of those in the field of philosophy (in the English-speaking world at least) seem to have quite completely abandoned a function accepted formly for the present-day, strictly disciplinary approach to their work. Of course, this latter development (i.e., more of a disciplinary approach to their work) was actually a direction followed by many other disciplines to a greater or lesser extent during the past several decades. In the 1960s, for example, a similar disciplinary orientation occurred in educational philosophy and then, during the 1970s, this trend spread to sport and physical education philosophy as well. To confuse the issue even further, the general public has incorporated such words as pragmatism, idealism, realism, and existentialism into their vocabulary, thereby distorting the original meaning of these philosophic schools or stances beyond recognition. The result is that correct use of any of these terms today now requires extensive qualification.

All of this adds up to the conclusion that society has now moved to the point where unanimity is largely lacking in regard to "what's good," "what's bad," or whether such distinction makes much difference any more. This conclusion may seem somewhat extreme, but it is true that the distinction between the concepts of 'good' and 'bad' has indeed become blurred at present no matter what phase of life is under consideration. This point was brought home forcibly by Cogley writing in the early 1970s as follows:

> every major institution in the land and most of the
> minor ones as well seemed to have been caught up
> in an identity crisis. Upheavals in the church
> were front-page news for almost a decade. The
> revolt against the prevailing idea of a university
> which began in Berkeley in 1964 kept erupting with
> dismaying frequency. Veteran army officers found

themselves at a loss as to how to deal with rebellious troops. The Democratic debacle at the Chicago convention four years ago dramatized a widespread disillusionment with the political parties. The once sacrosanct public school systems came under severe attack. Working newsmen who took to producing their own underground newspapers after hours voiced bitter disenchantment with the established press employing them. So prevalent was the discontent within the academic and professional communities that the 'radical caucuses' within them were given semi-official status. Bishops, university presidents, military brass, publishers, politicians, school principals, and other established 'leaders,' it became increasingly clear, were no longer leading. . . . (1972, p. 2).

In retrospect we now appreciate that the values, morals, and ethical standards of the 1960s were indeed undergoing an identity crisis that has carried on through the 1970s into the 1980s despite some swing of the pendulum in the other direction. Now many of the same problems are beginning to "heat up" in the 1980s (e.g., the "non-nuke group" and the "pro-life group"). No one can deny that the area of personal and professional ethics is indeed in a constant state of flux and warrants careful monitoring at all times.

If it is indeed true that the world seems to be more "rudderless" than previously, and who can argue this point, the implications for sport and physical education as a microcosm of the culture are that this field will continue to interact daily with present society. Thus, "waves will flow" in both directions for better or worse. It seems obvious that we in this field should become involved with the subject of ethics and morality in a serious way. Further, unless society becomes far more tranquil than it appears to be at present, such concern for ethics will be with us for a long time to come.

References

Baker, Russell.   Good bad sports.   The New York Times Magazine, Feb. 1, 1976.

Blumenthal, W. Michael. Business morality has not deteriorated --society has changed. The New York Times, Jan. 9, 1977.

Bok, Derek C. Can ethics be taught? Change 8 (9), October, 1975, 26-30.

Burtt, E. A. In search of philosophical understanding. New York: The New American Library, 1965.

Chace, James. How "moral" can we get? The New York Times Magazine, May 22, 1977.

Cogley, John. The storm before the calm. The Center Magazine, V (4), July/August, 1972, 2-3.

Dennis, Ann B. A code of ethics for sociologists and anthropologists. Social Sciences in Canada, 3 (1-2), 1975, 14-16.

Encyclopedia of Philosophy, The (Paul Edwards, Ed.). New York: The Macmillan Company and The Free Press, 8 vols., 1967.

Etzioni, Amitai. Do as I say, not as I do. The New York Times Magazine, Sept. 26, 1976.

Fairlie, H. The seven deadly sins today. Washington, D. C.: New Republic Books, 1978.

Hazard, G. C., Jr. Capitalist ethics. Yale Alumni Magazine & Journal, XLI (8), April, 1978, 50-51.

Hechinger, F. M. Whatever became of sin? Saturday Review/ World, Sept. 24, 1974.

Hospers, John. An introduction to philosophical analysis. Englewood Cliffs, N. J.: Prentice-Hall, Inc., 1953.

Johnson, H. M. The relevance of the theory of action to historians. Social Science Quarterly, June, 1969, 46-58.

Maeroff, G. I. West Point cheaters have a lot of company. The New York Times, June 20, 1976.

Martens, R. Kid sports: a den of iniquity or land or promise. Proceedings of the 79th Annual Meeting, NCPEAM, Gedvilas, L. L. (Ed.), Chicago, IL, 1976.

New York Times, The. The growing dishonesty in sports: is
    it just a reflection of our American society? Nov. 7,
    1976.

New York Times, The. The ethical imperative. News of the
    Week in Review Section, Feb. 26, 1978.

Nowell-Smith, P. H. Ethics. Harmondsworth, England, 1954.

Saturday Review Special Report. Watergating on Main Street,
    SR 3 (3), Nov. 1, 1975, 10-28.

Zeigler, E. F. and Spaeth, M. J. (Eds.). Administrative theo-
    ry and practice in physical education and athletics.
    Englewood Cliffs, N. J.: Prentice-Hall, Inc., 1975.

CHAPTER 2
THE 'GOOD' AND THE 'BAD' IN HISTORICAL PERSPECTIVE

In a volume such as this, there isn't space to review the problem of the 'good' and the 'bad' (and also the 'right' and the 'wrong') in great detail; thus, what follows will be an extremely brief outline history in the Western world of that branch of philosophy known as ethics. Further, the study of ethics and morality in the East is only a mystery to us in the West and is deserving of special treatment in its own right.

The primary focus at this point will be on metaethics and its central questions. What is meant when one searches for the "good" or the "bad?" What guarantee is there that any such intent is correct? Can there be right standards for use in judging actions or things to be good or bad? If such value judgments are indeed made, how do they differ--if at all--from judgments that are value free (or value neutral)? In any such search or investigation, it is also difficult to know whether to proceed from the general to the specific or vice versa (i.e., from the good in general to right conduct or justice in particular, or in the opposite direction).

Even a cursory examination of the history of ethics substantiates that it is a description of "irregular progress toward complete clarification of each type of ethical judgment" (Encyclopedia of Philosophy, III, p. 82). It is indeed difficult to judge even generally how much "irregular progress" has been made since the development of Greek ethics starting with the fifth century B.C. contributions of Socrates. It could be argued that the changing political, economic, and other social influences of the time required the development of a new way of conduct--just as there is a need for altered standards of conduct today. The emergence of professional teachers of philosophy were in a sense the by-product of greater civilization. As Sidgwick explained,

> If bodily vigour was no longer to be left to nature and spontaneous exercise, but was to be attained by the systematic observance of rules laid down to professional trainers, it was natural to think that the same might be the case with excellences of the soul (Outline of the History of Ethics, p. 21).

In this orientation section there will not be a detailed consideration of the ideas of Socrates, Plato, and Aristotle, nor later Hellenistic and Roman ethical tendencies that have come to be known as Epicureanism, Stoicism, and Neoplatonism.   Socrates began the development of standards for the qualities of goodness, justice, and virtue.   Plato gave a spiritual orientation to such thought as he believed that these timeless qualities or idea(1)s had been defined in a world beyond the ken of man. Conversely, Aristotle sought his answers typically in what now have been designated as the sciences and social sciences. Plato's approach to goodness was through comparison with universal idea(1)s, while Aristotle's "happiness" resulted from the accomplishment of more natural goals.   Individual good was related to social good, but the ideas of moral responsibility and free will were not viewed with the same importance as was to be the case later with Christian thought.

One might conclude from historical analysis that for the next two thousand years ethical thought was oriented much more to practice than to theory.   This explains why the meanings of the various ethical terms or concepts were not altered to any significant extent, even though moral codes and life purposes were viewed quite differently.   The Hellenistic and Roman ideas were lacking in the necessary insight required to advance beyond the intellectual genius of the earlier Greeks.   It was during this period that the seedbed of later, all-encompassing Christian philosophy was established.   As a result the Western world went into a long period during which time philosophy and religion were most closely interwoven.   During this somewhat dormant period in the history of ethics, there was one system in which man's reason and God's purpose for man were combined to produce one ultimate purpose for the human being-- ultimate union with the Creator.

During this period of medieval ethics Thomas Aquinas brought together Aristotle's scientific and philosophic thought with the theology of St. Augustine.   A highly significant and fundamental concept of the ethical system created by St. Thomas was his doctrine of natural law.   Here he invented an accommodation of two different ethical systems so that there was a "natural domain" and a "theological realm."   Reason and conscience were somehow fused inherently in man's nature; natural law contained God's ethical standards to which man could elevate himself by the application of God-given reason.   Religious dogmas at this point were considered infallible, however, and they could thereby negate what some might deem to be valid scientific advances.

Ethics in the Early Modern Era

During the marked period of social change of the six-
teenth and seventeenth centuries, what might be called more
modern ethics began to flourish. This philosophical watershed
seems to have occurred immediately after a series of major social changes had occurred. Of course, many considered the
prevailing ethical system to be in a state of disarray, but at
that time various attempts at reconstruction began. Thomas
Hobbes made a strong effort to release ethics from its complete
servitude to theological law. He postulated that ethics was
unreliable unless it was grounded on the objective laws of biology and psychology. If it turned out that the experimental
analysis of nature was to be ethically neutral, then he argued
that ethics should indeed be contrasted with science. Such
radical thought brought reaction and counter-action from the
early intuitionists (e.g., Henry More), Benedict Spinoza, John
Locke, Bishop Butler, David Hume, and the so-called Common-
sense Intuitionists (e.g., Thomas Reid). A similar "theoretical
struggle" was being carried on in eighteenth century France
through the ideas of Voltaire, Jean-Jacques Rousseau and the
Encyclopedists (e.g., Diderot), although it has been argued
that their varied political orientations often distorted the objectivity of their philosophical arguments. Montesquieu, the
French jurist and political philosopher, did add to the discussion, however, by viewing values more as sociological and historical facts or data.

Special mention must be made of the monumental role
played by Immanuel Kant, the "little professor" from Königs-
berg, Prussia, within what has been called the German enlight-
enment. His highly complex and often perplexing non-utilitari-
an analysis based moral principles on a priori laws by which
man's "practical reason" is guided. He postulated that the human feels no obligation to obey laws of nature, but that he or
she does sense subjectively a duty to respond to moral laws
that are inherent in the universe. Kant's ethical system had
three basic premises: (1) analysis of the evidence of moral experience, (2) consideration of the underlying logic, and (3) the
construction of metaphysical principles undergirded or presupposed by ethical analysis that is in contra-distinct to generalizations from science. Thus, he distinguished most sharply
between naturalistic ethics and moral law. His categorical imperative implied a moral code above and beyond any law of nature (e.g., man's strong desire for happiness). He postulated
a universalizability criterion as the most fundamental moral
principle ("Act only on that maxim which you can will to be a
universal law"). This more precise statement of the "golden

rule" represents perhaps Kant's greatest addition to the theory of ethics--despite its apparent weakness. Lastly, he envision-ed an autonomy of the will which placed man in a position to defy causal determinism grounded in regulative scientific prin-ciple. Humans were conceived as part of, and yet distinct from, the laws of nature and science.

The nineteenth century in the Western world witnessed a sharp struggle between the two great traditions of utilitarian-ism and idealism, the former looming large in England and France and the latter predominant in Germany. Thus, it is not sur-prising that both developing systems met with favorable re-sponses from different quarters in the United States. The ideal-istic position was welcomed by certain philosophers and literary figures and, of course, the Christian Church. Utilitarianism blended with the drive for greater technological advancement, and then was joined--and to a degree supplanted-- by the prag-matic ethics of Peirce, James, and Dewey.[1]

With a pragmatic approach, ethical considerations were extended to relate to all of human knowledge. The aim here was to avoid the almost ageless, perennial distinction between value and fact. This was accomplished by a reinterpretation that blurred the controversial issues for those who were willing to disavow Kantian ethics and the traditional outlook toward scientific knowledge as including only value-free facts. There-fore, it was argued that ethical judgment was simply a matter of applying reason to the results of scientific (empirical) inves-tigation by ascribing value to those human acts so designated as valuable.

The Situation in the Twentieth Century

By now the reader may aree that there are almost as many views of ethics and/or moral philosophy as there are phi-losophers--an obvious exaggeration, of course, but a definite indication that there is no single, non-controversial foundation stone upon which the whole structure of ethics can be built. In fact, it can even be argued that the nature and function of the subject are themselves topics upon which there is vigorous dispute. This is not to say that there are not some aspects of

---

[1] The subsequent developments in England, Germany, and the rest of the Continent will not be catalogued here. The es-sential "battle lines" had already been drawn and were men-tioned briefly above.

this branch of philosophy upon which there is fairly wide consensus. For example, in the past moral philosophers sought to
offer general guidance as to (1) what to do, (2) what to seek,
and (3) how to treat others (Nowell-Smith, 1954).

Philosophers as a rule have not tried to preach to their
adherents, although many have made strong efforts to offer
fairly practical advice that included important pronouncements
on the subject of good and evil. Many early philosophers believed that there was indeed a true moral code--a normative
ethical system upon which people could and should base their
conduct. In this sense, therefore, philosophers saw their task
as the enunciation of basic principles of morality (usually with
supporting justification). What is good? What is the good life?
What are the limits of moral justification? How shall people live
their lives? These were the types of questions to which philosophers spoke.

Others have offered advice freely down through the years
as well. Theologians, dramatists, novelists, poets, and even
comedians have offered considerable insight into the question of
good and evil, but such counsel was often viewed as dicta or
pronouncements, and usually differed from distinctly philosophical accounts in that it was specific, unsystematic, and typically
lacking in proof.

As explained previously, there is strong disagreement
within the traditional conception of the philosopher's task.
Some believed that philosophers should not or could not discover new truths (e.g., Kant), while others felt just the opposite to be the case (e.g., Bentham). There was an effort to
systematize the knowledge that men already have and to demonstrate the ultimate rationale for these beliefs. Some were concerned with objective justification of any moral claims, whereas
others (known as subjectivists) argued that true objectivity was
simply not possible or reasonable. One group was extremely
skeptical, therefore, about any body of knowledge which purported to tell people how they should live. Their opponents,
the objectivists, worked away toward the achievement of their
goal--the creation of a true moral code. In this struggle the
German iconoclast, Nietzsche, was a true revolutionary in that
he contradicted previous objectivistic thought violently--and
even the common-sense moral principles unchallenged by most
skeptics. In summary, therefore, the battle lines were drawn:
one group of ethical theorists agreed with the traditional task
of the philosopher, while the other denied that moralists could
ever hope to achieve such an objective goal as a truly justifiable moral code.

It is difficult but not impossible to gain some historical perspective on the philosophical trends and developments of the past seventy-five years. What is now called "the analytic movement" or "philosophical analysis" has been a most interesting and important development during this period of time. Thus, despite the fact that scholars in the Western world have been engaged in philosophical thought for more than two thousand years, there is still controversy over the exact nature of philosophy--what it is or should be. And so into the struggle between the ethical objectivists and the ethical subjectivists came a third combatant--the contemporary analytic philosopher of the twentieth century who asked himself or herself the question, "What kind of activity am I engaging in?"

Searching for the answer to the above question, the philosophers began to develop three different analytic approaches that became known as (1) logical atomism, (2) logical positivism, and (3) ordinary language philosophy. Each looked at analysis somewhat differently, but there was agreement that philosophy must be approached through the medium of language analysis to a greater or lesser extent. Logical atomists sought to rearrange our ambiguous language so that more logically arranged sentences would become crystal clear. Logical positivism's aim was to subject statements to a verifiability principle. This meant that regular language statements were to be arranged in logical, consistent form to see if they were empirically verifiable either through mathematical reasoning or scientific investigation. The main goal of so-called ordinary language philosophy was to decide what the basic philosophical terms were, and then to use them correctly and clearly so that all might understand. Obviously, these developments were a far cry from the efforts of the ethical subjectivists who were striving to keep the objectivists from strengthening their claims for superiority!

Finally, in the last quarter of the twentieth century with the world in such a turmoil of "hot and cold" wars, at the very time when people of all ages are highly concerned about ethical values--about "what to do, what to seek, and how to treat others"--brilliant philosophers are relatively silent, avoid the rational (public) justification of any type of moral system, and spend their professional time and energy analyzing the meaning and function of moral concepts and statements (or some other so-called analytic approach to the doing of philosophy). The result is that there has developed a sharp distinction between the normative ethics of the avowed moral philosophers and the analytic (or critical or theoretical) approach of that branch of philosophy now known as metaethics.

The reader may agree at this point that it is of considerable importance to those of us interested in sport and physical
education philosophy to ascertain in quite exact fashion what
we think the relationship between normative ethics and metaethics should be. For example, with the increasing emphasis
on violence in sport and the development of coaching certification programs, professionals in sport and physical education
don't receive much guidance from a metaethical statement like
"much more careful delineation of the concept of 'violence' is
needed at this time." However, normative statements like
"harsh coaching methods have no place in amateur sport" provide strong guidance at a time when such counsel seems absolutely necessary.

By the above statements, we do not for a moment mean
to imply that metaethical analysis is unimportant--far from it.
There are extremists on both sides, but a more reasonable approach would seem to be one in which a moral philosopher or
ethical theorist engages in metaethical analysis if he or she
wishes, but at the same time also works toward the elimination
of irrational ethical beliefs while searching for as much normative consensus as possible in an effort to find the best ethical
system consonant with an evolving democratic state. A variation of this might be a situation where departments of philosophy would deliberately engage scholars with strong inclinations
in one direction or the other, the end result of which tend to
strengthen both the sub-disciplinary and sub-professional aspects of the field (i.e., both the metaethical and normative aspects of philosophy). Although some might argue against the
seeming incompatibility of such an approach, in the final analysis the worth of the field could well be more readily recognized
by all.

Having made the above pronouncement, we do nevertheless recognize--as you, the reader, will also recognize shortly
--that the task of normative inquiry is most difficult, especially when people are confronted with most complex issues and
thus conclusions tend to stray into the realm of metaethics.
For example, when a normative ethical theory such as hedonism
(the position that a person's primary moral duty lies in the
pursuit of pleasure) includes a statement such as, "Competitive
sport is good because it brings pleasure," the non-hedonist
might challenge this statement solely on the meaning of the
terms "good" and "pleasure." The obvious difficulty of justifying a normative ethical theory brings to the fore questions about
about metaethical relativism and subjectivism, questions which
when pursued clearly point up the severity of the "subjectivist
threat."

   Basically and fundamentally, then, justification of an
ethical theory, or even an incomplete set of ethical statements
about sport and physical education (or any other aspect of life),
revolved around the ability of the theorist to state correctly,
elucidate sufficiently, and defend adequately his or her moral
and/or ethical claims and arguments. Is a moral judgment objective or subjective? Does a moral judgment differ from a factual judgment? Is an ethical statement about right or wrong
conduct in sport, for example, "publicly warrantable?" In other
words, is there some publicly acceptable procedure for verification which reasonable people would be willing to accept? Finally then, as you move ahead with this course experience, you
must decide for yourself to what extent you wish ethical claims
or judgments to be (1) objectively verifiable, (2) universalizable, (3) practical for use in everyday life, and (4) autonomous in the sense that the structure of their statements--its
very fabric--does not rest solely on non-normative statements.
You may not appreciate it at this point, but--both personally
and professionally--this experience with ethical decision-making
could well be extremely important to you in the years that lie
ahead.

References

Burtt, E. A. In search of philosophical understanding. New
    York: The New American Library, 1965.

Encyclopedia of Philosophy, The (Paul Edwards, Ed.). New
    York: The Macmillan Company and The Free Press, 8
    vols., 1967.

Sidgwick, Henry. Outline of the history of ethics. London:
    Macmillan Company, Ltd., 1960. (Published originally in
    1886).

Warnock, Mary. Ethics since 1900. New York: Oxford Uni-
    versity Press, 1966.

CHAPTER 3
ETHICAL OUTLOOK -- AN IMPLICIT/ EXPLICIT EXPERIENTIAL APPROACH

Having stated how important it is for a young person to learn to make rational ethical decisions, we should consider briefly how a child's personality develops in early life. It is important to understand what happens prior to the time when a young person gets an opportunity in our society to learn through education how to make ethical decisions in his or her life.

Rand offers us an interesting analysis of what occurs in the life of a young person before any semblance of a rational philosophy develops. Western world religions often impress upon the young child the idea that God is "watching over" him or her, and that He knows and makes note of every misdeed through some sort of supernatural recorder. Rand explains how she regards this as a myth, but that interestingly this myth is true, not existentially, but from a psychological standpoint.

Thus, the human possesses a "psychological recorder" which is truly the integrating mechanism of a person's subconscious. This so-called sense of life "is a pre-conceptual equivalent of metaphysics, an emotional, subconsciously integrated appraisal of man and existence. It sets the nature of a man's emotional responses and the essence of his character" (1960, p. 31). This human being is making choices, is forming value judgments, is experiencing emotions, and in a great many ways is acquiring an implicit view of life. All of this young person's conclusions or evasions about or from life represent an implicit metaphysics.

As people interested in the entire educational process-- our own and that of others with whom we might come into contact--our hope is that all young people will have the change to develop their rational powers. If this occurs, reason can then act as the programmer of the individual's "emotional computer" with a possible outcome that the earlier "sense of life" will develop into a reasonable logical philosophy. If the maturing child does not have the opportunity to develop a degree of rationality, or somehow evades the opportunity, then unfortunately chance takes over.

What are we faced with then? We have a person who has matured chronologically, but who is "integrating blindly, incongruously, and at random" (p.33). (And don't we all know people where this occurs daily to the extreme?) Thus, we can see how really important it is that in the development of a fully integrated personality the young person's sense of life match his/her conscious, rationalized convictions? As individuals we can either drive this powerful integrating mechanism, or be driven by it! Accordingly, we should inquire as to the role of philosophy in our lives, asking ourselves how a sound philosophy can help in the formation of a fully integrated personality. Further, can we deny that the goal of education is an individual whose mind and emotions are in harmony, thereby enabling the maturing person to develop his/her potential and achieve maximum effectiveness in life?

Taking the matter of the individual's development one step further, we need to keep in mind that we are dealing with a social animal, a person who in all probability will need help to bridge the gap from an early sense of life where embryonic, plastic value integrations occur, to the making of ethical decisions in life's many activities involving social, communicative, physical, aesthetic and creative, and more traditional learning interests (including educational hobbies). We should be helping this young person to develop conscious convictions in which the mind leads and the emotions follow.

Our concern is primarily with developmental physical activity in sport, dance, play, and exercise and the many ethical decisions that will have to be made based on the daily occurrences in these activities. For example, the varsity or intramural athlete involved in highly competitive situations that are charged with strong emotions should be so guided along the way that reason will take over as the "programmer of his or her emotional computer" as a "machine with a driver" develops.

The key concept in the formation of a person's sense of life is the term "important" (and not necessarily the term "good"). Rand argues that it is a metaphysical term that serves as a bridge between metaphysics and ethics while the young, immature person is learning what values are important. Thus, "the integrated sum of a person's basic values is that person's sense of life" (p. 35). During the period of adolescence, typically a certain amount of rebellion occurs, and we have on our hands a situation characterized by either quite frantic irrationality or a set of adult-imposed values.

What the young person needs at this crucial point in his
or her development is "an intellectual roadbed for one's course
of life" (p. 36).   The eventual goal, we trust, will be a fully
integrated personality, a person whose mind and emotions are
in harmony a great deal of the time.   When this occurs, we
have helped to create a situation where the individual's sense
of life matches his or her conscious convictions.   In this struggle that takes place to a great or lesser extent in each person's
life, a sound philosophical approach can help in the setting of
criteria for emotional integration.   If the young person's view
of reality has been carefully defined and is consistent, then we
will witness a gradual, but steady growth and development from
implicit, emotionally based reactions to problems to reactions
that are truly explicit, conceptually derived value-judgments.
This is undoubtedly the goal for which we must strive both as
individuals guiding our own lives, as well as for those times
when we are guiding others either as offspring or as young
people in our charge when we are serving as professional physical educator/coaches.

Reference

Rand, Ayn.   The romantic manifesto.   New York and Cleve-
    land: The World Publishing Company, 1960.

CHAPTER 4
MAJOR ETHICAL ROUTES EXTANT IN
THE WESTERN WORLD

Inasmuch as we have arrived at the point where I have stated that a young person in our society should be so educated that there is an opportunity to develop rationality as a "life competency," it is time to consider what major alternative routes are available for use in the Western world.

There should be no difficulty in reaching agreement on the position that it is most important for a young person to bridge the gap between immaturity and maturity insofar as ethical understanding is concerned. Further, we would expect that the opportunity to achieve such comprehension within reasonable limits would be readily available to all aspiring young people in North American life today. Unfortunately, I am forced to state that nothing is farther from the truth based on my experience with young people over a number of decades. I must agree, therefore, with Rand's assertion that on all sides we find young people "integrating blindly, incongruously, and at random" about all aspects of life (1960, p. 33). No matter whether the question is one of taking drugs for presumably heightened experiences, or cheating on examinations or term papers, or breaking the letter or the spirit of the rules in competitive sport in one or more of a dozen overt or covert ways, the evidence points to an upbringing in which the young person has not received educational experiences in which an "ethical competency" could be developed or been the result.

With this dilemma in mind, I set out to determine what major ethical routes of a philosophical nature are available to the physical educator/coach today. A careful analysis of many sources indicates great variation in terminology and emphases. Terms that appear include ethical naturalism, ethical non-naturalism (or intuitionism), and emotivism (Hospers, 1953, p. 485); authoritarianism, relativism, and scientific ethics (Fromm, 1967, p. 37); the legalistic, the antinomian, and the situational (Fletcher, 1966, pp. 17-18); and religious absolutism, conventionalism, rational absolutism, and utilitarian relativism (Abelson and Friquegnon, 1975). Further, Titus and Keeton use a threefold classification, but they do their best to avoid an "ism" nomenclature by stating that there are (a) those who live under the aegis of codes (e.g., God's word); (b) those who thrust aside codes and prescribed laws; and (c) those who seek to establish ethical norms through the application of reflective moral judgment (1973, pp. 59-60). Finally, Patterson stated that we can delineate correctly two divisional categories of ethical theories--where the knowledge comes from, and the motive that prompts action (1957).

To add to this review of what might be called secondary listings, pertinent work of a primary nature was examined as follows: John Dewey (1929, 1932, 1946 and 1948); G. E. Moore (1948); Simone de Beauvoir (1964); A. J. Ayer (1946); C. L. Stevenson (1947-48); Joseph Fletcher (1966); Kurt Baier (1958); and John Rawls (1971). As a result of this analysis, six presumably different approaches were selected for inclusion in this volume. Each approach or "ethical route" is describe according to (a) underlying presupposition, (b) criterion for evaluation, (c) method for determination of ethical decision, and (d) presumed result. The six ethical theories or routes are as follows: (a) authoritarianism (or legalism); (b) relativism (or antinomianism); (c) situationism; (d) scientific ethics; (e) "good reasons" approach; and (f) emotivism. No strong argument is being made here for six approaches as opposed to any other number. It could be argued that this analysis represents only what might be called a consensual tabulation. (See Table 1).

Authoritarianism (or Legalism)

Underlying Presupposition. Absolute good and rightness are either present in the world, or have been determined by custom, law or code.

Criterion for Evaluation. The criterion is conformity or compliance with rules, laws, moral codes, established systems and customs in the society or culture.

Method for Determination of Ethical Decisions. Ethical decision-making is carried out by application of the prevailing normative standard or law.

Probable Result. The solution to any ethical dilemma can be readily determined by strict application of the evaluative criterion.

Note: Legalism has dominated Christianity (and many other orthodox religions) since its early days; thus, it is usually a question of blind obedience to rigid rules and/or laws. For example, homosexuals were burned to death in the Middle Ages, and condemned to death through some torturous means

Table 1.

MAJOR PHILOSOPHICAL APPROACHES TO ETHICAL DECISIONS

Ethical Approach	Underlying Presupposition	Criterion for Evaluation	Method for Determination of Ethical Decision	Probable Result
I. AUTHORITARIANISM (or Legalism)	Absolute good an rightness are either present in the world, or have been determined by custom, law, or code.	Conformity to rules, laws, moral codes, established systems and customs.	Application of normative standard (or law) to resolve the ethical dilemma or issue.	The solution to any ethical dilemma can be readily determined and then implemented (or acted upon).
II. RELATIVISM (or Antinomianism)	Good and bad, and rightness and wrongness, are relative and vary according to the situation or culture involved.	Needs of situation there and then in culture or society concerned.	Guidance in the making of an ethical decision may come either from "outside"; intuition; one's own conscience; empirical investigation; reason, etc.	Each ethical decision is highly individual since every situation has its particularity; there are no absolutely valid principles or universal laws.
III. SITUATIONISM (with certain similarity to #1 above)	God's love (or some other summum bonum) is an absolute norm; reason, revelation, and precedent have no objective normative status.	"What is fitting" in the situation is based on application of agapeic love; subordinate moral principles serve to illuminate the situation.	Resolution of ethical dilemma results from use of calculating method plus contextual appropriateness; act from loving concern; benevolence=right.	The best solution, everything considered, will result when the principle of God's love is applied situationally.
IV. SCIENTIFIC ETHICS (scientific method applied to ethics)	No distinction between moral goods and natural goods; science can bring about complete agreement on factual belief about human behavior.	Ideas helpful in solving problematic situations are therefore true; empirical verification of hypothesis brings union of theory and practice.	Use of scientific method in problem-solving; reflective thinking begets ideas that function as tentative solutions for concrete problems; test hypotheses experimentally.	Agreement in factual belief will soon result in agreement in attitude; continuous adaptation of values to the culture's changing needs will result in social change.
V. "GOOD REASONS" APPROACH (the "moral point of view")	Implies that ethical action should be supported by best reasons (good reasons—facts superior to others; moral reasons superior to other types.	Same rules must be for good of everyone alike; unselfish decisions to be made on principle that can be universalized.	Two stages: (1) determining which facts are relevant; (2) weighing facts to determine relative weight for consideration; a hierarchy of reasons needed.	Assumption is that each person can reason why through to a satisfactory method of ethical decision-making using a class of good reasons.
VI. EMOTIVISM (analytic philosophy's response to ethical problems that arise)	Ethics is normative (i.e., moral standards) and therefore cannot be a science; the term "good" appears to be indefinable.	An ethical dispute must be on a factual level; value statements must be distinguished from factual ones.	Involves logical analysis of ethical (normative standard) terms; factual statements referred to social scientists; analyze conflicting attitudes to determine progress.	Ethical dilemmas can be resolved through the combined efforts of the moralist and the scientist; common beliefs may in time change attitudes.

in the Old Testament descriptions. This sort of treatment is probably what led Henry Miller to write of the "immorality of morality," and Gloria Steinem to remark that "the Moral Majority are the people our ancestors came from Europe to escape."

Relativism (or Antinomianism)

Underlying Presupposition. Good and bad, and rightness and wrongness, are relative and vary according to the situation or culture involved.

Criterion for Evaluation. The needs of a situation there and then in the culture of society concerned are the determining factors as to the values or norms to be applied to a problematic situation.

Method for Determination of Ethical Decisions. Guidance in the making of an ethical decision may come from "outside," intuition, one's own conscience, empirical investigation, reason, etc.

Probable Result. Each ethical situation is highly individual, since every situation has its particularity. There are no absolutely valid principles or universal laws.

Note: It is important not to confuse ethical relativism with cultural relativism. The former denies the presence of any one basic moral principle in the universe, whereas the latter relates to cultural mores (e.g., the South Sea tribes situation where elders are killed so that their bodies will still be in good condition for their after-life).

Situationism (an eclectic "new morality")

Underlying Presupposition. God's love, or some other summum bonum is an absolute norm. As a result, reason, revelation, and precedent have no objective normative status.

Criterion for Evaluation. "What is fitting" in any problematic situation is based on the application of agapeic love (Christian love or God's love). There are subordinate moral principles that serve to illuminate the situation further, so that the most accurate evaluation of the problematic situation is made.

Method for Determination of Ethical Decisions. The resolution of an ethical dilemma results from the use of a calculating method in addition to what might be called contextual appropriateness. The individual should act from loving concern for others (i.e., what is benevolent is right).

Probably Result. The best solution, everything considered, will result from the application situationally of the principle of God's love.

Note: Agapē can be manifested only when (a) there is awareness of the relevant facts; (b) the likely consequences are calculated; and (c) the guidance of traditional norms is considered.

Scientific Ethics

Underlying Presupposition. With the application of scientific method to an ethical situation (to the greatest possible extent), there is no distinction between moral goods and natural goods. The presupposition is that scientific method can bring about complete agreement in due time based on factual belief about what constitutes the most efficient and effective behavior.

Criterion for Evaluation. Ideas that are helpful in the solution of problematic situations are therefore true. Thus, the empirical verification of a given hypothesis brings a theory and practice union.

Method for Determination of Ethical Decisions. The scientific method is applied to ethical problem-solving; reflective thinking begets ideas that function as tentative solutions for concrete problems. These hypotheses are then tested experimentally--to the greatest possible extent keeping in mind that humans are involved.

Probable Result. The assumption is that agreement in factual belief resulting from the application of scientific method will soon bring about agreement in attitude on the part of the majority of the people. Thus, we would have continuous adaptation of values to the culture's changing needs, and this over-time would effect the directed reconstruction of all social institutions as necessary.

Note: This approach should receive serious consideration, since it is apparent that there is indeed a "crisis of human values" at present, and that the earlier confidence in religion and philosophy has been greatly undermined. Science and technology has brought mankind to the point where human life on the planet could be destroyed permanently.

The "Good Reasons" Approach

Underlying presupposition. Baier's "good reasons" approach, which has also been called the "moral point of view," implies that ethical action should be supported by the best reasons (i.e., good reasons, or facts some of which are superior to others). Moral reasons (good reasons) are superior to reasons of immediate pleasure and reasons that are selfish.

Criterion for Evaluation. All must be subject to the same rules, and rules must be for the good of everyone alike. In the making of an ethical decision, one should not be selfish; one should make a decision on principle; one should be willing to universalize this principle; and one should consider the good of everyone alike. Ethical rules developed in this fashion quite frequently would require people to make genuine sacrifices.

Method for Determination of Ethical Decisions. This approach may be implemented in two stages: (1) by surveying the facts to determine which are relevant, and (2) the weighing of the facts to determine the relative weight of the considerations. First, we are confronted with "consideration-making beliefs" or "rules of reason." These are the major premises of "inference-licenses" to be considered. The minor premises are other facts, which when matched with the above, help the person to conclude which are the best reason(s). The presence of a specific fact as a consideration accordingly implies the context or outline of a course of action that is being planned by someone. Second, we move to the weighing of the various "best" reasons that seemed relevant to us at the first stage. These reasons are "weighed" or evaluated according to what is believed about the superiority of one type of reason over another. Here the hierarchy of reasons is as follows: (a) reasons of self-interest are superior to reasons of momentary pleasure; (b) reasons of long-range interest outbalance reasons of short-range interest; and (c) reasons of law, religion, and morality outweigh reasons of self-interest.

Probable Result. The assumption with this approach is that the invididual can reason his or her way through to a satisfactory method of ethical decision-making. The plan, that implies a class of good reasons, moves progressively from reasons of immediate pleasure, to those that are selfish reasons, and finally to so-called moral reasons that correlate with the person's long-range interests.

Note: Morality, for Kurt Baier, involves doing things on principle and, as a result, a condition of universal "teachability" could well prevail. Further, The rationale is that moral rules are meant for everyone, and thus they must be for the good of everyone alike. Thus, the "moral point of view" has a relationship to Kant's thought in that the individual should be willing to universalize the principle underlying the planned secaction.

Emotivism

Underlying Presupposition. Some have identified emotivism as analytic philosophy's response to the problems of ethics. In this approach ethics is normative in that there are indeed moral standards. This means, of course, that ethics can never be approached scientifically. The emotivist starts with a real problem in that the term "good" appears to be ultimately indefinable. This leads some to claim that use of the word "good" in an ethical sense merely reflects an emotion of the user's part.

Criterion for Evaluation. An ethical dispute must be on a factual level. It is vital that value statements be distinguished from factual ones.

Method for Determination of Ethical Decision. Typically, an emotivist approach involves logical analysis (to the extent that this is possible) of ethical (or normative standard) terms, whereas the factual statement in the argument would be based on the most current findings of social science. Then there would be an analysis of conflicting attitudes to determine to what extent programs had been accomplished.

Probable Result. The assumption is that ethical dilemmas can be resolved reasonably through the combined efforts of the moralist and the social scientist. The hope is that the presence of commonly accepted beliefs will in time change conflicting attitudes.

Note: This approach has much to offer and merits serious consideration. Its practicality for the average professional person (not trained in analytic philosophy) seems questionable. However, one may not have much choice if he or she is having difficulty accepting a specific definition of that elusive term "good."

Concluding Statement

After arguing that it is most important for a developing young person to achieve a level of competency that will enable him or her to employ rationality in arriving at ethical decisions in life, I proceeded to outline six ethical routes that are available. I must reiterate that these are not the only approaches available; nevertheless, a case could be made that they represent a consensual listing.

At this point some would argue that I owe the reader an indication of which approach I would personally recommend. There was a time when I made every effort to avoid any such recommendation, because I believed that it was somewhat unfair to take a strong stand in a society where pluralistic philosophies were permitted and known to prevail. However, the decade of the 1960s seemed to change all that--for the time being at any rate--and students argued that they "paid their money and had a right to know" where the instructor stood on such-and-such an issue.

In keeping with that attitude then, a stance that I adopted always with the caveat that I would make every effort to avoid so-called brainwashing, I freely confess my belief that the application of scientific method to ethical analysis seems necessary at present. I argue this way because many of us are discovering that there is indeed a "crisis of human values" at this time, and that the confidence that we had previously in religion and philosophy has been seriously undermined. Daily we hear on the one hand that onrushing science and technology are our great benefactors. Then in the next moment we learn that science and technology have shown people ways to actually destroy life on this planet permanently--at least in the sense that we have known evolution to this point (Saturday Review Special Report, 1977, p. 13).

Further, we have learned that the 20th century is a transitional one, that the old order has most definitely been replaced by the new! Additionally, what is not generally appreciated is that the rate of change in society appears to be gradually accelerating, and that this acceleration will probably continue to increase. All of this has led me to conclude that in the Western world we must as soon as possible eliminate the persisting dualism that has separated investigation about the physical world from the study of human behavior in relation to moral values and virtues.

Frankly, in this evolving democratic society, I cannot personally find a strong rationale for any authoritarian or legalistic doctrine governing ethical behavior to prevail--one in which <u>ironclad conformity</u> is required because of presumed <u>absolute good</u> and rightness in the world.   Such an assumption on my part is a personal one, of course, but I find myself increasingly repelled by the many "greater or lesser 'ayatollahs'" who seek to invade our lives.   It is fortunate for me that our society guarantees individual freedom in such matters as long as the laws of the land are not abrogated.   (This is not to imply for a moment that the struggle for individual freedom can be given up even momentarily.)

Still further, I have considered the antinomial, relativistic position as well.   As pleasant as it may be on occasion to rebel against society in a radical manner, antinomianism to me appears to be so far to the left on an authoritarian-anarchistic freedom spectrum as to be fundamentally out of key in a political society such as ours.

Despite the appeal of the emotivist approach, including application of the logic of the language analyst, it is my position that society's present plight requires <u>more</u> than just the implementation of this technique alone to life's many, everpresent ethical problems.   Baier's "good reasons" approach (the so-called "moral point of view") is highly appealing and obviously has much to offer.

The above notwithstanding--and I realize fully the impossibility of invoking any one approach at this time--I believe strongly that our failure to employ scientific method in the realm of so-called <u>moral</u> goods, as well as in the realm of so-called <u>natural</u> goods, will keep society in a position where changes in values have come about accidentally or arbitrarily.   Social theory has warned us continually about the powerful, controlling influence of societal values and norms.   I believe that we should work in the near future to obliterate the idea that there is a difference <u>in kind</u> between what we have called "human nature" and what <u>we have</u> identified as the "physical world."   When such a change in attitude is accomplished, we would then really be able to bring the sources of science to bear more effectively on <u>all</u> human behavior.

Dewey explained more than 50 years ago that what we need, therefore,

> . . . is intelligent examination of the consequences
> that are actually effected by inherited institutions
> and customs, in order that there may be intelligent
> consideration of the ways in which they are to be
> intentionally modified in behalf of generation of
> different consequences (1929, pp. 272-273).

Thus, we need a faith that (a) science can indeed bring about
complete agreement on factual belief about human benavior;
(b) such agreement in factual belief will relatively soon result
in agreement in attitudes held by people; and (c) resultantly
a continuous adaptation of values to the culture's changing
needs will eventually effect the directed reconstruction of all
social institutions (Dewey, 1948, p. xxiii).

At this point, I will bring this chapter to a close by
stating that perhaps what has just been stated in occurring already despite the efforts of many to hold back the hands of
time. A practical application of how this might work is offered
for your consideration in Chapter 18 (see p. 226). In the next
chapter I will introduce the idea of professional ethics as a
necessary supplement to personal ethics for the professional
person. And then in Chapter 6 you will be asked to consider
one plan of attack to ethical decision-making (what I am calling
a "triple-play" approach) that should receive quite ready acceptance at the present.

References

Abelson, R. and Friquegnon, M. Ethics for modern life. New
York: St. Martin Press, 1975.

Ayer, A. J. Language, truth, and logic. (Revised edition).
New York: Dover Publications, Inc., 1946.

Baier, Kurt. The moral point of view. Ithaca, New York:
Cornell University Press, 1958.

de Beauvoir, Simone. The ethics of ambiguity. New York:
The Citadel Press, 1964.

Dewey, John. The quest for certainty. New York: Minton,
Balch and Co., 1929.

Dewey, John and Tufts, James H. (Eds.). Ethics. New York:
    Holt, Rinehart & Winston, Inc., 1932. (Revised edition).

Dewey, John. Problems of men. New York: Henry Holt &
    Co., 1946.

Dewey, John. Reconstruction in philosophy. (Enl. & upd.
    ed.). Boston: The Beacon Press, 1948.

Fletcher, Joseph. Situation ethics: The new morality. Phila-
    delphia: The Westminster Press, 1966.

Fromm, Erich. Man for himself. New York: Fawcett World
    Library, 1967.

Hospers, John. An introduction to philosophical analysis.
    Englewood Cliffs, N. J.: Prentice-Hall, Inc., 1953. See
    2nd edition also dated 1967.

Patterson, C. H. Moral standards: An introduction to ethics.
    New York: The Ronald Press, 1957.

Rand, Ayn. The romantic manifesto. New York & Cleveland:
    The World Publishing Company, 1960.

Rawls, John. A theory of justice. Cambridge, Mass.: Har-
    vard University Press, 1971.

Saturday Review. Watergating on Main Street. This is a spe-
    cial report that appeared in Vol. 3, 3 (November 1, 1975),
    19-28. It includes separate articles by Max Lerner, Tom
    Braden, Irving R. Kaufman, Alexander B. Trowbridge,
    Abraham J. Briloff, Roy M. Fisher, Franz J. Ingelfinger,
    and Fred M. Hechinger.

CHAPTER 5
FROM PERSONAL
TO PROFESSIONAL ETHICS

Up to this point the emphasis has been on the need for the young person in our society to be so educated that there is ample opportunity for him or her to develop rationality as a life competency. The particular concern in this text has been to provide a means whereby a young person might bridge the gap between immaturity and maturity especially insofar as ethical understanding is concerned. Of course, I have been particularly concerned further that the young person be able to apply such "ethical competency" to problems that arise in the course of human motor performance in sport, dance, play, and exercise. Now, however, it is time to introduce the idea of professional ethics as a necessary supplement to personal ethics for the professional person.[1]

On the assumption that we as a profession are no better or worse than most others in regard to the application of ethics to our professional endeavors, it is not difficult to describe our present status. We are confused! As Miller pointed out in "The Tangle of Ethics,"

> Instead of having an impossible ideal confronting
> a practical necessity, we have such a diverse in-
> heritance of ethical ways that no matter which one
> we choose, the others are, at least to some de-
> gree, betrayed" (Ethics for Executive Series, n.d.,
> p. 51).

He points out further that the complex of moral systems that we have inherited (e.g., Hebraic, Christian, Renaissance, Industrial) has undoubtedly contributed to this confusion.

I could argue that this confusion has been gradually, but steadily carried over into all aspects of life. Further, we are now beginning to understand that the twentieth century has indeed become one of marked transition from one era to another,

---

[1] This chapter is based partially on material presented originally as the Dudley Allen Sargent Commemorative Lecture to the National Association for Physical Education in Higher Education, Indianapolis, Indiana, January 8, 1983.

and that our quite blind philosophy of optimism about history's malleability and compatibility in keeping with North American ideals has gradually turned out to be very shortsighted. The weapons stalemate between the two leading powers in the world --which both sides are seeking to maintain--has brought to prominence the importance of non-military determinants (e.g., politics and ideologies). Additionally, a vast ecological crisis has developed, a dilemma that is causing severe financial and health problems to the highly industrialized nations.

In the economic realm, economic collectivism is becoming steadily more apparent with an accompanying drift away from a more primitive, pure form of economic capitalism. Add to this the steady increase in size of what has been termed the welfare state and the expense involved with the spiralling military bu- reaucracy as recessions come and go, not to mention a vast so- cietal transformation that occurred as a result of the multitudi- nous series of protests that arose in the 1960s, and it doesn't take much imagination to understand why the subject of both personal and professional ethics came to the fore sharply in the 1970s.

I wish that it had been possible to tell you that the field of education, and specifically that the field of physical educa- tion and sport, was ready to meet the challenge of the 1970s-- and now the 1980s!--in this regard. However, as Chazan state stated, "Civil, political, and educational leaders frequently cite education's crucial role in the transmission of those 'moral and spiritual values' necessary for life in today's complex world; yet few educational systems make formal provision for such value education . . ." (1973, p. 1). In the profession of sport and physical education, several efforts have been made to iden- tify what our ethical concerns should be. The first such re- port appeared in 1930, and it was the findings of a committee chaired by the late Harry Scott (p. 19). Then in 1950 the Committee on Professional Ethics presented a "suggested code" for use by members of the Association (pp. 323-324, 366). Due to the nature of the profession at that time, these guidelines were based to a very large extent on those recommended for all teachers by the National Education Association. They were only marginally related to physical education and not applicable at all for coaches either within education or serving at other levels of society.

In 1973, under the leadership of the late Leona Holbrook, the (then) American Association for Health, Physical Education, and Recreation sponsored a Working Conference on Ethics prior to the Annual Convention itself. These fine papers were sup- plemented in 1975 by a second series of papers, arranged for

once again by Professor Holbrook, by members of the American
Academy of Physical Education (M. G. Scott, Ed., 1975, pp.
59-79).

Values of a Liberal Society

These were interesting developments, but such sessions
have obviously been too few and too far inbetween. If our
profession is to serve society more effectively in the years
ahead, it is absolutely vital that we be attuned to the greatest
possible extent with the values and norms of our evolving democratic society in North America. Values represent the highest
echelon of the social system level of the entire social action
system. These values may be categorized into such "entities"
as artistic values, scientific values, educational values, social
values, etc. Of course, all types or categories of values must
be values of personalities. The social values of our social system are an integral part of a hierarchy of control and conditioning that exert pressure downward along with the established
norms of the social structure. Together they work to maintain
the pattern consistency of the entire system with a reasonable
degree of flexibility.

Thus, the social values of our system are those values
that are conceived of as representative of the ideal general
character that is desired by those who ultimately hold the power
in our social system. Arguing from the premise that we are
reasonable people, we can accept that "the chief values relevant to professional ethics are (1) governance by law, (2) freedom, (3) protection from injury, (4) equality of opportunity,
(5) privacy, and (6) welfare" (Bayles, 1981, p. 5).

Norms, which are developed in societies as a result of
the values that are consensually held, are the shared, sanctioned rules which govern the second level of the social structure. The average person finds it difficult to separate in his
or her mind the concept of values and norms. Some examples
of norms in the United States are (1) the institution of private
property; (2) private enterprise; (3) the monogamous conjugal
family; and (4) the separation of church and state (Johnson,
1969, 46-58).

The Professions--Yesterday and Today

Granting that important professions need to be attuned
with a society's values and norms, the physical education and
sport profession needs to take a hard look at itself from this

standpoint. There are many who would still argue that our field is not a profession in its own right, that we are really part of the teaching profession, and that therefore the die is cast for us by whatever model is acceptable for the teacher in our society. However, I believe that this truncated version of our field has been abandoned by most who view our professional responsibility in a much broader fashion. To place this topic in brief historical perspective, we recall that the idea of professions and rudimentary preparation for such occupations in life originated in the very early societies. Centers for a type of professional instruction were developed in Greece and Rome as elementary bodies of knowledge became available. It wasn't until about the mid-point of the Middle Ages, however, that universities were organized when the various embryonic professional groups banded together for convenience, power, and protection. The degree granted at that time was in itself a license to practice whatever it was that the graduate "professed"--a practice that continued during the Renaissance at which time the instruction offered became increasingly secularized. However, the term "profession" was not used commonly until relatively recently (Brubacher in Henry, 1962, 46 et ff.).

Such historical background is interesting and provides a perspective, but what is a profession today? Many different meanings are offered, but a profession is usually described as a vocation which requires specific knowledge of some aspect of learning before the prospective practitioner is accepted as a professional person. The now legendary Abraham Flexner recommended six criteria as being characteristic of a profession as long ago as 1915 (Flexner, 1915, 578-581), but Bayles maintains that there is still no definition of the term that is generally accepted at present. He stresses that it is impossible to "characterize professions by a set of necessary and sufficient features possessed by all professions and only by professions (1981, p. 7). Keeping in mind that there are categories of recognized professions such as consulting, scholarly, performing, etc., Bayles suggests an approach whereby necessary features are indicated along with a number of other common features that would tend to elevate an occupation to professional status.

The three necessary aspects or components of a profession that are generally recognized are (1) the need for an extensive period of training, (2) a field where there is a significant intellectual component that must be mastered before the profession is practiced, and (3) a recognition by society that the trained person can provide a basic, important service to its citizens. Professions tend to have other features that are common to most vocations, but they don't seem to be absolutely necessary for such recognition. For example, there may be some sort of licensing by the state or province, or perhaps actual certification by the professional body itself. Members of professionals almost invariably establish professional organizations or societies, but membership may not be mandatory or enforceable. Further, most professional typically have a good deal of autonomy in their work, but those who work in large organizations characterized by considerable bureaucracy often feel constrained in their efforts by too much red tape. Finally, there are other salient features that characterize professions (e.g., near monopoly of services, research and publication) (Ibid.).

We need to keep in mind further that some professions are immediately recognized as such (e.g., law); some groups are striving for such status (e.g., management); and some groups tend to call themselves professionals (e.g., physical educators--when they feel that they are often separate and distinct from school teachers and wish recognition of this assertion). In the course of their development, the various, embryonic professional groups have gradually become conscious of the need for a set of professional ethics--that is, a set of professional obligations that are established as norms for practitioners in good standing to follow. These standards of virtue and vice, principles of responsibility, and rules of duty have usually conformed to one of two types or patterns than have been handed down over the centuries. As Hazard explains:

> One pattern is that of a creed or affirmation of
> professional belief. The ethical principles of med-
> icine or social work, for example, are stated this
> way. The creed is short and obscure, but lofty,
> expressing the aims of the profession and adjur-
> ing personal commitment to them--a kind of oath
> of vocational office. The other pattern is the
> legal code. Not surprisingly, this is the ethical
> format in the legal profession; to an increasing
> extent it is being adopted in accountancy. It
> may be described as a set of detailed administra-
> tive regulations . . . (Hazard, 1978, 50-51).

Hazard explains further that in some cases the regulations are spelled out by the profession itself, whereas in others it is a governmental or public policy that takes the lead. In the final analysis, however, the creed seems to have been accepted as a better approach than the code, perhaps because it is general and less confining to the professionals concerned.

Unfortunately, neither the creed nor the code has spoken too "intelligibly to the fundamental ethical problems arising in the professions in question" (Ibid.).

A Plan for the Future

We may be willing to grant that there is indeed a "tangle of ethics" as explained by Miller above. We can grant also that the field of education has been wary about the introduction of ethical and moral values in the school curriculum because of the separate of church and state tradition that has prevailed on this continent. Nevertheless, in my opinion there is no sound reason for us not to introduce a required course in professional ethics for every prospective teacher/coach specializing in our field at the first possible moment. There are literally hundreds of training programs offered by colleges and universities in every state and province on this continent. By this point you, the reader, may well agree with the stance being taken here. I sincerely hope so. Knowledge of the sport sciences is basic and fundamental. A knowledge of right and wrong ethical behavior for an athlete, teacher, or coach is vital.

For those people already out in the field, we should arrange interesting programs on an annual basis at professional meetings--programs where matters of serious ethical concern and import are placed up front for in-depth consideration, deliberation, and decision. Regional and state (or provincial) clinics on ethical topics are another means whereby we can make up for lost time, for our possible sins of omission in this regard. Still further, we should make an effort to have discussions on ethical matters of all types included in the coaching certification programs that are being made available increasingly for professionals, semiprofessionals, and amateurs (volunteers).

We can obtain some assistance with any such plans from several directions. For example, the American Association of University Professors produced a "Statement on Professional Ethics" that was endorsed by the membership at the Fifty-Second Annual Meeting of the Association. It is very brief and is, in essence, a creed rather than a code (as discussed earlier). It was "necessarily presented in terms of the ideal" and refers (1) to the responsibilities placed upon the professor as the advancement of knowledge is pursued, (2) to the need to encourage "the free pursuit of learning in his students." (3) to the "obligations that derive from common membership in the community of scholars," (4) to the obligation to seek "above all

to be an effective teacher and scholar," and (5) to the fact
that he/she has "the rights and obligations of any citizen"
(American Association of University Professors, 1969, 86-87).
Obviously, this is a fine statement of a creed, but how often
is it referred to, and what are the standards, principles, rules,
and duties that flow from the professional obligations of a professor?

Other assistance could come from the statements that are
made available periodically by the national, state, and provincial education associations. These statements are somewhat
more specific than that by the AAUP above, and therefore
probably more useful. For example, one such document contains five "principles," and each is followed by a series of general and (at times) specific "obligations" that the professional
educator is admonished to observe (NEA-MEA Code of Ethics,
n.d.). Further, The Journal of Higher Education in 1982 devoted an entire issue to "Ethics and the Academic Profession,"
a publication that I commend to you for purchase (1982, 243-
381). As stated, "these articles suggest ways in which aca-
demia might remedy its studied neglect of professional ethics"
(Ibid.). Additionally, the latter part of the issue is devoted
to an in-depth review of the 1980 Report by the Hastings Center that studies the teaching of ethics in higher education
(Ibid., 358-381).

We may all reasonably ask at this point, "Fine, but where
do we in sport and physical education go from here?" To this
I can only respond with the hope that many of you agree that
there is a real need for us all to become better prepared to
face the many ethical and moral issues with which we are being
confronted now and which will undoubtedly continue into the
indefinite future. Of course, I can't prove to you that experiential instruction in ethics and morality will result in a more
ethically minded teacher/coach, but I can state that the odds
are that such would be the case.

Further, there is no doubt in my mind but that we ur-
gently need a teaching/coaching creed that specifically applies
to work in sport and developmental physical activity, not to
mention a carefully devised ethical creed for athletes themselves
that is given prominent attention. These should be developed
as separate but complementary statements. It may even be that
an ethical code will be necessary because of the steadily increasing complexity of the ethical issues and problems with
which both athletes and coaches are being confronted. Which-
ever approach is followed, any such creed and/or code should
be supplemented by carefully developed professional norms--

that is, criteria or acceptable behavior for both teacher/coaches and athletes that can serve as evaluative standards for all who are in a position to be concerned with such evaluation. Such evaluation may also serve as the basis for disciplinary action against those who violate recognized norms.

To become more specific, we would have to ask ourselves what the leading issues or problems of an ethical nature are in today's competitive sport. From the standpoint of the athlete, we encounter such problems as (1) what constitutes fair play or sportsmanship; (2) excessive amounts of violence; (3) excessive use of power over another person (coach or other player); (4) cheating, by deliberately not living up to the rules—or the "spirit" of the rules; (5) use of drugs and similar substances to enhance performance; (6) stealing of equipment; (7) breaking of established training rules; (8) subsidization in universities and colleges (where there is no financial need), etc.

Conversely, what problems or issues of ethical import arise from the actions of coaches? Here we are dealing with items or issues that might well be included in a canon or code of coaching ethics. Here there are problems such as (1) use of overt or covert interpersonal power for selfish reasons; (2) not providing the athlete sufficient opportunity for self-expression and growth; (3) character defamation against another coach or athlete; (4) breaking a contract to take another position; (5) character development by demonstration of illegal or negative traits or actions; (6) withdrawal of services (i.e., should a coach ever strike or work to rule?); (7) undue prejudice in selection of team members, etc.

From a professional standpoint, therefore, there is every reason to support the development within the field of sport and physical education of a "professional arsenal" of ethics and morality. Such a code or canon of ethics—on the assumption that a creed might not ultimately be sufficient—could be a bulwark against the evils, vices, vicissitudes, sins of omission, and sins of commission that tend to creep into our everyday pattern of operation either as athletes involved in highly competitive sport or as volunteers, part-time coaches, or fully professional coaches.

Such a plan is needed because there is too much confusion and vacillation on matters of ethical import. Too many athletes have not received adequate training in this respect, and too many professional coaches and teachers are using common sense, an approach that breaks down typically when foresight and future planning are really needed. Hence we too often find our colleagues taking a very narrow, ill-considered approach when controversial issues of ethical concern arise. This is often highly damaging to our field's public image and gives the public a hazy occupation of what our highest aims and objectives are.

Today we hear much about the pursuit of excellence in North America and how our standards are declining somewhat. To me this means that we do indeed want to develop outstanding students, but it also means that we want all students, regardless of their inherent potential, to be motivated by a desire for excellence (insofar as this is possible for each individual). However, over and above such "excellence" we must have students with a sound ethical approach personally who then go on to their lifelong careers with the necessary knowledge and attitudes that will result a sound professional ethics as well. Failing this, any outstanding person at any given moment could deliberately or unwittingly undo by dishonesty or lack of positive action any technical excellence gained in a traditional classroom environment.

This brings us to a close with Part I on this text. In Part II, you will be presented with one plan of attack to ethical decision-making with which you will be asked to experiment for a substantive part of this course experience.

References

American Association of University Professors. Statement on professional ethics. AAUP Bulletin 55 (1), March, 1969, 86-87.

Bayles, Michael D. Professional ethics. Belmont, CA: Wadsworth Publishing Company, 1981.

Brubacher, J. S. The evolution of professional education. In Proceedings (Part II) of the National Society for the Study of Education (N. B. Henry, Ed.). Chicago, IL: The National Society for the Study of Education, 1962.

Chazan, B. I. and Soltis, J. F. (Eds.). Moral education. New York: Teachers College Press, 1973.

Committee on Professional Ethics. Suggested code of ethics for teachers of physical education. Journal of Health, Physical Education, and Recreation 21 (6), June, 1950, 323–324, 366.

Flexner, Abraham. Is social work a profession? In Proceedings of the National Conference on Charities and Corrections. Chicago, IL: Hildmann, 1915.

Hazard, G. C., Jr. Capitalist ethics. Yale Alumni Magazine and Journal XLI (8), April, 1978, 50–51.

Hospers, John. An introduction to philosophical analysis. Englewood Cliffs, N. J.: Prentice-Hall, Inc., 1953.

Johnson, Harry M. The relevance of the theory of action to historians. Social Science Quarterly, June, 1969, 46–58.

Journal of Higher Education (The). Ethics and the academic profession. 53 (3), May–June, 1982, 243–381.

Miller, S. H. The tangle of ethics. In Ethics for executives series. Boston, MA: Harvard Business Review, n.d.

NEA-MEA Code of Ethics. Lansing, Michigan, n.d. 3 p.

Scott, Harry A. (Chairman). Preliminary report of the Committee on Professional Ethics. Journal of Health and Physical Education 1 (11), November, 1930, 19.

Scott, M. Gladys (Ed.). Realms of meaning (The Academy Papers). Washington, D.C.: The American Academy of Physical Education, 1975.

PART II
ONE PLAN OF ATTACK

CHAPTER 6
A TRIPLE-PLAY APPROACH:
FROM KANT TO MILL TO ARISTOTLE

In Chapters 6 and 7 of Part II, a two-part plan of attack for ethical decision-making in sport and physical education will be recommended for your consideration.[1] When you are confronted with an ethical problem to be resolved--if indeed a person recognizes it as such--initially the first reaction is to state (perhaps implicitly) "What should I do?" Earlier in this text I have argued that typically one hardly knows where to turn for some basis upon which to formulate an answer or a response.

In Chapter 4 six major ethical routes extant in the Western world were presented for your review and consideration. Of this number I expressed a personal preference for what might be called a scientific ethics approach. Nevertheless, here in Part II I am first going to call upon three names of philosophers who were mentioned in Chapter 2 in the brief history of philosophical ideas about the "good" and the "bad"--Immanuel Kant, John Stuart Mill, and Aristotle. I am doing this because I am now convinced that some of their basic thought on ethical matters provide an "easy entrance" into this topic for most young people in this culture at present.

In case you should think that I am encouraging you to become a "philosophical sophist or charlatan" because it's the simplest way to get at a difficult subject, let me hasten to add that I have great respect for these men and the contributions that each one of them has made to the history of philosophy. I must admit also that we are all creatures of our own culture, and that therefore their ideas have considerable appeal to me despite my steadily growing inclination toward a scientific ethics approach as the 20th century has progressed.

The progression of major ideas to be presented moves from certain underlying principles that each has expressed, so

---

[1] The basic approach in Chapter 6 (not the term "triple-play," however) was recommended by Professor Richard Fox of the Department of Philosophy at Cleveland State University. We superimposed this approach on Toulmin's "layout for a jurisprudential argument" in Chapter 7 to round out the "plan of attack."

it occurred to me that it might be helpful to draw an analogy
with the sport of baseball. Thus, I decided to call the first
phase of this overall "plan of attack" by what is considered to
be one of the most skillful and fortuitous maneuvers in baseball, the triple-play. Thus, we have the triple-play approach,
or an approach to ethical decision-making that progresses from
Kant, then to Mill, and finally to Aristotle. Or, in other words,
it moves from Kant's test of consistency, to Mill's test of consequences, and then to Aristotle's test of intentions. In the
pages that follow, then, each of these steps will be discussed
in some detail. Then, in Chapter 7, I will demonstrate how I
believe these three steps can be "neatly superimposed" on
Stephen Toulmin's layout for a jurisprudential argument.

(Note: Although I will not discuss this topic specifically,
I should make mention that there are various forms of ethical
egoism. If this approach were to be followed, one might introduce a "test of reward for the agent." Here adherents emphasize the goal of a person's own self-interest; e.g., Epicureanism, Rand's rational self-interest theory.)

Kant's Test of Consistency (Step 1)

Without going into any detail about Kant's overall position (see p. 16), it should be explained here that he did distinguish sharply between naturalistic ethics and moral law.
His categorical imperative implied a moral code above and beyond any law of nature (e.g., man's strong desire for happiness or gratification). Kant postulated a universalizability criterion as the most fundamental moral principle, and it is this
that we are using for Step 1 or our test of consistency. In
other words, we should "act only on that maxim which you can
will to be a universal law."

The similarity between this and our culture's Golden Rule
is, of course, immediately apparent to most. Kant's more precise statement of the "golden rule" may well in time be considered to be his greatest contribution to the subject of ethics
--despite what some draw to our attention immediately as its
obvious weaknesses. George Bernard Shaw's cryptic retort to
this was to suggest the following: "Don't do unto others as
you would have them do to you--their tastes might be different." Kaufmann felt that the negative formulation of the Gold-
en Rule was far superior to the original, but it too had serious
deficiencies (1973, p. 188). In an ABC-TV political discussion
recently, George Will quipped, "Do unto others as fast as they
do unto you" (Jan. 16, 1983). We can appreciate that there
are maxims that could not be universalized, and also that there

are ones that it might not be desirable to universalize. Thus, we must ask ourselves by what criterion are we to tell which maxims should be universalized, and this takes us right back to the starting point.

Admitting that there are weaknesses to the test of consistency, or the criterion of universalizability, I am nevertheless recommending that your first question to ask when considering one of the many ethical problems soon to appear be the following: IS IT POSSIBLE TO "UNIVERSALIZE" THE ACTION TO ALL PEOPLE ON EARTH? Now we will proceed to Step 2.

Mill's Test of Consequences (Step 2)

Step 2 of our "triple-play approach" has been taken from our heritage of philosophic utilitarianism. For the maxim "Act so as to bring about the greatest good possible," we are in the debt of John Stuart Mill, as well as another significant philosopher, Jeremy Bentham. Here we have what may be called a "test of consequences" to invoke--that is, what the total effects of your action be? Further, we should be concerned with the promotion of the maximum amount of net, not gross, happiness. Such thoughts come to mind at this point as whether an action is fair, just, beneficient, and permits autonomy on the part of the other person(s) involved. Here we should presumably act in accordance with the best available evidence.

Recalling that with ethical considerations we are concerned with good and bad, and right and wrong, consider for a moment Mill's famous definition of "what is wrong?"

> We do not call anything wrong, unless we mean to
> imply that a person ought to be punished in some
> way or other for doing it; if not by law, by the
> opinion of his fellow creatures; if not by opinion,
> by the reproaches of his conscience. This seems
> to be the real turning point of the distinction be-
> tween morality and simple expediency (Utilitarian-
> ism, V).

What then is the logic of this second step we are offering for your use in this three-step approach? Kalish and Montague offer the following formal definition: "An argument is valid if it is possible for its premises to be true and its conclusion false" (1964, p. 3). Well and good; however, one tends to say "Huh?" at first reading to this statement. So let's try something like, "If all the premises are true, then the

conclusion will be true." Using basic modus ponens logic,
then, the following premises and conclusion apply in this instance:

1. The act that--on the basis of the best evidence available at the time of acting--pro-
   duces the greatest total good is right.

2. This act will produce the greatest total good.

3. Therefore, this act is right. (modus ponens)

This, then, is the basic utilitarian approach for what has subsequently been called act-utilitarianism. (A second utilitarian
approach called rule-utilitarianism will be described immediately
below.)

"So far, so good," you may be saying, "this second step
seems quite simple compared to the first one recommended."
Unfortunately, this is not quite true, because a number of
questions may be raised to show that--as usual--things are
never as simple as they seem at first glance. For example,
suppose you have made a solemn promise to your best friend,
and suddenly you realize that by keeping that promise you
won't be doing the most good? Or, to consider another problematic situation, suppose you had a worthless son and a really
intelligent, hard-working nephew both of whom needed assistance to attend college, should you help your nephew before
your own son on the assumption that you could do more good
that way? The archetypic example of the bind that one could
find himself in when attempting to follow act-utilitarianism to
the letter would be something like the following situation: You
are living with your crippled father, a wonderful old person,
in the family home. To help with finances, you have taken in
a roomer, a brilliant, young cancer researcher. One evening
you return home late, and you find your home ablaze. You
know that both your father and the young researcher are
sleeping on the second floor. Question: whom do you attempt
to rescue first?

Rule-Utilitarianism. There is a second type of utilitarianism known as rule-utilitarianism that you may find more
appealing than the approach just described. With this approach
your are admonished not to judge the rightness of an act by
act's consequences. Now you are to judge the rightness or
wrongness of an act by the consequences of adopting the rule
under which the particular act falls. Following the consequences of a rule instead of a particular act often colors a

problematic situation markedly.   One reason for this, of course, is that it is often extremely difficult to find the best rule!

Let us suppose, for example, that you are fully convinced that the world has seen too much killing and bloodshed. Accordingly you vow that you personally would never take another human life.   Then two days later you find yourself in a situation where, if you don't act quickly and decisively to harm an attacker, you undoubtedly stand a good chance of being killed yourself.   So you take a knife from a drawer and plunge it into the attacker's body.   He dies before the ambulance arrives, and somewhat later you realize that you broke your vow about the sanctity of human life.   Can you think of a better rule?   How about pledging that you would never initiate violence of a serious nature against another, but that you do see the validity of self-defense?   What we have with rule-utilitarianism, therefore, is an approach where you search for the best rules to adopt in human relations of an ethical nature--that is, rules that will ultimately do the most good.

There are undoubtedly other examples that you can think of to show that this second step, the test of consequences, is not infallible no matter whether you base your actions on the consequences of the individual act, or on the consequences of adopting the best rule to follow prior to ethical action.   Nevertheless, the test of consistency (or universalizability) first, and now this test of consequences, do offer a person some criteria infinitely better than mere common sense upon which to proceed when it is necessary to arrive at the best possible ethical decision under a given set of circumstances.

(Note: Before continuing with Step 3, the test of intentions, it should be mentioned that there are also theories of conduct not based on consequences only known as deontological theories.   This unfortunate choice of a term to describe an approach (deontological) contrasts with that of teleological theories where they are based on consequences only.   With deontological theories we often need to consider some of the probable consequences of an act (a future orientation), and often certain of the conditions also in which an act was out (a past orientation). These are referred to as duties of justice, or fidelity, or gratitude, for example.   A duty of justice would be based on acting fairly by providing equal treatment, whereas a duty of fidelity would be a situation where you had made a vow or promise to another person.   The duty of gratitude obviously needs no fur further explanation.)

Aristotle's Test of Intentions (Step 3)

Step 3 of the triple-play approach we may call the test of intentions. For this advice we turn to the ancient Greek philosopher, Aristotle, who asked in the Nicomachean Ethics, "What were the conditions under which the act was performed?" Virtue, as defined by Aristotle, "is concerned with emotion and action, and emotions and actions that are voluntary are objects for praise or blame, while those that are involuntary are objects for pardon and sometimes for pity" (Aristotle in Loomis, 1943, p. 113). Aristotle is arguing here that in a study of virtue, it is essential to know whether actions were voluntary or involuntary. He points out further that this knowledge would be especially useful for lawmakers. For example, an act carried out under compulsion or from ignorance would be considered involuntary and perhaps pardonable.

A very practical example of these ideas would be a situation where a person has committed a crime (e.g., murder), and we certainly would not wish to see such an act "universalized" and carried out against all people on earth. Further, this particular act (murder) had most serious consequences and did not contribute to the greatest (net) good or happiness of anyone (in fact, the opposite was the case). Thus, if we wish to judge this seemingly heinous crime as good, bad, or neutral, it can be argued that we need to know under what conditions the act was carried out. Here also, then, as was noted above at the end of Step 2, a person may have done something that would typically be judged as being wrong--and yet we might forgive him or her completely of partially because of the conditions under which the act was carried out. For example, we occasionally read in the newspaper that someone has done harm to or killed another person who had earlier committed a major crime against that person's relative. In such cases we might feel that justice had been done even though a law had been broken. Or we might, conversely, feel very sorry for the original perpetrator of a crime upon whom revenge had been carried out. Thus, even though this person had originally committed what we would call a major crime, we might still feel sympathetically inclined to him because we owed him a debt of gratitude, or because we had been very close friends to him in the past.

The question of the intentions of the person who commits what is determined to be a wrong is evidence when a law court considers a case of murder. A premeditated case of murder is called first-degree murder, whereas a so-called crime of passion that results in the death of another may be identified as second-degree murder and presumably less blameworthy. Further, if someone kills another by hitting him accidentally with an automobile in a street accident, this is designated as manslaughter. Finally in this vein, we have read about the extremely low percentage of convictions in Italy when a husband commits murder in the case of his wife's accused lover. Evidently many feel this is justifiable homicide in certain countries!

In regard to the topic of intentions, or behavior motivation, Aristotle stated that people acted according to one or more of the following reasons: chance, nature, compulsion, habit, reason, passion, and desire. An examination of this proposed list leads one to conclude that there are some acts where it is questionable whether an act is indeed involuntary or voluntary. When such doubt arises, Aristotle designated such an act to be of a "mixed character." Some actions, then, "are voluntary, although in the abstract they may be called involuntary, because no one would choose any such act in itself" (Loomis, 1943, p. 114).

Concluding Statement

In bringing Chapter 6 to a close, we should explain that the utilitarian theory of punishment is retributive--that is, the offender deserves to be punished according to the severity of the crime committed. Presumably society has advanced beyond the Old Testament's "eye for an eye" dictum; nevertheless, a thief in Iran may still have his hand cut off! Also, changing times have brought about many cries for capital punishment in countries where the death penalty had been abolished--for terrorists, police killers, etc.

In the 1970s John Rawls presented a conception of "justice as fairness," and this was considered by some as a "rescue attempt" for what has been called distributive justice (Rawls, 1971). Shortly thereafter, however, Walter Kaufmann argued that "distributions can never be just" no matter how carefully we may try. In his Without Guilt and Justice: From Decidophobia to Autonomy, he attempts to lead us one step farther away from retributive and distributive justice. Explaining that he envisions four cardinal virtues (honesty, courage, humbition --a fusion of ambition with humility, and love involving the sharing of plights of others), he states that a person's life goal should be what he calls "creative autonomy" (1973).

Finally, then, as we move along to Chapter 7, I am recommending that you approach each ethical situation with which you will be confronted in this experiential approach to ethical decision-making by first applying these three tests, 1, 2, and 3, in sequential order. Next, as will be explained in the following chapter, I will be asking you to employ Stephen Toulmin's layout for a jurisprudential argument in combination with the application of the three tests explained in this section.

References

Aristotle. Nicomachean Ethics (Book III, Chapter 1). In Aristotle (L. R. Loomis, Ed.). New York: W. J. Black, 1943. (Translated by J. E. C. Welldon).

Hospers, John. An introduction to philosophical analysis. (2nd edition). Englewood Cliffs, N. J.: Prentice-Hall, Inc., 1967. Earlier this book was most helpful, and ideas from it undoubtedly are evident in Chapter 6.

Kalish, D. and Montague, R. Logic: Techniques of formal reasoning. New York: Harcourt, Brace & World, Inc., 1964.

Kant, Immanuel. Fundamental principles of the metaphysics of ethics. Translated by O. Manthey-Zorn. New York: D. Appleton-Century Company, 1938.

Kaufmann, Walter. Without guilt and justice: From decidophobia to autonomy. New York: Peter H. Wyden, Inc., 1973.

Mill, John Stuart. Utilitarianism (V), 1861.

Rawls, John. A theory of justice. Cambridge, MA: Harvard University Press, 1971.

CHAPTER 7
DEVELOPING THE LAYOUT FOR
A JURISPRUDENTIAL ARGUMENT

Now that the tests of consistency, consequences, and intentions have been outlined in some detail for you to employ in sequential order as you confront a problem in ethical decision-making, I am asking you to superimpose these steps (1, 2, and 3) on what Stephen Toulmin has called his "layout for a jurisprudential argument" (Toulmin, 1964, p. 95). This is a formally valid argument in proper form that is similar to arguments employed in jurisprudence and mathematics and is "laid out in a tidy and simple geometrical form" (Ibid.). (For a detailed treatment of this argument layout, as it might be employed in an ethical situation, the reader is encouraged to refer at this point also to Chapter 20, pp. 253-273. Here the "bare bones" of the argument will be employed for illustrative purposes.)

In discussing the layout of arguments, Toulmin explains that "an argument is like an organism," and then he proceeds to designate the "chief anatomical units of the argument--its 'organs', so to speak" (p. 94 et ff.). I believe that Toulmin's logical apparatus--the logical form of a valid argument as one in which there is a combination of a formal, procedural argument in proper form with a straightforward, elementary geometrical form--has considerable merit for future use by sport and physical education philosophers.

In Chapter 20 this type of jurisprudential argument is employed to explain, not prove, the possible misuse of interpersonal power that a coach may exert over a recruited, subsidized athlete (and vice versa to a lesser degree). Then I went on to demonstrate the gradual development of an argument that should lead one to the conclusion that society would normally be expected to control the abuse of such power by coaches.

Step 1 (From Data to Conclusion)

The reader must understand that this is not being presented as formal logic in which D (Data) by definition leads us to C (Conclusion). This is not a modus ponens situation. It is simply the beginning of a rational argument that one might expect to hear in a court of law. I am simply asking you to

56

move forward gradually, steadily, and reasonably from D to C, from the data to what seems to be a reasonable conclusion. In this particular example taken from U. S. intercollegiate athletics, these initial steps might appear as follows:

A head coach in the U.S. is in a position to exercise undue interpersonal power over recruited, subsidized athletes So Universities should control undue use of such power in this society

From there (see p. 257 et ff.) I went on to explain nine different ways that a head coach might employ the interpersonal power that he or she has at hand, elements that in my opinion must be employed very carefully if at all. One example of this is that the head coach has fear as a source of power--fear that can be overt, subtle and is often irrational.

Step 2 (Warrants)

Step 2 in the Toulmin argument layout involves the creation of "general hypothetical statements, which can act as bridges, and authorize the sort of step to which our particular argument commits us" (Ibid., p. 98). Such statements are called Warrants (W) so that they may be distinguished from both Data (D) and Conclusions (C). A warrant may be explained further as a sanction, justification, practical standard, canon or argument, value, or norm. So, on our way to the conclusion of the argument started in Step 1, I am now asking you to add a warrant (a "How do you get there?" if you will) to the basic question mandated initially ("What conclusion might you draw from the facts on hand?"), or the data and the conclusion.

With the present argument, therefore, the warrant (W) can be a statement such as "In a democratic society it is considered morally wrong to use another person as a means to an end entirely or largely through the employment of deception, exploitation, and/or treachery." If I were now to symbolize the relationship among the three elements (D, W, and C, it could look as follows:

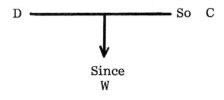

Or, to carry the present example through Step 2:

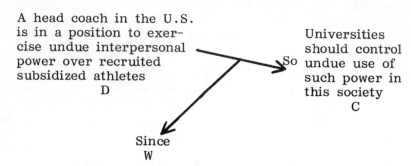

A head coach in the U.S.
is in a position to exer-
cise undue interpersonal
power over recruited
subsidized athletes
D

So

Universities
should control
undue use of
such power in
this society
C

Since
W

In a democratic society it
is considered wrong to use
another person as a means
to an end entirely or largely
through the employment of
deception, exploitation, and/
or treachery

The warrant here is designated as "incidental and explanatory," its function "being simply to register explicitly the
legitimacy of the steps involved and to refer it back to the
larger class of steps whose legitimacy is being presupposed"
(Ibid., p. 100). Thus, warrants are general, but data are
specific. Warrants are needed in all fields of endeavor, if we
wish to judge any ideas or arguments on a rational basis.

Step 3 (Modal Qualifier and Condition of Exception)

Of course, there are categories of warrants, because it
is often necessary to convey different degrees of intensity or
force. Therefore, we often find it necessary to make use of a
qualifying term just prior to the statement of the conclusion
(e.g., necessarily, presumably, probably, under "x" condition).
All of this makes the development of a valid argument more difficult and complex, because any such distinction or qualifier
will affect the import of the conclusion (C) that may be drawn.
For example, in the argument that has been developed so far,
I might ask myself whether D necessarily (interpreted as needfully or essentially) leads to C on the basis of the W that has
been provided.

This qualifying term is designated as a <u>Modal Qualifier</u> (Q), and it obviously helps to both clarify and make more complex the nature of the argument.   Q relates to W, yet it is distinct from it in that it speaks about W's "ability" to sound authoritative (or not) about the relationship between D and C. In this example I am bold enough to recommend that the modal qualifier (Q) should be interpreted to mean "necessarily." (The reasoning for this is explained on p. 263.)

The second part of Step 3 relates to the warrant also. It is called a <u>Condition of Exception</u> (R), and it too may influence the strength of the warrant markedly.   In fact, the condition of exception (R) can offer particular circumstances of greater or lesser import that might negate or even refute the authority of the warrant (W).   However, it negates the warrant in a somewhat different manner, and I must be careful to characterize the degree of force or intensity that each condition of exception (or rebuttal) (R) can exert on the conclusion (C) being drawn.   For example, some coaches in the present environment almost seem to be arguing for complete freedom of action such as the "survival of the fittest" approach put forth by Plato in the Gorgias (1961, p. 73).   (For a fuller discussion of this point, see p. 264.)

In Step 3, therefore, I can now symbolize the relationship among a total of five elements (D, C, C, Q, and R) as follows:

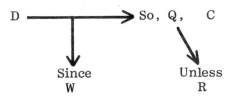

Or carrying the present argument literally through Step 3, I might have something like the following:

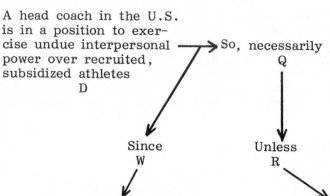

A head coach in the U.S. is in a position to exercise undue interpersonal power over recruited, subsidized athletes
D

So, necessarily
Q

Universities should control undue use of such power in this society
C

Since
W

Unless
R

In a democratic society it is considered wrong to use another person as a means to an end entirely or largely through the employment of deception, exploitation, and/or treachery

1. Athlete is actually not hurt by use of such power
2. Athlete doesn't believe he/she is being used
3. Athlete is not unhappy about being used
4. Coach didn't fully appreciate the extent to which he was using the athlete
5. Coach was being pressured inordinately to win
6. Society is unwilling to curb undue use of such power

Step 4 (Backing)

In Step 4, which is the final step to be discussed in the "rounding out" of the argument that I have been developing, we return to a further consideration of the nature of a warrant. The warrant, as explained in Step 2, is a general, hypothetical, bridge-like statement used to authorize or justify the conclusion being drawn on the basis of the data (evidence) provided. The warrant suggested here explained that it is wrong in this society to use a person through some form exploitation, deception, and/or treachery.

The above notwithstanding, an inquiry should be made as to the applicability of the warrant as stated in <u>all</u> cases in a democratic society. This is why I raised some possible conditions of exception (R)--and also some possible delineations of the coach's intentions. (The question of <u>intentions</u> will be

treated shortly, but further discussion of the conditions of rebuttal and exception is included on p. 265).

One condition of rebuttal (R) pointed out that North
American society seems unwilling to curb the undue use of interpersonal power by the coach. Why this seems to be so is
also explained elsewhere (p. 266), but this argument may also
be placed in another context altogether--say, for the sake of
this discussion, in another society or culture. This warrant
may be relevant and applicable in what is called the Western
world; however, I must also ask to what extent it would be
relevant and applicable in all countries in other cultures. Of
course, I hope it is most relevant and applicable there too, but
then I must ask myself if society "looks the other way" there
too--as it seems to do all too often in the United States.

At any rate, in Step 4 my aim is to present the idea of
providing Backing (B) for the warrant that I chose to use in
developing the pattern or layout of this argument. Here the
backing (B) supplements or strengthens the warrant even further. Thus, I state that the strength of the warrant becomes
even greater when it is appreciated that the use of interpersonal power through deception, exploitation, and/or treachery
typically involves entrapment and manipulation as well! As a
result I am able to add the following backing (B), preceded by
the words "On account of," to strengthen the warrant (W) even
further: "The written and unwritten rules, and laws of the
society. Manipulation of this type usually involves deception
(or even coercion) to which there is a moral reaction because
of the effort to control or elicit behavior through interference
with another's operative goals and thereby to destroy or seriously damage his/her personal dignity."

The taking of Step 4 ends the presentation of a recommended layout to be employed in the ethical analysis of a jurisprudential argument. Of course, it is recognized that there is
a "field-dependence" for backing of this type (i.e., it matters
a great deal whether one is dealing with ethics, physics, or
law, to name three). It might have been sufficient simply to
state the warrant (W) and leave it at that without adding the
backing (B). As Toulmin argues, "the warrant itself is more
than a repetition of these facts; it is a general moral of a practical character, about the ways in which we can safely argue in
view of these facts" (p. 106). Finally, in this pattern of argument (that started as "D, so C"), it ought to be possible to
turn it around and move from right to left (or "C, because D").

In Step 4, then, a sixth element called backing (B) has been introduced. Thus, D, W, B, Q, R, and C are all worked into the presentation of the complete argument and are symbolized as follows:

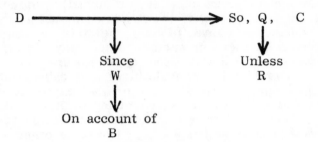

Or, to carry the present argument forward in detail through the final Step 4:

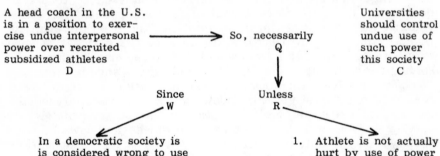

A head coach in the U.S. is in a position to exercise undue interpersonal power over recruited subsidized athletes
D

So, necessarily
Q

Universities should control undue use of such power this society
C

Since
W

Unless
R

In a democratic society is is considered wrong to use another person as a means to an end entirely or largely through the employment of deception, exploitation, and/or treachery

On account of
B

The written and unwritten rules, regulations, and laws that exist in our society. Manipulation of this type usually involves deception (or even coercion) to which there is a moral reaction because of the effort to control or elicit behavior through interference with another's operative goals and thereby to destroy or seriously damage his/her personal dignity

1. Athlete is not actually hurt by use of power
2. Athlete doesn't believe he/she is being used
3. Athlete is not unhappy about being used
4. Coach didn't fully appreciate the extent to which he was using the athlete
5. Coach was being pressured inordinately to win
6. Society is unwilling to curb undue use of such power by coach

Superimposition of Triple-Play Approach

Now that the recommended layout for an argument has been discussed in detail, it is appropriate to continue with the "blending" of the two phases of our "plan of attack" to employ in the resolution of ethical problems in sport and physical education. It can be readily seen that Toulmin's layout for an argument can be used to resolve just about any type of argument, theoretical or practical, in any field of endeavor. However, the primary concern here is with ethical decision-making, so it is necessary for you, the reader, to determine the ethical merits or demerits of the situation at hand. Accordingly, you are being asked to approach the controversial debates in Part III first by applying the tests of consistency (universalizability), consequences, and intentions and, second, by using this technique for the development of an argument layout.

When these two steps have been completed, it will then be a relatively simple matter to superimpose the elements of consistency (universalizability), consequences, and intentions upon the layout diagram that you have developed. In an effort to make this point most clearly, the following points may be made:

1. Consistency (Universalizability)--we certainly would not wish to universalize a situation where one person would use another as a means to an end entirely or largely through the employment of deception, exploitation, and/or treachery.

2. Consequences--if such misuse of interpersonal power were consistently carried out in a society, the consequences of such continued activity would not promote the greatest (net) good or happiness.

3. Intentions--the intentions of the person(s) misusing others in this way must be considered. Can he/she(they) argue that it is being done for the other's ultimate good? Is there a lack of awareness on the part of the coach, for example, or is the coach being pressured inordinately to win by some element in society?

Keeping the above in mind, then, as you begin the series of debates about controversial issues in Part III, your task-- depending upon whether you are on the affirmative or the negative team--will be to devise the "best fit" between the argument layout (for your side) and the tests explained above. You and your partner will then carry through with the debate as best you can in an effort to convince the class that you are the best debaters and that your ethical decision on one specific, controversial issue is the right one. (Subsequently, in Part IV, your task will become somewhat more complex. There you will be presented with a series of ten case problems that actually occurred in sport and physical education. This will add another dimension to the total experience that should make your reflection eminently practical.)

Concluding Statement

To round out this chapter (and Part II as well), the following is a symbolic description of how this merging of the triple-play approach and the argument layout will fit together:

Symbolic Description of Merger

Key:

D = <u>data</u> (a statement of a situation that prevails, including evidence, elements, sources, samples of facts)

C = <u>conclusion</u> (claim or conclusion that we are seeking to establish)

W = <u>warrant</u> (practical standards or canons of argument designed to provide an answer to the question, "How do you get there?")

Q = <u>modal qualifier</u> (adverbs employed to qualify conclusions based on strength of warrants--e.g., necessarily, probably)

R = <u>condition of exception</u> (conditions of rebuttal or exception that tend to refute the conclusion)

B =   backing (categorical statements of fact that lend further
           support to the "bridge-like" warrants)

An Example of "One Plan of Attack"
for Ethical Decision-Making

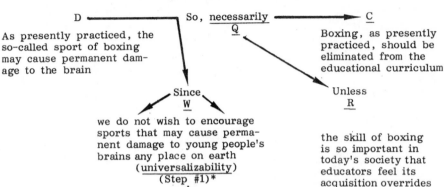

D ●────────────   So, necessarily ●────────▶   C

As presently practiced, the   Q   Boxing, as presently
so-called sport of boxing   practiced, should be
may cause permanent dam-   eliminated from the
age to the brain   educational curriculum

                          Since   Unless
                            W   R

                   we do not wish to encourage
                   sports that may cause perma-   the skill of boxing
                   nent damage to young people's   is so important in
                   brains any place on earth   today's society that
                   (universalizability)   educators feel its
                   (Step #1)*   acquisition overrides
                                                   the possibility of
                   On account of   brain damage
                        B   (intentions)
                                                   *(Step #3)
                   there is mounting evidence
                   and expert opinion indicating   and/or
                   that such damage occurs and
                   is cumulative   means are provided
                   (consequences)   whereby the skills
                   (Step #2)*   of boxing may be
                                                   learned with suffi-
                                                   cient protection
     * Step #1, Step #2, and Step #3   against possible
       apply to the "triple-play approach"   brain damage
       being recommended for possible use
       in ethical decision-making (i.e.,
       from universalizability to conse-
       quences to intentions--or from Kant
       to Mill to Aristotle)

References

Plato.   Gorgias.   In Masterpieces of world philosophy.
      (F. M. Magill, Ed.).   New York: Harper & Row, 1961.

Toulmin, S.   The uses of argument.   New York: Cambridge
      University Press, 1964.

PART III
DEBATING CONTROVERSIAL ISSUES

CHAPTER 8
PROPOSED DEBATING PROCEDURES

The value of competitive debating in the professional preparation of sport and physical education teacher/coaches has not been generally recognized. After using this teaching technique for a number of years at both the undergraduate and graduate levels of instruction, I have become thoroughly convinced that it can be an interesting, intellectually stimulating, and beneficial experience for all concerned. It is for this reason that I decided to employ this technique as part of the experential involvement planned for the course in ethics and morality.

A Communication Pro

Teachers in general, and especially teachers in our field, are going to spend the rest of their lives defending their beliefs, especially about controversial issues, as they seek to make as strong a case as possible for the various phases of their work. Our teacher/coaches are usually extroverted individuals who love to talk in the gymnasium, the swimming pool, or on the athletic field. (In fact, we are usually admonished to talk less and to keep our charges moving to a greater extent!) However, when they are forced to break away from the vernacular and speak somewhat more formally in the class, at a teachers' meeting, or at a local service-club luncheon, they often find the transition somewhat difficult.

After working in the field for more than 40 years, I am continually amazed to find out how little experience young people have in getting up on their feet and talking seriously and constructively about a topic or issue to their peers. It is really interesting, but also discouraging, to watch personalities change before my very eyes--and usually for the worse. They want to read a prepared statement--usually monotonously with little voice inflection. I practically force them to speak from notes organized in outline fashion; in fact, I urge the members of the audience (the class) to mark them down for such rote procedure on the individual evaluation sheets that are handed in anonymously at the end of the class session.

Thus, I am thoroughly convinced that giving students the opportunity to organize their thoughts in a logical sequence,

to work cooperatively with a partner to decide who will say
what, to then present the material interestingly in front of a
group of peers, and finally to attempt to refute the arguments
of an opponent under a certain amount of pressure can be one
of the finest experiences that a professional student can have
in his or her undergraduate career. It has been interesting to
note as well that many graduate students, even those who have
taught for several years, seem to need this experience almost
as much as do the undergraduates.

A Procedural Pattern

Debates such as these should not be overly formalized,
but there are certain rules that should be established. Typically, there is a chairperson appointed in advance (if the teacher doesn't fulfill this function). The topic is written on the
blackboard, as are the names, order of involvement, and team
of each speaker (affirmative or negative). There are usually
two teams with each team generally consisting of two speakers.

If possible, it is advisable to have a student on the affirmative team once and on the negative team once. Coeducational
debating is even more interesting than dividing the sexes, although for certain topics such a division provides for natural
rivalries between the sexes. Students should be allowed to express preferences in sequential order for topics, and then the
instructor does as best possible to involve people where they
want to be. Of course, this is not always possible, and I
often find myself flipping coins or suggesting to students that
they ask someone to change topics or dates with them (if absolutely necessary). This can be a nuisance, so the instructor
should be careful not to distribute a "final" schedule too soon.

The teacher may have to use his or her judgment to prevent one team from being stacked against another, as uneven-
ness of ability tends to destroy interest in the actual debate.
It is fun sometimes to hear a student debating against a position that everyone knows he accepts in everyday life. The
quality of the debate depends, of course, on the ability of the
speakers and the preparation they have made. Although the
quality of the debates improves markedly as students learn from
their experience and that of their classmates, the teacher
should be prepared to guide people to, or actually provide,
helpful items of information.

(Note: Since students had neither debated nor been involved with ethical analysis previously, I found it to be most
helpful to them if we all five met together the day before the

debate for about thirty minutes to make certain that all was
"on track." I even encouraged students to telephone me that
evening if necessary.)

Usually in a debate each team has two constructive
speeches and two rebuttal speeches. This procedure was modified for the typical 50-minute period by eliminating one of the
rebuttal speeches from each team's format. The suggested time
schedule, therefore, would be as follows:

1. First affirmative – 7 minutes

2. First negative – 7 minutes

3. Second affirmative – 7 minutes

4. Second negative – 7 minutes

5. Negative rebuttal – 5 minutes

6. Affirmative rebuttal – 5 minutes

Following the above format would consume approximately
38 minutes of a 50-minute class period, allowing a bit of time
at the beginning of class for organization, and some time at the
end for the gathering of evaluations from the class members.
These evaluations or appraisals serve a most useful purpose,
since most students are anxious to have a critical appraisal of
their efforts. As instructor I filled one out too and then later,
if I discovered that the large majority of the students rated
one or more students significantly higher or lower than I did,
I would make some alteration in my personal assessment. Usually we had some further discussion about the debate before
the class ended. First, however, I asked the students to complete their evaluation sheets, and then we took a vote (by
hand) to see which team was the winner. (While the voting
was being carried out, the debaters were asked to bow their
heads and "pray silently" to avoid embarrassment on anyone's
part.)

The use of students not involved in the debate to serve
as judges by recording their constructive criticism and decisions worked out very nicely. The debaters usually stayed for
a few moments after class to look over the written evaluations,
and often people came by my office later to read them carefully. People were very good sports about the whole affair, all
accepting the principle that the team that debates best should
win. If the affirmative does what the proposition requires, it
should win. The decision whould be based on whether the affirmative has shown that it is advisable to adopt the proposed
plan, or whether the negative has refuted the plan. With the

debates on ethics and morality, the discussion revolved about whether present practice in regard to such-and-such is unethical or illegal.

It should be stressed that the judges (the students and the instructor) should base their final vote only on the material presented by the debaters--material which seems to be reasonable proof and usually based on documented evidence. If a team violates the rules of debate, there is a penalty of a sort. If, for example, one side introduces new constructive arguments during its rebuttal period, the judges are obligated to ignore any such evidence. Hence, this side has merely wasted its time thereby weakening its total case.

A sample of the judges' appraisal form appears immediately below. These can be mimeographed blank at the beginning of the term, and then retained in sequential order for ease of reference at a later time. These may be placed on a chair near the door where students enter so latercomers won't disturb the proceedings.

JUDGES' APPRAISAL FORM

Date: Dec. 10, 198-

Debate Topic: Resolved that coaches have too much interpersonal power over athletes in today's competitive sport.

Affirmative   Jim Beals   (name)

Positive   Constructive

1. Good sense of humor   1. Stay on the topic; avoid side comments
Grade B-   2. Plenty of illustrations   2. Develop your points more quickly
3. Voice inflection fine   3. Organize material better

Rebuttal:
            This was much better than opening presentation; you argued well with good emphasis.

Affirmative   Beth Snow   (name)

1. Well organized   1. Show more dynamism
Grade   B   2. Well-modulated voice   2. Overdressed for the occasion
3. Some good points   3. Speak up a bit

Negative   Garth Poston   (name)

1. A really good start; established your   1. Maintain your pace throughout
    stand
Grade B+   2. A lot of good material   2. A few times I wasn't sure which side
                                         you favored
3. You have a good voice   3. Use best studies only

Rebuttal:
            You won the debate here by really refuting their arguments very well.

Negative   Trish Scannel   (name)

1. Excellent manner   1. Try to sound more authoritative
Grade B+   2. Well prepared   2. Work on voice inflection a bit
3. Several really good points   3. A bit brief

Winner: The Negative Side
               (affirmative or negative)

Strategy and Tactics

The actual proposition to be debated should be worded as a proposed policy, and the affirmative is required to support a definite action or stand by a person, group, or society. The topic should not be one-sided, and it should be interesting to the majority of the listeners. Be careful to insure that the topic expresses one main idea clearly.

The affirmative should make a sensible definition of the various terms included in the topic. This does not mean that the negative must accept this definition. They may give their own interpretation, but they should do this at the first opportunity. If they seem to agree on the affirmative's interpretation of the question at the outset, they can't object to it later on. The judges have to accept the interpretation that makes the most sense to them.

The next obligation of the affirmative is to demonstrate that the proposed policy or plan would be desirable if adopted. They cannot be expected to prove that the necessary approval for any plan could be obtained. They should be careful to stay within the limits of the topic and not recommend too much, since the burden of proof rests with them. The negative has to show the loopholes and defects of the plan. If they can show the disadvantages of such a proposal or policy outweigh the advantages, they have a good chance to win. Remember that any counterplan or counterproposal offered by the negative must be proved to a certain extent as well.

Logic and evidence are important in debating. Judges may not agree with a team's arguments, but they have an obligation to assess fairly how well the various speakers make their points. The debaters, also, should be scrupulously honest in the presentation of their facts. If a debater quotes any remarks of his opponent, they should be accurate.

The first affirmative speaker addresses his audience, explains the proposal or plan, lists its advantages over the present situation and discusses each, and then summarizes his or her position by enumerating them again. A few crucial questions may be posed as a challenge for the opposition to answer.

The first negative speaker then lists his or her team's objections to the proposed plan and discusses each of the claimed defects. It may be well to summarize the defects briefly after discussing them. Then this person may wish to refute the various advantages that the first affirmative speaker has given for the proposal. Obviously, it is wise to attack the opposition's strongest points first. Finally, the speaker may conclude by reiterating the disadvantages that were mentioned at the outset.

The second affirmative speaker has a somewhat more difficult task than the first speaker. Initially he or she may reiterate the advantages offered by the proposed plan by listing them in order. But then it is a question of refuting the points and repairing the damage that the first negative speaker may have done by rebuilding the original arguments. After this, he or she may wish to refute some of the disadvantages mentioned by the first negative speaker. If there is time, the advantages of the proposal may be restated in as favorable a light as possible.

The second negative speaker follows the pattern of the second affirmative speaker almost exactly, except that he or she is on the other side. This speaker lists the objections, strengthens them if and when necessary, lists them briefly in outline form, refutes the claimed benefits of the proposed plan or proposal, and finally summarizes the defects once again.

The speaker chosen for the rebuttal speech--in this instance it should probably be the first speaker on either team--plays a key role. The negative rebuttal speaker tells about the defects of the affirmative proposal, and then tells how the advantages explained by the affirmative speakers have been refuted. If this person's teammate immediately preceding him or her left anything important out of the basic negative argument, gaps may be filled in at this point. Following this, the negative rebuttal speaker explains as clearly and concisely as possible how the negative team negated the purported advantages of the affirmative proposal. Finally, the disadvantages of the affirmative plan should be pointed out in the strongest possible manner in keeping with debate decorum.

The last speaker of the debate, the affirmative rebuttal speaker begins by outlining the advantages of the proposed plan over the presently prevailing situation. This person next tells how the points made by the negative speakers were refuted, and also fills in any possible loopholes in the affirmative team's arguments. Then he or she summarizes the benefits of the basic debate proposition, explains how the alleged defects were refuted, and concludes by listing the advantages of the proposition being proposed strongly.

The final talks of each side should combine refutation and summarization; the only thing new that might be added is when some direct question has been left unanswered.

Reference

Certain of this material was adapted originally from Musgrave, G. M. Competitive debate. (3rd Edition). New York: The H. W. Wilson Company, 1957, Chaps. 1 and 3. A number of suggestions and changes were added based on experience when debates were employed in a classroom setting.

CHAPTER 9
PROPOSED DEBATE TOPICS

In Chapter 8 the proposed debating procedures were reviewed for your consideration. Now in Chapter 9 you will find a listing of ten proposed topics that have been used successfully. Additionally, I have included eight possible debate topics that were designated as supplemental. At this point the instructor and class members may find it desirable to make some changes from one listing to the other, or even to substitute some topics of your own choosing. Whatever you decide do to, choose topics that are interesting to the large majority of the class, are controversial, and have strong ethical/moral implications.

The first listing immediately below is identical with that included in the proposed course outline (see Appendix A). This is followed by the provision of a listing of ten other topics for supplementary purposes (e.g., substitution, length of course).

Course Outline Topics

1. "Resolved that an unacceptable level of violence is an inevitable concomitant of contact/collision sports"

2. "Resolved that living up to the 'spirit' of the rules is outmoded and incongruent in today's highly competitive sport"

3. "Resolved that coaches have too much interpersonal power over athletes in today's competitive sport"

4. "Resolved that the use of all stimulants, pain-killers, and body-builders and developers should be banned and carefully monitored by officials administering sports competitions"

5. "Resolved that highly competitive sport develops desirable personality traits"

6. "Resolved that a teacher/coach should never go out on a strike"

7. "Resolved that a high standard of coaching ethics should be developed and enforced by the profession"

8. "Resolved that athletic scholarships should be banned in colleges and universities"

9. "Resolved that the physical education profession should take a strong stand against elite sport at all levels of education"

10. "Resolved that a student's scholastic average should have a bearing on his/her athletic eligibility"

Supplemental Debate Topics

1. "Resolved that post-season tournaments and play-offs should be potentially available for all high school and college athletes"

2. "Resolved that coaches should strongly enforce specific rules prohibiting smoking, drinking, and use of similar substances by varsity squad members"

3. "Resolved that student fees for physical activities should be used proportionately to support intercollegiate/interscholastic athletics and intramural athletics and physical recreation in direct relation to the number of students typically involved in these respective phases of the total program"

4. "Resolved that there should be less money spent on women's intercollegiate/interscholastic sport than on men's programs"

5. "Resolved that contact/collision sports should be eliminated from the physical education and sport program at the middle-school level (app. Grades 5-8)"

6. "Resolved that the concept of 'amateur' sport is a hopeless ideal in highly competitive sport at any level in the world"

7. "Resolved that sex education should be taught coeducationally as part of all middle-school and high-school physical and health education programs"

8. "Resolved that specific aspects of military training can be an adequate substitute for elements of the physical education program within the educational system"

9. "Resolved that body-building through weight-training should be an integral part of every physical education program for both men and women (and boys and girls)"

10. "Resolved that all agencies sponsoring competitive team sports should be required to hire certified coaches"

Analysis of Individual Debate Topics

In the remainder of this chapter, each of the ten recommended debate topics will be analyzed in a limited fashion according to the triple-play approach and the layout for an argument as presented in Chapters 6 and 7, respectively. You are urged to keep in mind that these analyses should be challenged by you in all respects (except for the data statement taken directly from the debate topic itself). Thus, you may find that you don't agree with the conclusion drawn or the modal qualifier (Q) in one or more instances. The affirmative team should work primarily on the left side of the argument layout page, although they will need to be fully aware of the rebuttal, exceptions, and intentions. You are cautioned not to accept this information blindly.

DEBATE TOPIC: RESOLVED THAT AN UNACCEPTABLE LEVEL OF VIOLENCE IS AN
INEVITABLE COMPONENT OF CONTACT/COLLISION SPORTS

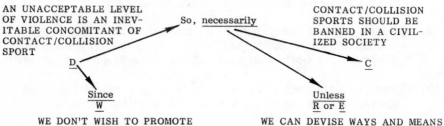

AN UNACCEPTABLE LEVEL
OF VIOLENCE IS AN INEV-   So, necessarily
ITABLE CONCOMITANT OF
CONTACT/COLLISION
SPORT
D

CONTACT/COLLISION
SPORTS SHOULD BE
BANNED IN A CIVIL-
IZED SOCIETY

C

Since
W

WE DON'T WISH TO PROMOTE
SPORTS ON A WORLDWIDE
BASIS WHERE PEOPLE ARE
PUT INTO SITUATIONS WHERE
VIOLENCE AND ANTI-SOCIAL
BEHAVIOR IS ENCOURAGED

Unless
R or E

WE CAN DEVISE WAYS AND MEANS
OF PREPARING PEOPLE FOR SUCH
INVOLVEMENT SO THAT THEIR
AGGRESSIVE TENDENCIES ARE
KEPT IN CHECK

Universalizability
  (Kant)   On account of
                     B

THERE IS MOUNTING EVI-
DENCE THAT VIOLENT PHY-
SICAL ACTIVITIES PROMOTE
ANTI-SOCIAL BEHAVIOR
THAT CARRIES OVER TO
OTHER ASPECTS OF DAILY
LIFE

and

WE CAN SO EQUIP PEOPLE WITH
UNIFORMS AND PROTECTIVE DE-
VICES THAT EXCESSIVE VIO-
LENCE AND CONCURRENT IN-
JURIES ARE KEPT TO AN ABOLUTE
MINIMUM

Consequences
  (Mill)   and

THERE HAS RESULTED AN
UNACCEPTABLE LEVEL OF
SERIOUS INJURIES THAT
CAUSE UNDUE PROBLEMS
NOW AND IN THE FUTURE

Intentions
  (Aristotle)

DEBATE TOPIC: RESOLVED THAT LIVING UP TO THE "SPIRIT" OF THE RULES
                 IS OUTMODED AND INCONGRUENT IN TODAY'S COMPETITIVE
                 SPORT

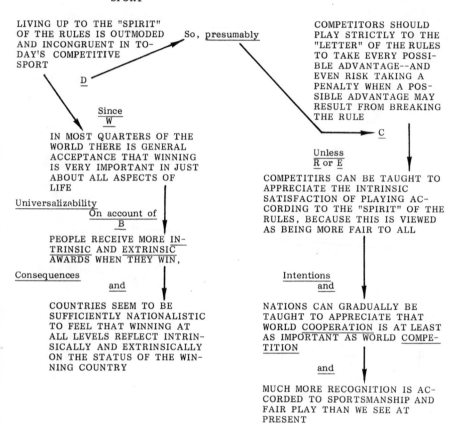

LIVING UP TO THE "SPIRIT"
OF THE RULES IS OUTMODED   So, presumably
AND INCONGRUENT IN TO-
DAY'S COMPETITIVE
SPORT

D

Since
W

IN MOST QUARTERS OF THE
WORLD THERE IS GENERAL
ACCEPTANCE THAT WINNING
IS VERY IMPORTANT IN JUST
ABOUT ALL ASPECTS OF
LIFE

Universalizability
                On account of
                B

PEOPLE RECEIVE MORE IN-
TRINSIC AND EXTRINSIC
AWARDS WHEN THEY WIN,

Consequences
                and

COUNTRIES SEEM TO BE
SUFFICIENTLY NATIONALISTIC
TO FEEL THAT WINNING AT
ALL LEVELS REFLECT INTRIN-
SICALLY AND EXTRINSICALLY
ON THE STATUS OF THE WIN-
NING COUNTRY

COMPETITORS SHOULD
PLAY STRICTLY TO THE
"LETTER" OF THE RULES
TO TAKE EVERY POSSI-
BLE ADVANTAGE--AND
EVEN RISK TAKING A
PENALTY WHEN A POS-
SIBLE ADVANTAGE MAY
RESULT FROM BREAKING
THE RULE

C

Unless
R or E

COMPETITIRS CAN BE TAUGHT TO
APPRECIATE THE INTRINSIC
SATISFACTION OF PLAYING AC-
CORDING TO THE "SPIRIT" OF THE
RULES, BECAUSE THIS IS VIEWED
AS BEING MORE FAIR TO ALL

Intentions
                and

NATIONS CAN GRADUALLY BE
TAUGHT TO APPRECIATE THAT
WORLD COOPERATION IS AT LEAST
AS IMPORTANT AS WORLD COMPE-
TITION

                and

MUCH MORE RECOGNITION IS AC-
CORDED TO SPORTSMANSHIP AND
FAIR PLAY THAN WE SEE AT
PRESENT

<u>DEBATE TOPIC</u>:   RESOLVED THAT COACHES HAVE TOO MUCH INTERPERSONAL
POWER OVER ATHLETES IN TODAY'S COMPETITIVE SPORT

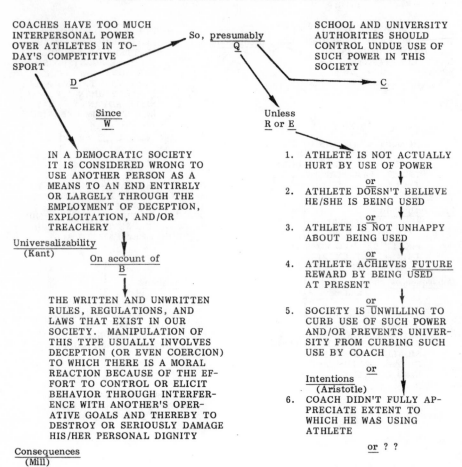

COACHES HAVE TOO MUCH
INTERPERSONAL POWER
OVER ATHLETES IN TO-
DAY'S COMPETITIVE
SPORT

D

So, presumably
Q

SCHOOL AND UNIVERSITY
AUTHORITIES SHOULD
CONTROL UNDUE USE OF
SUCH POWER IN THIS
SOCIETY

C

Since
W

Unless
R or E

IN A DEMOCRATIC SOCIETY
IT IS CONSIDERED WRONG TO
USE ANOTHER PERSON AS A
MEANS TO AN END ENTIRELY
OR LARGELY THROUGH THE
EMPLOYMENT OF DECEPTION,
EXPLOITATION, AND/OR
TREACHERY

Universalizability
(Kant)

On account of
B

THE WRITTEN AND UNWRITTEN
RULES, REGULATIONS, AND
LAWS THAT EXIST IN OUR
SOCIETY. MANIPULATION OF
THIS TYPE USUALLY INVOLVES
DECEPTION (OR EVEN COERCION)
TO WHICH THERE IS A MORAL
REACTION BECAUSE OF THE EF-
FORT TO CONTROL OR ELICIT
BEHAVIOR THROUGH INTERFER-
ENCE WITH ANOTHER'S OPER-
ATIVE GOALS AND THEREBY TO
DESTROY OR SERIOUSLY DAMAGE
HIS/HER PERSONAL DIGNITY

Consequences
(Mill)

1. ATHLETE IS NOT ACTUALLY
   HURT BY USE OF POWER
   or
2. ATHLETE DOESN'T BELIEVE
   HE/SHE IS BEING USED
   or
3. ATHLETE IS NOT UNHAPPY
   ABOUT BEING USED
   or
4. ATHLETE ACHIEVES FUTURE
   REWARD BY BEING USED
   AT PRESENT
   or
5. SOCIETY IS UNWILLING TO
   CURB USE OF SUCH POWER
   AND/OR PREVENTS UNIVER-
   SITY FROM CURBING SUCH
   USE BY COACH
   or
   Intentions
      (Aristotle)
6. COACH DIDN'T FULLY AP-
   PRECIATE EXTENT TO
   WHICH HE WAS USING
   ATHLETE
   or ? ?

DEBATE TOPIC: RESOLVED THAT THE USE OF ALL STIMULANTS, PAIN-KILLERS,
AND BODY-BUILDERS AND DEVELOPERS SHOULD BE BANNED AND
CAREFULLY MONITORED BY OFFICIAL ADMINISTERING SPORTS
COMPETITIONS

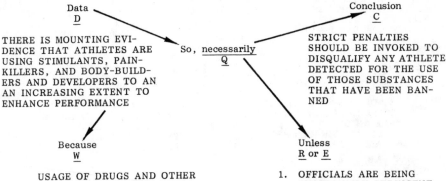

Data
D

THERE IS MOUNTING EVI-
DENCE THAT ATHLETES ARE   So, necessarily
USING STIMULANTS, PAIN-   Q
KILLERS, AND BODY-BUILD-
ERS AND DEVELOPERS TO AN
AN INCREASING EXTENT TO
ENHANCE PERFORMANCE

Conclusion
C

STRICT PENALTIES
SHOULD BE INVOKED TO
DISQUALIFY ANY ATHLETE
DETECTED FOR THE USE
OF THOSE SUBSTANCES
THAT HAVE BEEN BAN-
NED

Because
W

USAGE OF DRUGS AND OTHER
SUBSTANCES TO ENHANCE
PERFORMANCE IS UNFAIR TO
OTHER ATHLETES WHO ARE
COMPETING IN THESE EVENTS

Universalizability

On account of
B

MANY OF THESE DRUGS AND
SUBSTANCES MAY BE ULTI-
MATELY HARMFUL TO THE
ATHLETES WHO EMPLOY
THEM, NOT TO MENTION
THE CHARACTER DEFECTS
THAT ARE DEVELOPED IN
THE PROCESS

Consequences

Unless
R or E

1. OFFICIALS ARE BEING
   EXCESSIVELY STRINGENT
   IN THEIR ADMINISTRA-
   TION OF THE RULES

2. THE USE OF CERTAIN
   SUBSTANCES AND TECH-
   NIQUES CANNOT BE DE-
   TECTED, AND THUS CON-
   TROLS ARE INEFFECTIVE

3. IT IS IMPOSSIBLE TO
   DETERMINE AT WHAT
   POINT SUCH USAGE BE-
   COMES UNETHICAL

Intentions

DEBATE TOPIC: RESOLVED THAT HIGHLY COMPETITIVE SPORT DEVELOPS DESIR-
ABLE PERSONALITY TRAITS

D ➤   ➤ C

| HIGHLY COMPETITIVE SPORT PROVIDES EXPERIENCES FOR PEOPLE THAT RESULT IN THE DEVELOPMENT OF DESIRABLE PERSONALITY TRAITS | So, presumably | SOCIETY SHOULD EMPLOY ALL POSSIBLE MEANS TO PROVIDE SUCH EXPERIENCES FOR PEOPLE AT THEIR LEVEL OF SKILL AND ABILITY |

Q

Since W   Unless R or E

WE WOULD WISH THAT ALL   HIGHLY COMPETITIVE SPORT
PEOPLE IN SOCIETY SHOULD   HAS INADEQUATE LEADERSHIP
HAVE AN OPPORTUNITY TO   THAT RESULTS IN THE DEVELOP-
DEVELOP DESIRABLE PER-   MENT OF UNDESIRABLE PERSON-
SONALITY TRAITS   ALITY TRAITS

Universalizability
                                            and/or

Because B   SCIENTIFIC EVIDENCE EVENTU-
                                    ALLY DETERMINES THAT UN-
SUCH DEVELOPMENT OF   DESIRABLE TRAITS RESULT NO
DESIRABLE PERSONALITIES   MATTER HOW GOOD THE LEADER-
SHOULD RESULT IN AN   SHIP IS
IMPROVED SOCIETY
                                            and/or
Consequences
                                    IT IS DETERMINED THAT THE
                                    TEMPORARY AND PERMANENT
                                    INJURIES THAT RESULT FROM
                                    SUCH PARTICIPATION DO NOT
                                    WARRANT THE INVOLVEMENT

                                            and/or

                                    SOCIETY DISCOVERS A BETTER
                                    MEANS TO PRODUCE THE DE-
                                    SIRED RESULTS

                                            Intentions

DEBATE TOPIC: RESOLVED THAT A TEACHER/COACH SHOULD NEVER GO OUT ON
A STRIKE

D ────────────────────────────────────►C

A TEACHER/COACH IS A   Q   **A TEACHER/COACH**
MEMBER OF A PROFESSION,   So, necessarily   **SHOULD NEVER WITHHOLD**
NECESSARY FEATURES OF   **HIS/HER SERVICES FROM**
WHICH ARE EXTENSIVE   **HIS/HER STUDENTS AS**
TRAINING INVOLVING A   **SUCH ACTION WOULD BE**
SIGNIFICANT INTELLECTUAL   **CONTRARY TO TEACHING**
COMPONENT AND THE PRO-   **ETHICS AND WOULD DE-**
VISION OF AN IMPORTANT   **PRIVE CONSUMERS OF**
SERVICE TO SOCIETY AND   **THEIR RIGHTS**
ITS NORMAL FUNCTIONING

Since W   Unless R or E

HISTORICALLY THE PUBLIC   WORKING CONDITIONS BECOME SO
HAS "REGARDED PROFES-   UNACCEPTABLE THAT THE TEACH-
SIONALS WITH RESPECT   ER/COACH FEELS THAT HE/SHE IS
AND ENTRUSTED THEIR   NOT ABLE TO PRACTICE HIS/HER
LIVES AND FORTUNES TO   PROFESSION IN KEEPING WITH ITS
THEIR JUDGMENT"   HIGHEST TRADITIONS

Universalizability   and/or

Because B   THE REMUNERATION FOR HIS/HER
                                    SERVICES ARE SO INADEQUATE
BECAUSE PROFESSIONS HAVE   THAT HE/SHE CANNOT PROVIDE
BECOME INCREASINGLY CEN-   FOR HIMSELF/HERSELF WHAT ARE
TRAL TO THE FUNCTIONING   CONSIDERED TO BE THE ESSEN-
OF A SOCIETY THAT HAS   TIALS OF LIFE
BECOME INCREASINGLY MORE
COMPLEX AND DEPENDENT   and/or
UPON TECHNOLOGY WITH
VARIOUS CONTROLS SHIFT-   SOCIETAL CONDITIONS SOMEHOW
ING FROM THE INDIVIDUAL   CHANGE AND MEMBERS OF THE
TO PROFESSIONALS   TIME-HONORED PROFESSIONS ARE
                                    VIEWED DIFFERENTLY THAN THEY
Consequences   HAVE BEEN IN THE PAST

                                            Intentions

DEBATE TOPIC: RESOLVED THAT A HIGH STANDARD OF COACHING ETHICS
                 SHOULD BE DEVELOPED AND ENFORCED BY THE PROFESSION

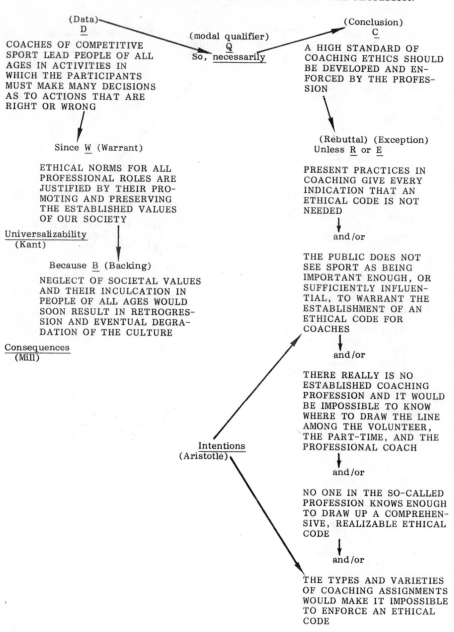

(Data)
D

COACHES OF COMPETITIVE
SPORT LEAD PEOPLE OF ALL
AGES IN ACTIVITIES IN
WHICH THE PARTICIPANTS
MUST MAKE MANY DECISIONS
AS TO ACTIONS THAT ARE
RIGHT OR WRONG

(modal qualifier)
Q
So, necessarily

(Conclusion)
C

A HIGH STANDARD OF
COACHING ETHICS SHOULD
BE DEVELOPED AND EN-
FORCED BY THE PROFES-
SION

Since W (Warrant)

ETHICAL NORMS FOR ALL
PROFESSIONAL ROLES ARE
JUSTIFIED BY THEIR PRO-
MOTING AND PRESERVING
THE ESTABLISHED VALUES
OF OUR SOCIETY

Universalizability
(Kant)

Because B (Backing)

NEGLECT OF SOCIETAL VALUES
AND THEIR INCULCATION IN
PEOPLE OF ALL AGES WOULD
SOON RESULT IN RETROGRES-
SION AND EVENTUAL DEGRA-
DATION OF THE CULTURE

Consequences
(Mill)

Intentions
(Aristotle)

(Rebuttal) (Exception)
Unless R or E

PRESENT PRACTICES IN
COACHING GIVE EVERY
INDICATION THAT AN
ETHICAL CODE IS NOT
NEEDED

and/or

THE PUBLIC DOES NOT
SEE SPORT AS BEING
IMPORTANT ENOUGH, OR
SUFFICIENTLY INFLUEN-
TIAL, TO WARRANT THE
ESTABLISHMENT OF AN
ETHICAL CODE FOR
COACHES

and/or

THERE REALLY IS NO
ESTABLISHED COACHING
PROFESSION AND IT WOULD
BE IMPOSSIBLE TO KNOW
WHERE TO DRAW THE LINE
AMONG THE VOLUNTEER,
THE PART-TIME, AND THE
PROFESSIONAL COACH

and/or

NO ONE IN THE SO-CALLED
PROFESSION KNOWS ENOUGH
TO DRAW UP A COMPREHEN-
SIVE, REALIZABLE ETHICAL
CODE

and/or

THE TYPES AND VARIETIES
OF COACHING ASSIGNMENTS
WOULD MAKE IT IMPOSSIBLE
TO ENFORCE AN ETHICAL
CODE

DEBATE TOPIC: RESOLVED THAT THE CANADIAN INTERUNIVERSITY ATHLETIC
UNION SHOULD BAN ATHLETIC SCHOLARSHIPS IN COLLEGES AND
UNIVERSITIES*

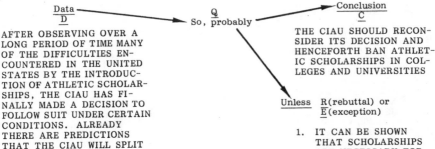

Data
D

Q
So, probably

Conclusion
C

AFTER OBSERVING OVER A
LONG PERIOD OF TIME MANY
OF THE DIFFICULTIES EN-
COUNTERED IN THE UNITED
STATES BY THE INTRODUC-
TION OF ATHLETIC SCHOLAR-
SHIPS, THE CIAU HAS FI-
NALLY MADE A DECISION TO
FOLLOW SUIT UNDER CERTAIN
CONDITIONS. ALREADY
THERE ARE PREDICTIONS
THAT THE CIAU WILL SPLIT
UP OVER THIS DECISION.

THE CIAU SHOULD RECON-
SIDER ITS DECISION AND
HENCEFORTH BAN ATHLET-
IC SCHOLARSHIPS IN COL-
LEGES AND UNIVERSITIES

Unless   R(rebuttal) or
E(exception)

1. IT CAN BE SHOWN
THAT SCHOLARSHIPS
ARE NECESSARY FOR
THE CONTINUANCE OF
A VIABLE INTERCOL-
LEGIATE ATHLETICS
PROGRAM

Because
W

and/or

THE VALUES AND NORMS OF
CANADIAN SOCIETY INDICATE
THAT THERE SHOULD BE
EQUALITY OF OPPORTUNITY
FOR ALL COLLEGE AND UNI-
VERSITY STUDENTS, NO MAT-
TER WHAT THEIR EXTRA-
CURRICULAR TALENTS MIGHT
BE.

Universalizability

2. ATHLETIC SCHOLAR-
SHIPS CAN BE ADMIN-
ISTERED IN SUCH A
WAY THAT ONLY THOSE
WITH FINANCIAL NEED
RECEIVE THEM--AND
OTHER TALENTED,
WORTHWHILE STUDENTS
ON CAMPUS WITH SIMI-
LAR NEED RECEIVE FI-
NANCIAL ASSISTANCE

On account of
B

Intentions

and/or

THIS DECISION CREATES AN ELITE
GROUP DISREGARDING THE QUES-
TION OF FINANCIAL NEED. THE
END RESULT WILL PROBABLY BE A
REPETITION OF THE U.S. SCENE
WHERE ALL SORTS OF CHEATING
AND DISHONESTY ARE PREVALENT,
AND THE INTEGRITY OF THE COL-
LEGES AND UNIVERSITIES THEM-
SELVES HAVE BEEN SERIOUSLY
DAMAGED

Consequences

3. PEOPLE ARE CONVINCED
THAT THE FEDERAL
GOVERNMENT'S SPORT
PROGRAM FOR THE ELITE
IS VITAL TO THE FU-
TURE OF THE COUNTRY
(AND THEREBY OVER-
RIDES THE PROBLEMS
THAT MAY ARISE)

and/or

* When this topic is debated in the
United States or elsewhere, the
name of the appropriate organization (e.g., NCAA, NAIA) should
be substituted.

4. CANADIAN COLLEGES
AND UNIVERSITIES CAN
SOMEHOW PROFIT FROM
THE MANY MISTAKES OF
THE U.S. AND SOMEHOW
DEVELOP A UNIQUE SYS-
TEM THAT SOMEHOW
WILL BE GOOD FOR ALL
CONCERNED

and/or

???

<u>DEBATE TOPIC</u>: RESOLVED THAT THE PHYSICAL EDUCATION PROFESSION SHOULD
TAKE A STRONG STAND AGAINST THE IDEA OF ELITE SPORT AT
ALL LEVELS OF EDUCATION

Data
<u>D</u>

Q

<u>Conclusion</u>
C

So, presumably

AT ALL EDUCATIONAL LEVELS
THE FIELD OF PHYSICAL EDU-
CATION THAT HAS A RESPON-
SIBILITY FOR DEVELOPMENTAL
PHYSICAL ACTIVITY IN SPORT,
DANCE, PLAY, AND EXERCISE
OF <u>ALL</u> STUDENTS HAS BEEN
CONSISTENTLY HAMPERED IN
THE ACHIEVEMENDS OF ITS
GOALS BECAUSE OF THE TIME,
ATTENTION, EMPHASIS, MONEY,
AND FACILITIES PLACED ON
ELITE SPORT WITHIN EDUCA-
TION IN THIS CULTURE

THE FIELD OF PHYSICAL
EDUCATION SHOULD NOW
TAKE A STRONG STAND
AGAINST THE IDEA OF
ELITE SPORT WITHIN ALL
LEVELS OF EDUCATION

<u>Unless</u>   R(rebuttal) or
E̲(exception)

Because
<u>W</u>

ONE OF THE VALUES OF A LIBERAL
SOCIETY IS EQUALITY OF OPPOR-
TUNITY, AND ELITE SPORT WITHIN
EDUCATION HAS CREATED A SITU-
ATION WHERE OPPORTUNITIES FOR
THE FINEST TYPE OF DEVELOP-
MENTAL PHYSICAL ACTIVITY EX-
PERIENCES ARE UNNECESSARILY
RESTRICTED TO AT LEAST 95% OF
THE EDUCATION POPULATION
<u>Universalizability</u>

On account of
<u>B</u>

THE PREVAILING SITUATION HAS
DEVELOPED TO THE POINT WHERE
EDUCATIONAL VALUES ARE NOT
BEING UPHELD FOR THOSE INVOLVED
IN ELITE SPORT, THEREBY TURN-
ING UNIVERSITIES AND COLLEGES,
AS WELL AS MANY JUNIOR AND
SENIOR HIGH SCHOOLS, INTO
ORGANIZATIONS SPONSORING DU-
BIOUS ENTERTAINMENT THAT ULTI-
MATELY NEGATES THE TRUE PUR-
POSE OF THE INSTITUTIONS AS
PATTERN-MAINTENANCE FORCES IN
SOCIETY
<u>Consequences</u>

1. ELITE SPORT IS MODI-
FIED TO THE POINT
WHERE THE PRESENT
ABUSES ARE REMOVED,
AND THE HIGHEST EDU-
CATIONAL VALUES ARE
RESTORED

and/or

2. SUFFICIENT TIME, AT-
TENTION, EMPHASIS,
MONEY, AND FACILITIES
ARE MADE AVAILABLE
TO MAKE A COMPLETE
PROGRAM OF DEVELOP-
MENTAL PHYSICAL AC-
TIVITY IN SPORT,
DANCE, PLAY, AND
EXERCISE POSSIBLE FOR
ALL WITHIN THE SYSTEM

and/or

3. ELITE SPORT BECOMES
COMPLETELY SELF SUP-
PORTING, AND THOSE
CONCERNED ARE SEPA-
RATED FROM THE LEGI-
TIMATE EDUCATIONAL
STREAM OF THE INSTI-
TUTION

and/or

4. ONLY A FEW GATE-
RECEIPT ELITE SPORTS
ARE RETAINED TO
SERVE AS PUBLIC EN-
TERTAINMENT AND
"CULTURAL MAXIMIZERS"
WITH THOSE INVOLVED
AS PARTICIPANTS EN-
GAGED AS SEMIPROFES-
SIONALS NOT TAKING
FULL ACADEMIC PRO-
GRAMS
<u>Intentions</u>

DEBATE TOPIC: RESOLVED THAT A STUDENT'S SCHOLASTIC AVERAGE SHOULD
HAVE A BEARING ON HIS/HER ATHLETIC ELIGIBILITY

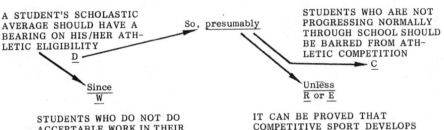

A STUDENT'S SCHOLASTIC
AVERAGE SHOULD HAVE A   So, presumably
BEARING ON HIS/HER ATH-
LETIC ELIGIBILITY
D

STUDENTS WHO ARE NOT
PROGRESSING NORMALLY
THROUGH SCHOOL SHOULD
BE BARRED FROM ATH-
LETIC COMPETITION
C

Since
W

Unless
R or E

STUDENTS WHO DO NOT DO
ACCEPTABLE WORK IN THEIR
ACADEMIC CURRICULUM
WILL NOT GRADUATE AT
ANY EDUCATIONAL LEVEL
Universalizability

IT CAN BE PROVED THAT
COMPETITIVE SPORT DEVELOPS
DESIRABLE PERSONALITY TRAITS

and

On account of
B

SOCIETY IS WILLING TO ACCORD
COMPETITIVE SPORT STATUS AS
A CO-CURRICULAR EXPERIENCE

GRADUATION DIPLOMAS AND
DEGREES ARE INCREASINGLY
NECESSARY FOR SUCCESSFUL
ENTRANCE INTO THE JOB
MARKET
Consequences

and

IT CAN BE SHOWN THAT THE
OPPORTUNITY TO PLAY IN
SPORTS HELPS TO KEEP YOUNG
PEOPLE IN SCHOOL LONGER

and

Intentions   and ? ?

ATHLETIC PROWESS RARELY
IS RESPONSIBLE FOR A PER-
SON HOLDING A JOB

and

TEST SCORES ARE INDICATING
THAT EDUCATIONAL COMPE-
TENCY HAS DECLINED IN RE-
CENT YEARS

Concluding Statement

If the class size is too large to schedule each student at least once for a debate, it may be necessary to make some adjustment to insure that this valuable experience is not missed. The following schedule was distributed--after the initial shakedown period when a few dropped and some students added the course--so that each person would have a copy for his subject file. Note that 16 people were involved in debates at a different class time. Thus, they were all expected to attend the 10:30 a.m. session only on those four Wednesdays. The schedule was limited to those days only because those were the topics in which they expressed interest. Each student was asked to hand in a slip expressing his/her first, second, and third preferences for topics, although it wasn't always possible to give each person his or her #1, #2, or #3 choice.

ETHICS & MORALITY IN SPORT & PHYSICAL EDUCATION (PE 393b)
The University of Western Ontario   Winter Term, 1982-1983

Listing of Debate Participants (9:30 - 10:20 a.m.)

Week	Topic	Affirmative		Negative (E.)
#3	Violence, etc.	Anschuetz-Carson (F.)	vs.	Bouwman-Clynick
#4	Spirit of Rules	Bouwman-Furry	vs.	Foster-Gerbsch
#5	Interpersonal Power	Garrett-Goldring	vs.	Henry-deBoer
#6	Use of Drugs	Herbin-Kinahan	vs.	Westaway-Lawson
#7	Personality Traits	Izzard-Lowe	vs.	January-Malloy
#8	Strikes	Jennings-Miller	vs.	King-Smet
#9	Ethics Code	Madge-Smith, C.	vs.	Morrison-Tong
#10	Scholarships	Hall-Van Maanen (B.)	vs.	Ladly-Oesch (E.)
#11	Elite Sport	O'Leary-Tuckey	vs.	O'Leary-Webster

(10:30-11:20 a.m.)
Room 204

Week	Topic	Affirmative		Negative
#3	Violence, etc.	Beatty-Caughlin	vs.	Hirai-Lodge
#4	Spirit of Rules	Horvath-McDonald	vs.	Sweazey-Merner
#5	Interpersonal Power	Venhuizen-Blair	vs.	Teed-Price
#6 ??				
#7	Personality Traits	Herd-Hoshoian	vs.	Whitfield-Easton

In the next chapter, Chapter 10, that begins Part IV of the text, we will get into the use of cases for ethical decision-making. These discussions typically occurred on Fridays, and another dimension was added to the plan of attack employed to this point.

PART IV
GETTING DOWN TO CASES

CHAPTER 10
ORIENTATION TO CASE DISCUSSION:
ADAPTATION TO ETHICAL
DECISION-MAKING

In 1959 the case method of instruction for the teaching of human relations and administration was introduced to the field of physical education for the first time (Zeigler, 1959). Since then this technique has been used in a variety of ways in this profession, as well as in health education and recreation administration.

Now in this text, I am recommending that it can be used most successfully as a teaching/learning technique in a class on ethics and morality in sport and physical education as well. Thus, Part IV of this volume is called "Getting Down to Cases," and shortly you will be presented with a series of 10 true-to-life cases that have been gathered for your use at this time. Each one of these cases depicts an actual situation that occurred at the high school or university level.

It isn't possible, of course, to move directly from a management case to a case about sport and physical education ethics, although it is true that many management cases included problems that were ethical in nature. Also, just as there was no fixed formula whereby one might analyze a management case correctly, you won't find that there is one way only to resolve any one of these cases involving sport and physical education ethics.

However, I feel it is possible to blend or meld the triple-play approach and the layout for an argument with the knowledge that has been gained over the years through the use of the case plan of instruction in some of the major professions (e.g., medicine, law, business). Help has been obtained also from the field of philosophy (e.g., Manicas and Kruger, 1968). With this plan in mind I will review some of the information available for using the case method of instruction. Finally you will be offered a step-by-step plan to use with the 10 cases presented in Chapter 11.

Developing an Ethical Frame of Mind

The primary objective of a course in ethics and morality as applied to sport and physical education is to help the prospective teacher/coach develop an attitude and a theoretical point of view toward ethical decision-making and practice. Such competency cannot be achieved by mere reading and discussion of the various assignments, although accomplishing this much certainly gives some increase in understanding. Through the application of the case method of instruction to ethical decision-making, students and instructor will meet new situations constantly. These situations cannot help but be characterized by facts, half-facts, and opinions.

You will most certainly not find "the answers" in these 10 case problems. There may be some opinions given which may be the best for the situations to which they apply. The answer that you come up with may be an answer, but you cannot state unequivocally that it is the answer. How you approach an ethical problem depends, of course, on which of the ethical approaches you decide to accept or experiment with. I have offered you "one plan of attack," but in Chapter 4 a number of other "ethical routes" were explained for your consideration as well.

A Supplement to Experience

Adapting the case method to the teaching of ethics and morality in sport and physical education may not be an infallible substitute for actual life experience--depending upon the quality of that life experience, of course. However, it does expose the student to a variety of cases taken directly from the field which he or she is preparing to enter. As the group faces these concrete, true-to-life (but disguised) situations, it is the responsibility of the instructor to guide each member in such a way that he or she arrives at a solution by constantly examining and re-examining all the relevant facts that are known. This should be carried out, of course, in keeping with the tenets of the ethical approach or route that the individual has accepted.

You are presented with an actual case situation where a young teacher/coach is seemingly forced to defend himself and decides to take the offender to the principal's office. Later the principal gives the teacher the feeling that he is being charged with prejudice against another race, and that he is "guilty until proven innocent" (Compton High Case). As you review the relevant facts, half-facts, and opinions of the situation, you are forced to ask yourself on what basis you will arrive at an ethical decision in this matter.

What would you do in a situation such as this seems to be? How do your personal and professional ethics enter into such a troublesome problem? Do you resign on the spot? Do you tell the principal in no uncertain terms that he is dead wrong in making such an assumption, and that your record will bear your position out if he will but check with other teachers and students. What can you do, and what should you do?

No Fixed Formulas

A word of warning may be necessary here, particularly if you feel that the making of ethical decisions is not so difficult after all. Possibly no other method of learning can be more demanding of your time, effort, and interest. There may be some ready-made theories--the extreme ones--that can be applied quite readily to a number of situations, but even in these instances subjective judgments must be made. A certain amount of confusion and frustration will often result from your efforts. The instructor also may have certain misgivings as you and other class members struggle with a particular case. You may indeed wonder about this approach and reflect longingly at your earlier "common-sense" approach that in retrospect seemed to be an easier way out.

However, after a few months you may feel that you are beginning to see the light and, perhaps for the first time, you may feel the satisfaction of independent, concrete, responsible thinking on your part consonant with the ethical route that you have decided is best for you.

An instructor may find the need to exercise restraint, because he or she has greater experience and accordingly may "know the answers" or, at least, the "best" approach. For this reason I believe that an instructor should not fall into the trap of giving you the answer unless it is made very clear from "which direction he or she may be coming."

Preparing the Ethical Professional Person

The thesis of this text is that ethical teacher/coaches can be best prepared through the use of experiential or laboratory techniques. I have recommended debating and case discussions as two excellent techniques to accompish this purpose. No matter whether professional practice at the higher, intermediate, or lower levels of education is being considered--or profession-- al practice in the semi-public and public sphere outside of edu- cation--all professionals in sport and physical education have duties and responsibilities where ethical situations arise. I be- lieve, therefore, that an experiential approach represents the best possible method of implementing the concept of "ethical awareness" that has been brought to the fore in recent years.

Somehow those responsible for professional preparation, as well as those who have been promoting so-called sport and physical education philosophy, have not generally been aware of what now appears to be an urgent need. Student teaching and field work experience may bring such matters to the at- tention of the prospective teacher/coaches, but rarely do they give students the opportunity to think and to reason about ethical problems. I believe that there is typically no time spent on ethical theory and practice, and I regard this as a serious shortcoming.

Even if it does become evident to those responsible for professional preparation that such experience is required or highly advisable, I am fearful that the best type of experi- ences for young people will not be made available. The fact remains that no amount of theoretical or factual knowledge passed on by a competent teacher can give the student wisdom and judgment about how to act most effectively as an ethical professional person. The teacher can explore the different ap- proaches or routes with you through lectures and discussions, but you must develop and use your own beliefs, your own knowledge, your own wisdom, and your own insight to pene- trate a difficult ethical situation.

What has impressed me in the past is that instruction by the case method has a democracy-in-action flavor that can never be approached by the more dictatorial method of "telling." Students, as members of the class, begin with the same facts as the instructor--the case situation at hand. Your task is to analyze the known facts and arrive at a solution based on the ethical approach that you have personally selected. Each one of you has exactly the same opportunity to offer a solution to the ethical problem area under discussion. All contribute to the development of a set of "currently useful generalizations" that may govern policy formation in this particular case. You should keep in mind that not even the instructor knows the answer, although he or she may have come up with what ap- pears to be the best solution of a number that are considered. When you are dealing with human relations, there is no set of answers that can be consulted. Some would disagree with this statement, of course, because of the authoritative nature of the route they have selected. Of course, it is quite possible that, because of the way the case has been presented, or for some other reason, the best answer has not yet come to light.

Through this experiential method of instruction, a new set of personal relations precepts may appear to each participant. The spotlight falls on the teacher as the star performer to a lesser extent. You begin to transfer your attention to the various other personalities in the group. In this type of class, you most definitely tend to be equals; hence, you should know what each is thinking. To achieve this there must be the chance for freedom of expression. Because each student realizes that he or she is part of this process, the individual thinks more and many are anxious to try out their wings. You begin to realize that others will come up with suggestions that you had not even considered. You acquire experience in expressing your own thoughts to a perceptive, perhaps critical audience.

The Role of the Instructor: Case Plan Format

You may wonder just what the instructor does when the case method approach is employed. There is no set formula for conducting classes by this method to the best of my knowledge. The instructor generally introduces the method and assigns the cases to be read for class discussion. In this particular situation, because we are adapting the case plan of instruction to a course in ethical decision-making where I have actually recommended one plan of attack for your initial use, and also because I introduced this approach to the field in connection with management training, a general format or formula is recommended as follows:

1. First, after consideration of the various sub-problems of the case at hand, determine what you believe the main ethical problem to be.

2. Second, determine through the employment of the triple-play approach--from Kant to Mill to Aristotle--the several aspects of the ethical or moral issue in the specific case at hand. In other words, you should proceed from universalizability (consistency) to (net) consequences to intentions in your consideration of what you have indicated is the main ethical problem. Keep in mind at this stage that you are concerned with any action that countermands the principles of autonomy, beneficence, and fairness.

3. Third, integrate the results of your application of the recommended triple-play approach with the layout for an argument as recommended by Toulmin.

4. Fourth, consider to your satisfaction the personalities involved in the case and their ethical relationships.

5. Fifth, develop your formulation of the most relevant, possible, and meaningful alternatives that appear to be available to one of the key participants in the case.

6. Sixth, outline your elaboration of the proposed alternative solutions by the framing of warranted prediction statements (both pro's and con's).

7. Seventh, select what you believe to be the preferred alternative solution. This should include initial tentative testing of the proposed solution prior to actual implementation. Such testing should indicate whether the proposed solution has more vital pro's than con's in its favor.

8. Eighth, determination of currently useful generalizations for possible future use as guidance in similar cases.

Note: This approach has been adapted from Zeigler's approach to the Harvard case plan of instruction, 1982 and an approach to ethical decision-making recommended by Manicas and Kruger, 1968.)

There does not appear to be any set remark for an instructor to make to open discussion. If a case seems to be very complicated, the instructor might ask, "What is the main ethical issue in this case?" Or simply, "Ethical issues aside, what do you think of this case problem?" might be sufficient. Experience has shown that some students feel able to bring the main issue into focus much sooner than others, or at least they think that they have such ability. Everything considered, I recommend that the class should work to identify issues of all types at first. Then subsequently an individual or the group can make a decision as to what the main issue really is.

At times the instructor will be tempted to redirect the thinking of the group, but he or she must decide if such action is appropriate. At first, even when a student appears to have misinterpreted some of the facts, the instructor must make a choice whether to speak out or to wait for others to challenge. Of course, it must be understood whether a student plans to follow the proposed format (triple-play approach, lay-out, etc.) exactly, or if one of the other ethical routes is be-ing adopted. At first it would seem best to follow the recom-mended format closely. Later after there have been lectures and assigned readings relating to other approaches available, the student will be better equipped to strike out on his own somewhat more capably.

With a mature group, perhaps at the upper undergradu-ate level but definitely at the graduate level, the instructor may give individual students the opportunity to chair certain discussions. Depending on the size of the class, students gen-erally sit in a circle, or have swivel chairs, in order to face each other when speaking. Name plates or "rigidly" folded pa-per with sufficiently large letters for first and last names help a great deal.

Some students who lead discussions for the first time tend to become quite "directive" or even dictatorial in their approach --but the rest of the class will usually not be denied. They tend to take over and make it a real group discussion. A chairperson should be careful to see that each person has a chance to express an opinion. Hand-raising is perhaps the best means to let the chairperson know that a person wishes to speak, although this may not be necessary in a very small class. The chairperson should keep track of the order in which three or four hands were raised. Coffee-drinking may help in the crea-tion of an informal atmosphere, but smoking is now against most fire regulations and is typically offensive to others.

The Role of Lectures. Most students have come to ex-pect that the answers will be handed to them in some form or other. To such individuals the case plan of instruction will come as somewhat of a shock. They may find that they have no background from which to draw material. In fact, the strain of such active thinking may be great, especially when their arguments are generally challenged "publicly." Others will sim-ply not choose to speak, and the instructor may find it advis-able to occasionally divide the class up for 10 or 15 minutes into groups of four or six. Even then instructors may find that group opinions are not forming, even though there has been much heated discussion. At that point he or she is best advised not to lecture, especially when the group does not ap-pear to be arriving at the instructor's personal conception of the "correct answer."

There is, however, a place for lecturing when these ex-periential techniques are employed. Typically, I lecture for the first class period each week so that students will get my slant on what may strictly be called the "knowledge component" of the course experience. If case discussions are confined to the usual 50-minute period (80 minutes is much to be preferred), the instructor may want to deliver a brief "lecturette" at the end of the period to pull some of the loose ends together. When other types of laboratory experiences are planned, such a brief introductory lecture could come at the beginning. However, when the lecturette comes at the end of a case discussion, the instructor must be careful not to disrupt the open relationship that is planned with this approach. This type of lecturing is not inconsistent with what has been suggested as the five-fold role of the instructor by Dearborn: discussion leader, resource person, helpful expert, evaluator or summarizer, and judge of performance (in McNair, 1954, pp. 128-132).

Students Undergo Phases. It was observed many years ago that the student new to the case method approach in business administration typically undergoes three clearly recognizable phases. First, he or she may think there is one answer only and is quite surprised at the great variety of suggestions that come from fellow students. About the end of the first eight to 10 weeks, students can generally accept help from others in good grace. Realizing that they can't know it all, they draw more heavily on the ideas of others. Although competition for grades is as keen as ever, no one seems too worried about giving or receiving assistance to a reasonable extent.

If all progresses well, intelligent students should realize toward the end of the course that their instructors may think that he or she has the answer, and it may indeed even turn out to be the best answer. But what is most important, they understand that they are entitled to their own opinions, so long as they are ready to substantiate their facts and to argue their opinions logically (Gragg in Andrews, 1953).

Case Method Not Perfect

Although fine development can be expected from use of the case method of instruction, as well as from the debating of controversial issues, these techniques are not the final answers to the teaching/learning process. There is a great difference between thinking about an ethical problem constructively on the one hand, and actually making a decision that may radically affect the professional task you are carrying out as well as your own personal life. I do believe, however, that the case method approach is the best substitute for actual guided experience

that has yet been devised. Understanding, judgment, and independent thought are some of the rewards to be gained from a
careful application of this approach to ethical decision-making.

Class Atmosphere Is All-Important. This point cannot be
stressed too much. It involves such intangibles as the relationship among you, the other students, and the instructor. The
instructor may quickly begin to call you by your first name.
Although it is not necessary that you address him or her so
familiarly, I always tell a new group of students to call me by
whatever name they feel comfortable with--first name, Dr.,
Professor, Mr., Ms., but not "Hey you!" I wouldn't feel comfortable with that. The main point is that you both feel that
you are discussing a problem as relative equals. Only then
will the student feel free to express all his or her ideas about
various aspects of the case at hand and its ethical analysis.
Everyone in the class, including the instructor, should gain
from this interaction.

Students Learn to Analyze

It is basic to this course experience that you learn how
to analyze ethical situations as carefully and completely as possible. Some may do this quite automatically, either because of
sheer intelligence and insight, or because of their implicit ethical philosophies. Many in the class will read through a case
quickly and rather carelessly. Some may even appear during
the discussion to wander far from what appears to the majority
to be the central issue of a problem. Presumably the instructor will try to ask "leading" questions to keep the class on approximately the right track.

Case Writing. Your instructor may ask you to "write up"
a case that you may have observed or experienced relative to
some aspect of sport and physical education. This can be an
extremely valuable experience in many ways. Perspective is
developed that can be most helpful. In writing a case, you
may wish to give an overall interpretation after the basic re-
porting has been finished. If you do this, it is advisable to
interpret the case from the standpoints of the various people
involved in the situation. At the very least it would seem to
be wise to include an ethical analysis at the end based on the
triple-play approach being superimposed on the layout for an
argument. Some may wish to follow through with a complete
analysis as outlined above, keeping in mind the ethical route or
approach that you have selected for your own use.

Subjective Opinions vs. Objective Facts.   Keep in mind that you must judge between a subjective opinion and an objective fact, as well as between relevant and irrelevant material. If a coach states, for example, that the athletic director was unethical to think that the team could get along with such poor equipment in a collision sport, you, as a careful analyst, must determine whether the coach was being unreasonable or whether ethical implications were present in the director's stand (not to mention legal implications as well!).

The truism "things are never as simple as they seem to be on the surface" is at the heart of the case plan of instruction.   Each person involved in a case problem is inescapably unique, for no two people see the same situation in exactly the same way.   When you realize this, your own discernment will greatly improve.   Then you will be on the way to a better understanding of human relations in this increasingly complex world.

When a Case Is Not What It May Seem to Be

This leads us to the conclusion that a case may not be what it seems to be on the surface.   Every student will analyze the problem through the "colored glasses" of his or her own ethical background and present attitudes.   A student with an authoritarian background may look at things as either black or white.   Thus, in one case because of this orientation, the coach will be his fair-haired boy, while the principal is the "rat."   Such a student's opinion is generally that if the principal is fired (by whom and for what?), everyone will live happily forever after.   Another student will be accustomed to having the instructor think for her, while a third tend to be a "knee-jerk radical" and won't let anyone think for him.   A fourth student may be looking for the approval of her classmates, and will tend to say what she thinks others want to hear.   An occasional student will simply "wander off into the night," and all will wonder if the same case is being discussed. And so it goes. . . .

Concluding Statement

One of the facts that I soon discovered upon beginning this method of instruction is that some students by nature talk a great deal more than others--perhaps nurture plays a significant role here too!   At any rate, we soon realize that these talkative ones are not necessarily the most intelligent and wise members of the group.   Thus, when the first set of written case analyses are turned in, you might be surprised to find that the young woman who spoke in class only when spoken to actually wrote the best ethical analysis. You might be further surprised to learn that the student who was always ready with a quick, facile answer has analysed the case problem only superficially.

Finally, it is difficult for instructors who are leading a discussion for the "umpteenth" time to avoid directive teaching and strong class guidance. I believe strongly that the instructor should not direct the discussion to follow a specific pattern because he and last year's class came up with a certain proposed solution to a case that seemed excellent. Although different ethical routes are possible, as was explained in Chapter 4, there is not any reason to be absolutely certain that a predetermined solution would work best. Some ethical routes may seem to prescribe "pat" answers, but even there we are faced with the human relations factor, an aspect of life that is typically most unpredictable. Thus, as an instructor I tend to "let the cards fall where they may," and there is always an opportunity to voice an opinion when the group seems to have "forged a tenable position" through discussion. In this way I believe most sincerely that everyone in the class will have a thoroughly enjoyable, useful experience from which much will be learned about ethical decision-making for both one's personal and professional life.

References and Bibliography

Anderson, C. R., Menning, J. H. and Wilkinson, C. W. Writing for business. Homewood, IL: Richard D. Irwin, Inc., 1960.

Andrews, K. R. The case method of teaching human relations and administration. Cambridge, MA: Harvard University Press, 1953. This includes many papers by different authors.

Brackenbury, R. L. Getting down to cases. New York: G. P. Putnam's Sons, 1959. This is one example of the use of a case problem approach in educational philosophy.

Bauer, R. C. Cases in college administration. New York: Teachers College, Columbia University, 1955.

Charan, R.   Classroom techniques in teaching by the case method. Academy of Management Review, July, 1976, 116-123.

Dearborn, D. C.   Observer's report on the role of instructors in case discussion. In McNair, M. P., The case method at the Harvard Business School. New York: McGraw-Hill Book Co., 1954.

Dooley, A. R. and Skinner, W.   Casing case methods methods. Academy of Management Review, April, 1977, 277-289.

Fraser, C. E.   The case method of instruction. New York: McGraw-Hill Book Co., 1931.

Gragg, C. I.   Because wisdom can't be told. In Andrews, K. R. The case method of teaching human relations and administration. Cambridge, MA: Harvard University Press, 1953.

Leenders, M. R. and Erskine, J. A.   Case research: The case writing process. 2nd Edition. London, Ontario: School of Business Administration, The University of Western Ontario, 1978.

McNair, M. P., Ed.   The case method at the Harvard Business School. New York: McGraw-Hill Book Company, 1954.

Manicas, P. T. and Kruger, A. N.   Essentials of logic. New York: American Book Company, 1968.

Towl, A. R.   Study administration by cases. Boston, MA: Graduate School of Business Administration, Harvard University, 1969.

Wernette, J.   The theory of the case method. Michigan Business Review, January, 1965.

Zeigler, E. F.   Administration of physical education and athletics: A case method approach. Englewood Cliffs, N.J.: Prentice-Hall, Inc., 1959.

Zeigler, E. F.   The case method of instruction as applied to the preparation of athletic administrators and coaches. In Proceedings, National College Physical Education Association for Men (C. E. Mueller, Ed.). Minneapolis, MN: The Association, 1968, 143-152.

Zeigler, E. F. Decision-making in physical education and athletics administration: A case method approach. Champaign, IL: Stipes Publishing Company, 1982.

CHAPTER 11
CASE PROBLEMS ABOUT
ETHICAL ISSUES

In Chapter 11 you are presented with the second of the two basic experiential techniques that are being recommended for your introduction to ethical decision-making in sport and physical education--a case method approach. The case problems that have been assembled are all based on real situations that occurred in the recent past. Of course, every effort has been made to disguise the real names and places in order to spare any possible embarrassment to those people who were involved in these situation.

To assist you with the analysis of these case problems, after the presentation of each of the 10 cases you will find a brief layout of the argument that has been developed with the triple-play approach in mind. Naturally, you should not accept the premises and tenets of any of these argument layouts without careful analysis and discussion. I suggest that you use each one for purposes of discussion and for purposes of comparison with your "embryonic" analysis. After the class discussion has been held, and you have then given the problem situation further consideration based on this discussion, I suggest that you then prepare your written case analysis based on the eight steps as outlined in Chapter 10, p. 92. Of course, if you decide to follow one of the other proposed ethical approaches with any of these case analyses, steps 2 and 3 of the recommended format should be omitted, and the key elements of that basic approach should be entered in their place. Some of the readings listed in the bibliography should be read carefully (e.g., Abelson and Friquegnon, 1975), and you may wish to discuss this with your instructor for any other suggested readings that he or she might recommend. Of course, you would be well advised to read Chapter 4 over again carefully, with special reference to the pages where your intended approach is reviewed briefly and presented in tabular form.

CASE A

"Discipline at Compton High"

Ralph Talbot was a physical education instructor, the wrestling coach, and an assistant football coach at a large metropolitan high school (Compton High School). One of his assigned duties was noon-hour supervisor of the school's indoor recreation area. This included checking on the boys' lavatory occasionally to prevent smoking which is against the state law.

On this particular day Ralph was walking across the room to shut off the record player because it was time to close up for the afternoon. As Bob Jones, a tall, quite well-built young man (a Black) saw him, he moved directly in his path in what was evidently a deliberate move. Ralph stopped and asked him what he wanted. Bob replied, "Nothing." Ralph asked him to move four times, and then stated that he was not going to tell him again. Bob simply smiled. Ralph grabbed his right arm and tried to move the student. One move led to another, and Ralph stated that they should go to the Principal's Office.

To Ralph's surprise he was hit in the face twice before he started to defend himself. Then Ralph took Bob to the floor with a wrestling maneuver. Bob scratched at Ralph's face from the bottom, so Ralph hit him in the face. Just then a black, ex-wrestler separated them, and Bob again came at Ralph and hit him again. So Ralph went behind Bob with a wrestling hold, dragged him to the Office, and threw him on the sofa there while continuing to hold him down. When Bob agreed to calm down, Ralph released him. However, Bob immediately started after Ralph again, but finally several students and teachers got control of the situation. So Ralph went to his next class.

A bit later Principal Thornton called Ralph to the office. He stated that nothing like this had ever happened there before, and that some of the students had stated that Ralph was prejudiced against Blacks. Ralph denied this vehemently, stating that he had no problems with Blacks either in wrestling or football. As Ralph left the office he had the feeling that in the eyes of the principal he was "guilty until proven innocent." That evening Bob's mother called Ralph asking why he had hit her son and also torn his clothes. She explained that she was a single parent with five children and really didn't have time to get overly involved with the entire situation. Ralph wondered what he should do, if anything.

As Ralph thought about the problem later that evening, he recalled that he had reported Bob at the beginning of the school year for smoking in the lavatory. Also, he had stopped Bob and a young woman from doing what he thought was an obscene dance during noon hour a bit later. The next morning Ralph learned that Bob had a reputation for fighting; that he had just received his report card with all failures; and that Bob was actually cutting a class at the time the fracas developed.

Argument Layout

D ———————————————→ C
                    Q
           So, presumably

KEEPING IN MIND THAT A TEACH-
ER SHOULD UNDERSTAND FULLY
WHAT DISCIPLINE IS PERMITTED
BY LAW, A TEACHER CLEARLY
HAS THE RIGHT TO DEFEND HIM-
SELF/HERSELF IN A REASONABLE
MANNER

RALPH HANDLED THIS
UNUSUALLY TROUBLE-
SOME DISCIPLINARY
MATTER IN THE BEST
WAY POSSIBLE, AND BOB
SHOULD BE PUNISHED

On account of
W

Unless
R or E

TEACHERS ARE EXPECTED
TO KEEP STUDENTS UNDER
CONTROL IN THIS SOCIETY
SO THAT THE NORMAL
EDUCATIONAL PROCESS
WILL NOT BE DISTURBED

RALPH SHOULD NOT HAVE LAID
HIS HANDS ON THE YOUNG MAN
FIRST

(Universalizability)

or

RALPH HAS BEEN UNREASONABLE
IN HIS EARLIER TREATMENT OF
THE YOUNG MAN

Because
B

or

PERMITTING A STUDENT
TO THREATEN AND THEN
TO ACTUALLY STRIKE
HIM OR HER COULD
CAUSE SERIOUS HARM TO
BOTH PARTIES CONCERN-
ED

RALPH HAD BEEN UNDULY VIO-
LENT IN HIS REACTION TO THE
YOUNG MAN'S CHALLENGE

or

(Consequences)

BOB WAS UNDER THE INFLUENCE
OF SOME DRUG AND WASN'T
FULLY AWARE OF WHAT HE WAS
DOING

Intentions

or

BOB WAS UNDER SEVERE STRESS
FOR SOME REASON AND NEEDED
PSYCHIATRIC HELP

CASE B

"Stealing at Chickamauga Township High School"

Chickamauga Township High School is situated in the sub-urbs, south of Los Angeles. It is a relatively new high school with an enrollment of approximately 3,500 students. The area's main business concern is automobile accessories, and there are a number of other minor industries. The high school's athletic facilities and equipment compare with the best in the state of California.

The varsity football team at Chickamauga has had an out-standing record, having won their conference six of the last seven years. Head Coach Brogan is 34 years of age and is in his eighth year there. He is assisted by Paul Duthie, who is in his fifth year. The players seem to hold them both in great respect.

This fall, once again, the football team is off to a great start, having won the first two games with most comfortable margins. Townspeople are already talking about another cham-pionship team.

On Monday morning after the second win, Coach Bragg was checking over equipment and noticed that several boxes of brand new "T" shirts were missing. That afternoon at prac-tice, he and Coach Duthie called the squad members together and explained the morning's discovery. He explained how only people related to the team had access to the equipment room and said how badly he and Paul felt that there must be one or more thieves on the squad. Finally, he stated that serious consideration would be given to cancelling the schedule for the year if the shirts weren't returned. Then both coaches left for the day.

The co-captains, Jeb Stuart and Harry Lee, immediately held a meeting of the entire group. Some felt that each squad member should chip in one dollar or so to pay for the missing equipment. Others felt that things like this happened all the time, and that it wasn't a "very big deal." Another faction wanted nothing to do with a pool to raise money to pay for the shirts; these team members felt that those who had snitched the shirts ought to own up to the theft.

Finally, it was agreed that the co-captains would sit in the room where chalk-board sessions were held, and that each person on the squad should report there individually and (in effect) take an oath about non-involvement. This plan was carried out, but no one confessed to guilt in the matter.

It was agreed further that each person should bring back anything that he might have stolen. When the coaches arrived for practice the next day, there was a huge pile of equipment on the locker room floor by the entrance--but no "T" shirts . . .

Argument Layout

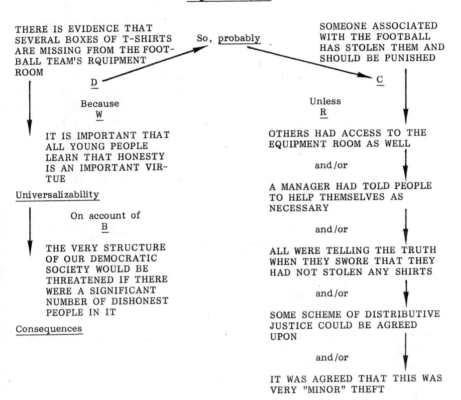

THERE IS EVIDENCE THAT
SEVERAL BOXES OF T-SHIRTS   So, probably
ARE MISSING FROM THE FOOT-
BALL TEAM'S RQUIPMENT
ROOM

D

Because
W

IT IS IMPORTANT THAT
ALL YOUNG PEOPLE
LEARN THAT HONESTY
IS AN IMPORTANT VIR-
TUE

Universalizability

On account of
B

THE VERY STRUCTURE
OF OUR DEMOCRATIC
SOCIETY WOULD BE
THREATENED IF THERE
WERE A SIGNIFICANT
NUMBER OF DISHONEST
PEOPLE IN IT

Consequences

SOMEONE ASSOCIATED
WITH THE FOOTBALL
HAS STOLEN THEM AND
SHOULD BE PUNISHED

C

Unless
R

OTHERS HAD ACCESS TO THE
EQUIPMENT ROOM AS WELL

and/or

A MANAGER HAD TOLD PEOPLE
TO HELP THEMSELVES AS
NECESSARY

and/or

ALL WERE TELLING THE TRUTH
WHEN THEY SWORE THAT THEY
HAD NOT STOLEN ANY SHIRTS

and/or

SOME SCHEME OF DISTRIBUTIVE
JUSTICE COULD BE AGREED
UPON

and/or

IT WAS AGREED THAT THIS WAS
VERY "MINOR" THEFT

etc.

Intentions

CASE C

"Breaking Training Rules at Slocom High"

The Slocom Board of Education was asked at its meeting last evening to rule on a petition by parents to overrule a recent action by the high school administrative and coaching staff to suspend 10 football players and a member of the track team from athletics for the remainder of the school year.

The disciplinary action against 9 seniors and 2 juniors was the result of a drinking party held after Slocom's 33-0 football victory over Dedham on Sept. 29. The 11 suspended athletes admitted that they had been drinking at a lakeside cottage, and also that 2 automobiles had been damaged by gunfire during the party.

Last night's special meeting of the school board was called at the request of Trustee Paul E. Munn, who asked President Howard Franszen to hold the session in response to mounting pressure for a more lenient policy from members of the community and parents of the affected boys.

Community concern appeared to be divided between alarm at the revelation that under-age teen-agers have been involved in such an affair and further alarm at the impending absence of the core of the varsity team from this year's highly rated football team. The latter group really began to protest after the junior varsity team--ten of whom would now automatically be elevated to the varsity squad--was able only to tie the winless Blanton High School football team last Thursday.

Thus, some 35 persons arrived at 7:30 p.m. for the meeting last night and waited for two hours in the high school library to learn what the decision of the appeal would be as a result of the closed, executive session of the Board being held in the school cafeteria. The Board gave no reason for its sudden decision to meet behind closed doors when leaving the room, but later explained that this was done because several newsmen were present. Franszen later denied that the closed session was held because there was evident disagreement among the members of the Board--and he wanted to present a united front after the final decision had been made.

At any rate, the meeting was begun officially at 9:30 p.m. Franszen stated, "This is not a pleasant topic." After clearing his throat, he continued: "We have discussed our policy, and

I am now ready to entertain a motion to resolve the petition that has been submitted to us by members of the community." At that point, Trustee Munn moved that the decision of the school staff should be upheld. During the ensuing discussion the chairman of the Board declared that members of the audience would be given up to 15 minutes to state their opinions. Many parents felt that the penalty imposed was too severe, even though the boys themselves felt that the decision was fair. Chairman Franszen wondered if he shouldn't urge the group to compromise.

Argument Layout

D ──► C

THERE IS EVIDENCE THAT 11
ATHLETES TOOK PART IN A   Q
DRINKING PARTY AFTER A   So, presumably
SUCCESSFUL FOOTBALL GAME
WHICH MEANS THAT TRAIN-
ING RULES WERE BROKEN

STRICT DISCIPLINARY
ACTION SHOULD BE
TAKEN AGAINST THE
OFFENDERS BY SCHOOL
ADMINISTRATOR (I.E.,
SUSPENSION FROM ATH-
LETICS FOR THE YEAR)

Because
W

Unless
R or E

THE BREAKING OF TRAIN-
ING RULES BY THE COM-
MISSION OF UNLAWFUL,
INJURIOUS HEALTH PRAC-
TICES IS CONTRARY TO
SOCIETAL VALUES AND
NORMS IN THIS SOCIETY
(Universalizability)

IT CAN BE PROVED THAT SOME
OF THE PRESUMED OFFENDERS
ARE INNOCENT

and/or

On account of
B

THE BOARD OF EDUCATION CAN
BE CONVINCED THAT THE
PUNISHMENT ENACTED IS TOO
SEVERE FOR THE OFFENSE

SUCH CONDUCT IF UN-
PUNISHED IS UNHEALTHY,
PROMOTES DISRESPECT
FOR SOCIETAL MORES, IS
INJURIOUS TO THE
SCHOOL'S REPUTATION,
AND PROMOTES A BREAK-
DOWN OF AUTHORITY IN
THE SCHOOLS AND IN SO-
CIETY GENERALLY

and/or

PARENTS OF TEENAGERS ELI-
GIBLE TO DRINK ALCOHOL SEE
NOTHING WRONG WITH THEIR
SONS' CONDUCT AND CAN HAVE
THE SUSPENSION LIFTED EITHER
BY THE BOARD OR THE COURTS

(Intentions)

(Consequences)

CASE D

"Drug-Taking at Midwestern University"

One of the aspects of highly competitive sport where coaches encounter problems today is that area where stimulants, painkillers, and/or body-building agents are being employed by the athlete, often through the advice and encouragement of the coach and/or athletic therapist, to improve the level of performance required for success in an increasingly competitive environment. Of course, this is only a part of a still greater societal issue--the use of marijuana, cocaine, amphetamines, LSD, heroin, alcohol, tobacco, and the variety of major and minor drugs being used daily by millions.

It goes something like this: "The night before a game, the guys will take some tranquilizers for "butterflies." Just before the game half the team will benny-up. Some might do some coke to help kick in the bennies. After the game, win or lose, they'll need about five mandarax to settle them down again."

Many college coaches, trainers, and doctors officially frown on the use of drugs, but they know that they're being taken. "We can't do much about it," they say. "The boys going from here (Midwestern) to professional draft situations will try building themselves up with everything they can," said Dr. C. P. James, a local physician who has followed sport closely. There are three basic kinds of drugs used typically in highly competitive sport: steroids for body-building while training, pep pills for energy, and painkillers for injuries.

Coach Dave Morentino was fully aware of these developments, but was committed to keeping such usage to an absolute minimum--and then only if something were medically prescribed by the team physician (e.g., a painkiller prior to a contest for the type of injury where participation could do no further harm to the player). Thus Morentino's football team was typically "clean" in this regard because the players respected their football coach. Further, as Trainer Joe LaRose stated, "Steroids may make a difference, but they can't change silver into gold!"

Midwestern University Beavers, Morentino's football team, was having a good season. They looked like they might be repeaters, and this was the Coach's last year at the helm of this typically most successful team. The pressure mounted as the season was drawing to a close, but Midwestern continued with its winning ways.   The word got around that some of Midwestern's key players--on both offense and defense--were using drugs.   However, this practice was most secretive, although LaRose was quoted as saying, "I know guys use steroids and some use amphetamines; believe me, I keep warning them about it."   Finally, Coach Morentino made a special point about addressing the entire squad about these rumors.

The entire season came down to the last game.   During the last week of practice, Midwestern was generally favored to win.   However, Boulder University was powerful, and there were relatively few injuried on the squad.   Thursday was to be a light practice day for Midwestern.   As Coach Dave and his assistants were dressing to go out on the field, there was a knock at the door.   The team manager stated that one of the local newspaper reporters had an urgent message for the head coach in the hall.

As the Coach went out in the hall, he immediately recognized Tom Jackson, the sports editor of one of the two newspapers in the community.   Tom said, "Someone has brought me what seems to be irrefutable evidence that your two co-captains have been picking up drug prescriptions from Wardle's Drugs in the east end of the city.   I can't sit on this story, unfortunately for you and the boys.   What do you have to say?   Also, what do you intend to do about it with your final game on Saturday?"

Coach Morentino was stunned.   By questionning he learned that these drugs were not the really "bad stuff"; they were merely what have been called "uppers" and "downers."   Nevertheless, he has only recently gone over the problem with the entire squad, and had made a point of stating that such usage would not be tolerated.   Not what was he to do, and when should he do it?   He realized that this thing could be blown way out of proportion.   He rationalized that to a large extent it was a private matter.   And yet he knew that many would argue that the university community and others had a right to expect that drugs were not being used.   What should Coach Dave do?

Argument Layout

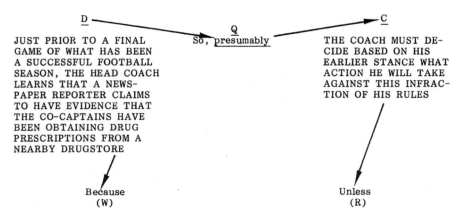

D ———————————————————————————————→ C

JUST PRIOR TO A FINAL
GAME OF WHAT HAS BEEN
A SUCCESSFUL FOOTBALL
SEASON, THE HEAD COACH
LEARNS THAT A NEWS-
PAPER REPORTER CLAIMS
TO HAVE EVIDENCE THAT
THE CO-CAPTAINS HAVE
BEEN OBTAINING DRUG
PRESCRIPTIONS FROM A
NEARBY DRUGSTORE

Q
So, presumably

THE COACH MUST DE-
CIDE BASED ON HIS
EARLIER STANCE WHAT
ACTION HE WILL TAKE
AGAINST THIS INFRAC-
TION OF HIS RULES

Because
(W)

Unless
(R)

WHEN THIS INFORMATION
BECOMES PUBLIC KNOWL-
EDGE, SOME DISCREDIT
WILL BECOME ATTACHED
TO ALL CONCERNED,
SINCE SOCIETY EXPECTS
ITS ATHLETES TO AP-
PEAR LIKE PARAGONS OF
VIRTUE

(Universalizability)

THE CO-CAPTAINS HAVE AN
ACCEPTABLE EXPLANATION
FOR THEIR ACTION

and/or

THE MEN CONCERNED APOLO-
GIZE FOR THEIR ACTIONS
AND REQUEST THE CHANCE
TO PLAY IN THEIR LAST
GAME

and/or

On account of
(B)

DRUG-TAKING OF A
GREAT VARIETY OF PROB-
LEMS HAS BECOME A SIG-
NIFICANT CULTURAL
PROBLEM THREATENING
THE NATION'S HEALTH
AND WELL-BEING, AND
YOUTH TEND TO COPY
PRACTICES OF ATHLETES

(Consequences)

THE COACH DECIDES WHAT
THEY HAVE DONE IS REALLY
A MINOR INFRACTION AND DE-
CIDES THAT SUSPENSION AT
THIS POINT WOULD BE UN-
REASONABLE

(Intentions)   etc.

CASE E

"Athletic Recruiting at Midwestern University"

Glen Mather, the elderly, successful head wrestling coach at Midwestern University, urged Bob Wood to apply for admission. Midwestern is a large prestigious state university with a fine tradition in many sports (including wrestling).

Bob had a fine record in high school wrestling, but his grades were not high because of the need for him to work at two part-time jobs during his senior year in high school. Thus, injury and illness brough his grade average down to the point where he barely graduated from high school. As it turned out, therefore, Coach Mather had to arrange for a special examination so that Bob was finally admitted to Midwestern.

There was an agreement that Bob would receive an athletic tender (grant-in-aid) to cover in-state tuition. If he maintained sufficiently high grades for athletic eligibility, and his performance in wrestling was satisfactory, Coach Mather stated verbally that Bob would shortly receive a "full ride" (room, meals, books, and tuition).

Bob was smaller than the top limit of the lightest weight class, which meant that he was always wrestling against heavier opponents both in practice and in regular competition. The coach arranged for some outside amateur competition, however, and was very pleased when Bob won the Olympic trials in his region. However, he injured his ankle and could proceed no further in the competition at that time.

At the beginning of his sophomore year, Bob did not receive the "full ride" that had been discussed because his grades "were not sufficiently high." As Bob was looking for part-time work, he learned that two other members of the team were getting the "full package" (even though they had lower averages than Bob!).

During Christmas break Bob had a minor operation that set back his conditioning program. Also, he had to miss the tournament that the team took part in traditionally over the holiday period. Bob was released from the hospital the day before classes started up again, and Bob dropped by practice on the opening day to explain the situation to Coach Mather. Realizing that Bob's operation was not of a nature to prevent him from practicing, the coach urged him to get started immediately.

As it turned out, Bob lost close matches on Friday and Saturday on that same week while competing for the team.

Two weeks later wrestling with a much heavier man at
the coach's suggestion, Bob received a severe dislocation of his
right elbow. Bob was in the hospital for two weeks and was
told by several doctors that his wrestling career was over.
Coach Mather visited Bob the day after the accident and was
very glum about the bad news. When Bob was released from
the hospital, he wasn't able to continue with his part-time work.
He asked Coach Mather if the University Athletic Association
could help him a bit financially. This was evidently not possible, and Bob became very discouraged. He had fallen behind
in his school work too, so there was nothing to do but drop
out of school.

For the next year and a half Bob worked to recover normal use of his arm. At the same time he took a full-time job
and saved every cent possible so that he could complete his
university education. Bob was determined to pay his own way
completely, because he felt that his coach hadn't treated him
fairly, and he didn't want to be obligated to wrestle for Midwestern if he ever went out for wrestling again.

When Coach Mather heard that Bob had returned, he called him and urged him to come out for the team again. However, Bob felt that he ought to re-establish himself academically first. This status was accomplished, and Bob was married
in August after the academic year had been completed. Bob
discovered at the beginning of what he thought was his final
year that he really had three semesters of academic work left
in order to receive his bachelor's degree. Coach Mathers knew
about this too and had made application so that Bob might have
two full years of eligibility left if he took the absolute minimum
of credit hours each semester.

Bob's former desire to make good at wrestling returned.
He realized further that a truly successful record in competition would help him obtain a better position as a teacher/coach.
The coach offered him a tuition waiver, but Bob and his wife
decided not to accept the help. She was working; they had
their savings; and Bob knew about a good part-time position
(two hours daily and ten hours over the weekend). It turned
out to be a very good year. Bob's academic average was better than ever before; he wrestled in all of the meets and placed
third in the conference finals. The future seemed bright again.

The summer before his senior year at Midwestern turned out disastrously. Bob could only find a minimum of part-time work, and his wife became ill and required hospitalization. So in August, with much hesitation and a great deal of regret, Bob asked his coach for the proverbial full ride (grant-in-aid). Others were receiving it, and Bob felt that he had truly earned such compensation. However, Coach Mather told him that all possible commitments had been made already, but that he might be able to put him on the "full-ride" roster for the second term. It turned out additionally that a new, lower weight class had been added, and Bob was the only man on the squad who could conceivably make the weight—by losing fifteen (!) pounds. Bob did it; he made the weight for the early meets. However, at the beginning of the second term Bob lost his quite lucrative part-time job. Then Coach Mather said that he was sorry, but that he simply could not put Bob on the roster.

Argument Layout

D ─────────────────────► Q ◄──────────────────► C

So, presumably

| IN A NUMBER OF WAYS, IT SEEMED LIKE COACH MATHER WAS EXPLOITING BOB BY NOT LIVING UP TO HIS PROMISES AND BY DESERTING BOB WHEN HE WAS BESET BY INJURIES AND FAMILY ILLNESS AND THEREFORE IN DESPERATE NEED OF FINANCIAL HELP | BOB SHOULD TELL THE COACH THAT HE SIMPLY COULD NOT CONTINUE WITHOUT FINANCIAL ASSISTANCE; IF THIS DOES NOT WORK, HE SHOULD CONSIDER AP- PROACHING THE ATH- LETIC DIRECTOR WITH A REQUEST THAT HIS CASE BE CONSIDERED |

Since
W

Unless
R or E

SOCIETY HAS COME TO UNDERSTAND THE ATH- LETIC SCHOLARSHIP PLAN, AND THE PUBLIC EXPECTS THAT SUCH AID IS GRANTED IN A FAIR AND EQUITABLE MANNER TO ALL WHO QUALIFY REGARDLESS OF SUBSEQUENT INJURY

(Universalizability)

IT IS DISCOVERED THAT BOB HAS MISREPRESENT- ED THE FACTS OF THE SITUATION AND WAS AC- TUALLY EXPECTING MORE THAN COACH MATHER SHOULD BE EX- PECTED TO PRODUCE FOR HIM FINANCIALLY

and/or

Because
B

THE COACH WAS NOT FULLY AWARE OF THE GREAT DIFFICULTIES THAT BOB WAS HAVING FINANCIALLY

ATHLETES BASE THEIR FINANCIAL PLANS ON SUCH AID AND, IF IT IS NOT FORTHCOMING, MAY BE FORCED TO LEAVE SCHOOL WITHOUT A DEGREE. AL- SO, THE UNIVERSITY'S REPUTATION WOULD SUFFER IF ALL WERE NOT TREATED FAIRLY WITH SUCH A PLAN

(Consequences)

and/or

THE COACH HAD OVER- COMMITTED HIMSELF AND WAS TELLING THE TRUTH WHEN HE ON SEVERAL OCCASIONS WAS NOT ABLE TO OFFER FINAN- CIAL AID

(Intentions)

and/or

THE COACH WAS BEING PRESSURED INORDINATE- LY TO WIN AND MADE WHAT HE CONSIDERED TO BE EMINENTLY FAIR DECISIONS ABOUT HOW THE GRANT-IN-AID MONEY SHOULD BE DISTRIBUTED

and/or ??

CASE F

"Sportsmanship at Midwestern University"

Midwestern basketball co-captain Sandy Slews was suspended from participating in any capacity for one full year for
alledgedly "spitting in a referee's ear," and then making antisemitic remarks Wednesday night after his fraternity, Mu Gu,
lost to Hi Phi in intramural basketball competition.

The action was taken by the Intramural Protest Board
Thursday afternoon after a lengthy session where a number of
witnesses were called to testify. The Board also voted to put
Mu Gu on probation for the remainder of the semester.

According to officials, a technical foul was handed Slews
early in the contest when he, in his capacity as Mu Gu's coach,
protested a referee's decision too vehemently.

Slews was said to have quieted down after the incident,
but erupted again late in the game as another technical foul
was called on him for walking on the court and using obscenities.

As the game ended with Mu Gu losing by two points,
Slews, according to several people present, chased one of the
referees, shouted a string of obscenities at him, and then made
a strong antisemitic remark at him. Finally, Slews grabbed the
referee and spit in his ear. Then he released him, rushed over
to the sidelines, picked up one of the benches, and threw it at
the basketball backboard. (Interestingly, the referee was of
Iranian heritage.)

Slim Paterson, Intramural Supervisor, stated that such
violent action was the worst that he had ever encountered. He
felt that Slews' most serious offense was "his antisemitic outcry
and action toward the referee. Religious or racial prejudice
has no place in IM activities on this campus," Paterson continued, "and it simply will not be tolerated."

According to the referee, there was some evidence of
liquor on the court, but he could not specifically attribute the
smell of alcohol to any one person.

The referees of the game agreed with Mu Gu's representatives at the meeting that the incident was really not the fault

of the team, and that therefore the house should not be su-
pended. Dave Spanich, Mu Gu's President, said, "The team
members were reasonably well behaved. There just wasn't anything that we could do with Slews at that point."

The following day Coach Cecil Smythe, Midwestern's head
basketball coach, decided that Sandy should sit out one varsity
game to think about his outburst at the intramural game. Stating
that "this has been a difficult season for us," Coach Smythe
stated, "this is the culmination of many things. Sandy still has
an opportunity to play in the last two games, and we expect
him to be at practice on Sunday. This is all very unfortunate."

Argument Layout

(D) ——————————————————————————→ (C)

A COACH OF AN INTRAMURAL
BASKETBALL TEAM, WHO HAP-
PENS ALSO TO BE CO-CAPTAIN
OF THE VARSITY BASKETBALL
TEAM, COMMITS A VARIETY OF
INFRACTIONS ON THE SIDELINE
DURING A GAME. THESE IN-
CLUDE SWEARING AT OFFICIALS,
GOING OUT ON THE FLOOR,
PHYSICALLY ABUSING OF OFFI-
CIALS AFTER THE GAME, CAST-
ING A RACIAL SLUR AT ONE
OFFICIAL, DESTRUCTION OF
PROPERTY, AND WAS POSSIBLY
UNDER THE INFLUENCE OF
ALCOHOL

Since (W)

SOCIETY EXPECTS SPORT
COMPETITION TO BE
CHARACTERIZED BY VIG-
OROUS, BUT BASICALLY
"GENTLEMANLY" BEHAV-
IOR ON THE PART OF
ALL CONCERNED--THE
EXPECTATION BEING
THAT SOME TRANSFER
OF TRAINING MAY OCCUR

(Universalizability)

Because (B)

SUCH BEHAVIOR THREAT-
ENS THE VERY STRUCTURE
OF COMPETITIVE SPORT;
THE RULES MUST BE OBEY-
ED, OR SUCH COMPETITIONS
SHOULD BE CANCELLED;
STUDENTS WILL REFUSE TO
TAKE PART IN SUCH UN-
PLEASANT EXPERIENCES

(Consequences)

Q
So, necessarily

THE INTRAMURAL PRO-
TEST BOARD SHOULD
TAKE SOME ACTION
AGAINST SUCH FLA-
GRANT MISBEHAVIOR

Unless (R or E)

THE CO-CAPTAIN WAS SO
DRUNK THAT HE TRULY DID
NOT KNOW WHAT HE WAS
DOING

and/or

THE CO-CAPTAIN FREELY
AND WILLINGLY APOLOGIZES
TO ALL CONCERNED FOR
HIS INEXCUSABLE BEHAVIOR

and/or

THE CO-CAPTIN WAS SOME-
HOW GOADED INTO SUCH
REASONABLE BEHAVIOR

and/or

THE CO-CAPTAIN WAS UNDER
SUCH STRESS THAT HE HAD
SOMEHOW BECOME MENTALLY
ILL (PSYCHOTIC)

(Intentions)

CASE G

"Grading Practices for Athletes at Midwestern University"

Note: The following letter was addressed to Dr. T. C. Collins, Undergraduate Professional Program Director, Department of Physical Education, Midwestern University on February 1, 198-:

Dear Dr. Collins:

As you know, Head Coach Courtney and I have just completed the teaching of PE 156 (Wrestling), a course that we have handled jointly for the past few years. This year I had developed a new grading scheme which we presented to the students at the first class period. We agreed that I would determine the written work to be completed, and the skills we were to teach were those that Tom stresses typically.

Both of us graded students at various times during the semester on their ability at the skills. Tom asked me, as usual, to grade all of the written work. This I did and all grades, including attendance, were listed on a large chart kept in Coach Tom's office. Near the end of the term, incidentally, many students were complaining to both Tom and me that he (Courtney) had been marking them absent incorrectly.

While grading the written work, I noticed that one student, a prominent Midwestern athlete, turned in someone else's notebook under his own name. I actually remembered grading it last spring. He also handed in several other assignments at this time--ones that were actually due at the middle of the semester. He explained that injury had prevented him from getting them in on time. Unfortunately, this was not his own work either. I notified Coach Tom immediately, since he is my superior. He suggested that I give him the papers and the notebook, and that he himself would confront the student and his coach together.

The following day Coach Tom informed me that, despite the young man's plagiarism, Courtney and Slaughter (the student's coach) agreed that the athlete should re-work his notebook and papers. As punishment he would be asked to complete an extra assignment suggested by me. In this way his failing grade could be raised sufficiently so as not to make it impossible for him to get off academic probation. The student came to see me; received the extra assignment; and was to return everything to me when it was completed. Then I would change the grade if his work merited such revision.

My complaint is that I never saw the results. I asked Coach Tom about it, and he explained that he had received the work, graded it, and had misplaced it at home. I checked out the grade submitted and learned that this person, and many other varsity athletes, received a grade of A in the course, while others more deserving received B's and C's. Regretfully, I must charge Coach Tom with dishonesty and a lack of professional ethics.

Very sincerely yours,

Wm. Sanders, Asst. Coach

Argument Layout

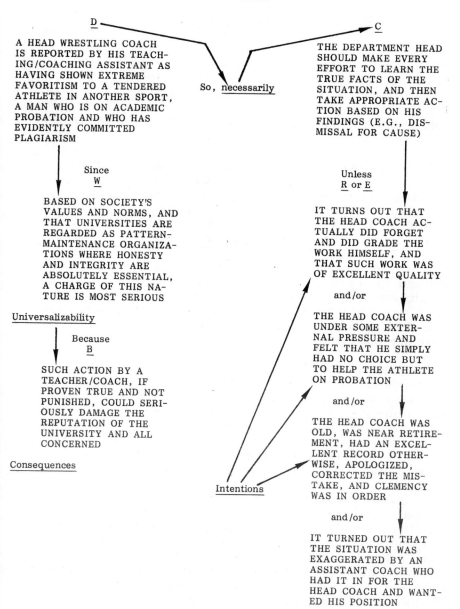

D

A HEAD WRESTLING COACH
IS REPORTED BY HIS TEACH-
ING/COACHING ASSISTANT AS
HAVING SHOWN EXTREME
FAVORITISM TO A TENDERED
ATHLETE IN ANOTHER SPORT,
A MAN WHO IS ON ACADEMIC
PROBATION AND WHO HAS
EVIDENTLY COMMITTED
PLAGIARISM

So, necessarily

C

THE DEPARTMENT HEAD
SHOULD MAKE EVERY
EFFORT TO LEARN THE
TRUE FACTS OF THE
SITUATION, AND THEN
TAKE APPROPRIATE AC-
TION BASED ON HIS
FINDINGS (E.G., DIS-
MISSAL FOR CAUSE)

Since
W

BASED ON SOCIETY'S
VALUES AND NORMS, AND
THAT UNIVERSITIES ARE
REGARDED AS PATTERN-
MAINTENANCE ORGANIZA-
TIONS WHERE HONESTY
AND INTEGRITY ARE
ABSOLUTELY ESSENTIAL,
A CHARGE OF THIS NA-
TURE IS MOST SERIOUS

Universalizability

Because
B

SUCH ACTION BY A
TEACHER/COACH, IF
PROVEN TRUE AND NOT
PUNISHED, COULD SERI-
OUSLY DAMAGE THE
REPUTATION OF THE
UNIVERSITY AND ALL
CONCERNED

Consequences

Unless
R or E

IT TURNS OUT THAT
THE HEAD COACH AC-
TUALLY DID FORGET
AND DID GRADE THE
WORK HIMSELF, AND
THAT SUCH WORK WAS
OF EXCELLENT QUALITY

and/or

THE HEAD COACH WAS
UNDER SOME EXTER-
NAL PRESSURE AND
FELT THAT HE SIMPLY
HAD NO CHOICE BUT
TO HELP THE ATHLETE
ON PROBATION

and/or

THE HEAD COACH WAS
OLD, WAS NEAR RETIRE-
MENT, HAD AN EXCEL-
LENT RECORD OTHER-
WISE, APOLOGIZED,
CORRECTED THE MIS-
TAKE, AND CLEMENCY
WAS IN ORDER

Intentions

and/or

IT TURNED OUT THAT
THE SITUATION WAS
EXAGGERATED BY AN
ASSISTANT COACH WHO
HAD IT IN FOR THE
HEAD COACH AND WANT-
ED HIS POSITION

CASE H

"Breaking a Teaching/Coaching Contract"

Charles Carson came to Central High as a physical education teacher and head football coach in the first year of the school's operation. Although from the first he was popular with the student body and most of the faculty and staff, Principal Twombly soon discovered that Carson could create problems.

Soon many policies and procedures were established, but Carson then caused embarrassment by refusing to do almost everything that was not to his liking. He skipped faculty meetings always because they conflicted with football practice; never showed up at PTA meetings; and never bothered to initial a sign-in sheet system that was started.

Carson was very outspoken about the importance of football and sports in general in the school curriculum. His philosophy was that anything worth doing was worth doing well, so he was most neglectful of any other assigned duties (such as a class sponsor, a dance chaperone, and as cafeteria supervisor one noon a week).

Finally, Twombly called Carson to his office regarding his persistent dereliction of duty. The principal was an experienced administrator, but he was somewhat baffled by Carson's quite good-natured refusal to live up to what Twombly had designated as his school duties. What made matters especially difficult was that Twombly merely tolerated athletics anyhow as a relatively unimportant aspect of what should characterize a high school's fine academic program.

Bob Dixon, the assistant principal, was a man who delighted in accepting responsibilities. He then had trouble carrying out his many responsibilities, but refused to give anything up and "hung on for dear life." He was also athletic director, director of school recreation, senior counselor, and golf coach. Duties conflicted with each other regularly, and all sorts of problems arose because of missed appointments, etc. His pleasing personality helped during the course of the many minor crises that arose.

During the school's second year of operation, Dixon intimated to Carson that he would be recommended for the post of athletic director when he (Dixon) relinquished the post in a

year or two. As it turned out, however, no changed has occurred by the end of Carson's fourth year at Central. (As a
matter of fact, the superintendent had quoted Dixon as saying
that he did not feel that Carson was really the right person to
become athletic director--presumably because it had become
clear that football would be emphasized at the expense of the
many other aspects of the athletic program.)

Superintendent Blosdell was an understanding man who
was anxious to support any reasonable request made by the
athletic department. In the spring of his fifth year, Carson
went to him to talk about his future. He mentioned that he did
not believe in "staying put" when he wasn't satisfied. Since
there seemed to be no immediate possibility of the athletic director's positions becoming available, he said that he had given
some thought to the possibility of getting into coaching at the
college level. Blosdell encouraged him to look for such a post
and thanked him for having discussed the problem with him.
Carson has a fine win-loss record, so the superintendent knew
that he ought to be "keeping an eye open" for other successful
coaches in the region.

Carson started looking in earnest for a college post. Although he was interviewed for several positions, he said nothing about this either to Blosdell or Twombly. He did not sign
his Central contract, intending to leave it unsigned as he had
done several times before. (This was known as a Teachers
Continuing Contract--a form of tenure which stated that the
position was permanent, and that he could be dismissed only
for cause.) On these occasions he hadn't signed it until late
in the fall. This year the office staff had been more efficient
in getting out contracts and having them turned in with appropriate signatures. Since Carson had heard nothing definite
about a new position, he signed the contract--with the intention of breaking it if a college post came through.

During the first week of July, someone called the Central
High School office and reported that Carson had been hired by
Lakeside Community College as head football coach. Superintendent Blosdell called and was only able to reach Mr. Dixon in
an effort to learn more about the situation. Dixon became up-
set because he didn't even know that Carson was thinking about
a move. When Carson heard about this turmoil, he called the
superintendent immediately and told him that he still planned to
return to Central. Blosdell thanked him, stating that he knew
Carson would not leave Central in such an embarrassing position at a late date.

On July 18 Carson was notified that he was the choice for the post at Lakeside, and the story broke in the afternoon edition of the newspaper. Late in the afternoon Superintendent Blosdell received a note from Carson indicating that he did indeed intend to break his signed contract. He wrote that he was sorry, but that--everything considered--he simply couldn't afford to let such an opportunity go by.

Argument Layout

(D) ──────────────→ ──── Q ──── ───────→ (C)
              So, presumably

(D) COACH CARSON, EVEN THOUGH HE HAD BEEN LOOKING ACTIVELY FOR A COLLEGE POST, SIGNED A CONTRACT FOR THE COMING YEAR. AS LATE AS THE FIRST WEEK IN JULY, WHEN SOMEONE REPORTED TO SUPERINTENDENT BLOSDELL THAT CARSON HAD BEEN HIRED ELSEWHERE, CARSON DENIED THIS RUMOR, STATING THAT HE FULLY INTENDED TO FOLLOW THROUGH WITH THE SIGNED CONTRACT. ON JULY 18, AFTER A STORY APPEARED IN THE NEWSPAPER, CARSON WROTE A NOTE TO BLOSDELL INDICATING THAT HE HAD ACCEPTED ANOTHER POSITION.

(C) CARSON SHOULD BE RE-PRIMANDED FOR SUCH UNETHICAL CONDUCT, AND THE SCHOOL AU-THORITIES SHOULD CONSIDER WHAT ACTION TO TAKE.

Unless (R)
or
(E)

CARSON REASONED THAT HE HAD BEEN TREATED UNFAIRLY IN HIS TENURE AT CENTRAL, AND THAT HE WAS SIMPLY EVENING THE SCORE

and/or

Since (W)

SOCIETY'S NORMS AND LAWS REGARD A SIGNED CONTRACT AS A LEGAL DOCUMENT, AND THERE IS EVERY REASON TO EXPECT THAT THE CONDI-TIONS OF THE CONTRACT WILL BE MET.

(Universalizability)

CARSON DID NOT TRULY UNDERSTAND THE SE-VERITY OF THE ACTION HE HAD TAKEN, LOOKING UPON THE SIGNING AS A FORMALITY AND NOT REALLY A BINDING CON-TRACT.

and/or

Because (B)

(Intentions)

SINCE OUR SOCIETY IS GOV-ERNED BY LAW AND ORDER, THE EFFECTS OF PEOPLE BREAKING SIGNED CON-TRACTS WITHOUT PERMIS-SION OF THE OTHER PARTY CONCERNED WOULD ULTI-MATELY BRING ABOUT AN UNTENABLE SITUATION WHERE PEOPLE COULD NOT RELY ON THE VERBAL AND/OR SIGNED AGREEMENTS OF THEIR FELLOWS. THUS, THE FABRIC OF THE SOCI-ETY'S MORALS WOULD BE THREATENED.

(Consequences)

CARSON HAD READ MANY TIMES ABOUT COACHES BREAKING CONTRACTS AND REASONED THAT MATTERS WERE DIFFER-ENT IN SPORT

and/or

CARSON DECIDED THAT THIS NEW POSITION WAS SO IMPORTANT TO HIM THAT HE DECIDED TO TAKE THE RISK OF BREAKING THE CON-TRACT NO MATTER WHAT THE OUTCOME MIGHT BE

and/or

CARSON REASONED THAT CENTRAL HIGH SCHOOL WOULD REALLY HAVE NO DIFFICULTY FILLING HIS POST EVEN IN MID-JULY

CASE I

"Poison-Pen Letters at Midwestern University"

Midwestern University was a large public university with a growing school of health, physical education, and recreation. After World War II the school continued its development and gradually became highly respected in the field. Sometime later Dr. Ramsay, who had a solid background experience in a large municipal system and subsequently in one of the country's foremost training institutions, was appointed dean of the entire school (It should be pointed out that both the intercollegiate and intramural athletic programs were under the general supervision of the school.)

In the years that followed Dr. Ramsay gradually became an even more highly regarded person at both the state and national levels. Ramsay was a solidly principled "health and physical education man." Thus, he regarded intercollegiate athletics as a program that should be worked into an overall, balanced program of health, physical education, and recreation. As part of this picture, he stressed the importance of required physical education and the intramural athletics program that reached the large majority of students at Midwestern. Further, he disliked athletic scholarships that gave "free rides," because he believed that they caused dissension between his department and others on campus. His philosophy embodied more of an "Ivy-League approach"--one in which financial aid was provided to any needy student who was also a bonafide student.

When an opening for a new basketball coach developed, Dr. Kyle Brammel was finally selected from the outside. Brammel had a strong, dynamic personality and was regarded as a highly effective coach. Players respected him, but feared him too because of an explosive temperament (often followed by a string of investives). Part of Brammel's responsibility was the teaching of theory and activity courses in basketball. It turned out that his philosophy of athletics was quite diametrically opposed to that espoused by Ramsay. Both faculty members and students increasingly argued for one position or the other, and the Brammel point of view easily gained the support of just about every other coach. Also, Brammel was younger and more dynamic than Ramsay. The latter eventually was regarded as a high-principled educator whose views were somewhat dated.

It became obvious to Dr. Ramsay that his leadership was being challenged in many ways, so he voluntarily stepped down from his dean's post "to concentrate more on writing and re-search"--an oft-heard phrase in university circles. Soon there-after Dr. Brammel was appointed by the President to succeed Ramsay as Dean, College of Health, Physical Education, and Recreation.

Due to prevailing social influences and the enthusiasm of Dean Brammel, the program of intercollegiate athletics received an increasing amount of emphasis at Midwestern. This is not to say that the other programs "suffered" by this development. (There are so many intangible factors to be considered in any analysis of this type.) However, when changes in emphasis occur, there are always those who are opposed to such change --and they show this disapproval in a variety of ways.

For example, the President and members of the Board of Trustees began to receive unsigned letters explaining that the faculty wanted a de-emphasis of intercollegiate athletics. These letters began about the middle of the football season and typical-ly extended well into the basketball season. The letters stated that football and basketball varsity athletes were presumably receiving a variety of types of employment--jobs for which they were paid but at which they never actually worked! As stated above, all of these letters were typed, but unsigned. They were postmarked "University Heights," the town where Midwestern was located.

As time went on, these letters kept coming to the same people about all types of irregularities and inconsistencies that presumably were occurring within the program of intercollegiate athletics at Midwestern. Eventually the governor of the state heard about these letters, and he called for an investigation. Within two months Dr. Ramsay was identified as the writer of a long series of "poison-pen" letters. All of the media picked up this interesting news. It became widely known that a Midwest-ern University professor had been sending unsigned letters about the vicissitudes of intercollegiate athletics at Midwestern. When asked to comment, Brammel simply stated that the charges were preposterous, obviously the work of a disgruntled person who had become almost psychotic about a perceived injustice.

The President appointed a special committee of the Univer-sity Senate to investigate the matter and to make recommenda-tions. Sometime later there was a brief article explaining that Dr. Ramsay had requested early retirement from Midwestern. The special committee struck was in accord with this request that went through appropriate channels rapidly. Nothing has been heard from Dr. Ramsay in professional circles since that time.

Argument Layout

D ——————————————————————→ C

So, necessarily

Q

DR. RAMSAY, DEAN OF THE SCHOOL OF HEALTH, PHYSICAL EDUCATION, AND RECREATION AT MIDWESTERN UNIVERSITY, WAS GRADUALLY SUPERSEDED BY DR. BRAMMEL, A SUCCESSFUL BASKETBALL COACH, WHOSE PHILOSOPHY WAS MORE IN ACCORD WITH A UNIVERSITY WHERE SUCCESS IN INTERCOLLEGIATE ATHLETICS WAS EVIDENTLY MOST IMPORTANT. UNIVERSITY OFFICIALS AND BOARD MEMBERS BEGAN TO RECEIVE A SERIES OF ANONYMOUS LETTERS CHARGING A MULTITUDE OF RULE INFRACTIONS AT MIDWESTERN INVOLVING ALL TYPES OF IRREGULARITIES AND INCONSISTENCIES IN CONNECTION WITH ILLEGAL AID TO ATHLETES IN SELECTED SPORTS.

Since $\underline{W}$

SOCIETY HAS DEVELOPED NORMS AND LAWS AGAINST LIBEL AND SLANDER THAT PROTECT PEOPLE FROM THE STIGMA OF UNFOUNDED ACCUSATIONS BY THEIR FELLOW CITIZENS

(Universalizability)

Because $\underline{B}$

LIFE WOULD SOON BECOME INTOLERABLE IN A SOCIETY WHERE PEOPLE COULD LIBEL AND SLANDER OTHERS AT WILL EITHER OPENLY OR SECRETLY. SUCH A SITUATION WOULD BREED INCREASING MISTRUST AND DISCORD.

(Consequences)

THE PERPETRATOR OF THESE POSSIBLY LIBELOUS LETTERS SHOULD BE DISCOVERED AND MADE TO PROVE THE CHARGES THAT HE WAS MAKING AGAINST DULY APPOINTED OFFICIALS AND ATHLETES AT MIDWESTERN. IF THE PERSON INVOLVED COULD NOT SUBSTANTIATE THE CHARGES, HE/SHE SHOULD BE CHARGED WITH LIBEL.

(RAMSAY WAS IDENTIFIED)

Unless $\underline{R}$ or $\underline{W}$

RAMSAY COULD PROVE THE CHARGES THAT HE HAD MADE

and/or

RAMSAY COULD PROVE THAT HE HAD BEEN SYSTEMATICALLY UNDERMINED IN AN IMPROPER WAY BY BRAMMEL AND THAT HE WAS SIMPLY ACTING IN RIGHTEOUS ANGER AGAINST SUCH TREATMENT

and/or

RAMSAY COULD PROVE THAT HE HAD NOT COMMITTED THE SLANDER WITH WHICH HE WAS BEING CHARGED

and/or

RAMSAY ADMITTED HIS GUILT AND ASKED TO BE ALLOWED TO RESIGN OR TAKE "EARLY RETIREMENT" BASED ON HIS SERVICE TO THE UNIVERSITY

and/or

RAMSAY WAS DISCOVERED TO BE MENTALLY ILL BY A PHYSICIAN WHO DIAGNOSED HIM AS PSYCHOTIC; HENCE THE UNIVERSITY URGED HIS FAMILY TO ACCEPT "EARLY RETIREMENT" ON HIS BEHALF

(Intentions)

CASE J

"Special Physical Education at Baker High School"

My name is Gerald Scanlon. I'm a physical education teacher/coach at Baker High School in Porterfield. I've been here for two years now, and I like my work. They keep me busy, but I expected that, and besides I'm not married. I'm in charge of all boys' physical education work, and I teach two classes in history (my minor). After school I coach three teams, one in each season during the year--from football to basketball to track and field.

I've had a good education. In addition to a pretty good background in the arts and social science areas, with a minor in history, my work in the sciences was also sound. I came from a school where they had a superior professional program in physical and health education. By the time I graduated I realized quite fully that there was a great deal to be done in our field. In addition to physical education work, I acquired some knowledge about school health education, recreation, and safety education. I thought at times that there was too much crowded into our curriculum, but at least my eyes were opened to the many areas for which we may be held responsible.

Most of my professional duties I can handle. However, as a professional person in this field of human motor performance in sport, dance, play, and exercise, I realize that the young people who come to Baker fall roughly into three categories: those who are reasonably normal, those who might be called "accelerated" in one way or another, and those who are "sub-normal" in the sense that they have temporary or permanent disabilities that tend to keep them from a "normal experience."

What can I, or should I, do about those boys or young men in my classes who need corrective exercise or adapted sports? Oh, I know it's now called "special physical education," and that's fine with me. From my study of the history of the field, I know that it has had a variety of names down through the 20th century. Originally I think it was "remedial gymnastics," but since then it has been designated as correctives, adapted physical education, adaptive physical education, individual physical education, special exercise, and (finally) special physical education. Call it what you will, however, but that does not escape the fact that this aspect of our work--of our built-in responsibility, if you will--is indeed a troubling matter for a person in this field with a "professional conscience." What do I do about it--look the other way because I don't have the time, energy, or special expertise to resolve the matter satisfactorily?

Of course, in my undergraduate program, I studied general biology, mammalian anatomy and physiology, human anatomy and physiology, kinesiology and biomechanics, physiology of exercise, adaptive physical education, and care and prevention of athletic injuries. Thus, even though I feel that I have a good background in this area, I now find that I am stymied when it comes to dealing with individual problems out on the job at Baker High.

Porterfield is like a lot of other towns. We have one high school with one gymnasium. There is one outdoor swimming pool operated by the Recreation Commission in the summer. Fortunately, there are folding doors in the gym, so that Ms. Collins, the girls' and young women's physical education teacher/coach, and I have two teaching stations. However, our total workload and schedule is so arranged that we don't have time to deal with any individual cases. Even if we did have time, there is no special room with equipment for exercise therapy (as it is sometimes called). Further, the way finances are right now, it would be almost impossible to get a special allotment of funds for such a purpose. Even if we did get some money, imagine what it would cost for a special room with equipment for remedial work.

Day after day I see youngsters who need special help-- help that they should have received at the elementary school level. I'm not talking about problems that need immediate attention; they usually get that at the time of accident or illness. One youngster has marked lordosis; another has obvious overcarriage. Kyphosis, lordosis, scoliosis, overcarriage, protruding abdomen, ankle pronation--you name it, and I see it every day. One boy returns after an abdominal operation for appendicitis; another has had a broken arm. John Ford, the halfback on my football team, had the cartilage removed from his knee the Monday after our third game. Andy Riordan, my basketball center, is still complaining about his elbow after last year's dislocation during practice. These young men are released by their physicians, and often the insurance doesn't cover any rehabilitation after two subsequent visits. They return to our physical education classes and our interscholastic and intramural sports, and what do we do with them then? Fortunately, Nature helps in many cases after a considerable period of time, but it takes so long. I am never certain when they can go "full speed" again. Much valuable class and sport time is lost, and all too often there is a recurrence of the original injury.

These cases just mentioned really aren't so bad. But then there is the case of Peter Sabo, a fine-looking, rugged lad with one withered arm as a result of a birth injury. Pete has all the attributes to make a successful athlete--except two good arms. He wants to be one of the boys and take part in everything, but it's difficult. Several weeks ago I noticed that Pete was doing some things with his bad arm. I questioned him about it and learned that he hadn't been to a doctor about it since the fifth grade. I gave him a few simple tests to see if he could flex, extend, supinate, etc. To my surprise a number of the muscle groups seemed to be working. So I immediately suggested--recognizing my own diagnostic limitation-- that Pete see Dr. Bailey, Porterfield's only orthopedic surgeon. Do you know what Dr. Bailey's professional opinion was? Pete should have been doing exercises for that arm all through his childhood days! Dr. Bailey said that there might have been a chance for seventy or eighty per cent efficiency, but now the improvement would undoubtedly be limited to a lesser amount. This really bothered me when I heard this news; somehow it troubled my conscience even though I was not responsible for Pete's condition in any way.

Who should be handling cases like this and the others? Should local doctors be referring youngsters to us for specific exercise. What is the responsibility of the physiotherapist and how far does it extend? Should there be someone on staff in the elementary school, middle school, and high school to help these boys and girls? If so, what qualifications should they have? With whom should they work cooperatively? Or should children and young people get special care only if their parents have the knowledge, interest, and money to see to it that such assistance is somehow provided?

I could go on and tell you about other youngsters whom we come across in our classes: Bill, who is overweight and miserable; Jack, who wants to gain weight so I'll consider him a good football prospect; Ken, who wants to change his image from the proverbial "98-lb. weakling"; and so on down the line.

If this is a matter of professional ethics for me (i.e., where do my responsibilities lie?), to whom do I turn? Does anyone else have a responsibility and duty here too? These are the kids that haunt me--whenever I have time to think

about it.   Maybe we in this field should declare publicly that
this is not part of our job.   Maybe that would help my conscience a bit.   I wish I knew . . .

Argument Layout

<u>D</u> ————————————————————————————→ <u>C</u>

D — GERALD SCANLON, A QUALI-
FIED PHYSICAL EDUCATION
TEACHER HAS BEEN TAUGHT
THAT HE HAS A RESPONSI-
BILITY FOR CORRECTIVE
EXERCISE AND ADAPTED
SPORTS FOR THOSE WHO ARE
NOT ABLE TO HAVE A NOR-
MAL EXPERIENCE, BUT THERE
IS NO TIME NOR ANY MONEY,
FACILITIES, OR EQUIPMENT
TO FILL THIS SEEMINGLY
URGENT NEED

So, <u>presumably</u>
Q

C — GERALD IS NOT LIVING
UP TO HIS PROFESSION-
AL OBLIGATIONS, EVEN
THOUGH HIS SUPERIORS
DON'T APPRECIATE THIS
FACT, AND DESERVES
CRITICISM IF HE DOESN'T
MAKE EVERY POSSIBLE
EFFORT TO RECTIFY THIS
SITUATION

Since
W

Unless
R or E

TAX-PAYING CITIZENS IN
A SOCIETY HAVE A RIGHT
TO EXPECT THAT TEACH-
ERS WILL LIVE UP FULLY
TO THEIR PROFESSIONAL
OBLIGATIONS IN ALL RE-
GARDS AND TO MAKE IT
KNOWN IF THEY ARE NOT
ALLOWED TO DO SO

UNLESS THE TAXPAYERS
MAKE IT CLEAR THAT THEY
DO NOT EXPECT ANY SUCH
ASSISTANCE TO BE PRO-
VIDED FOR A MINORITY

<u>Universalizability</u>

Because
B

A SIZEABLE MINORITY OF
THE STUDENTS ATTENDING
PUBLIC HAVE REMEDIABLE
PHYSICAL DEFECTS THAT
DESERVE ATTENTION, AND
THOSE WITH PERMANENT
DEFECTS SHOULD AT LEAST
HAVE AN ADAPTED SPORTS
EXPERIENCE

<u>Consequences</u>

and/or

IT IS DECIDED THAT THIS
TYPE OF ASSISTANCE
SHOULD BE PROVIDED BY
SOMEONE WITH SPECIAL-
IZED TRAINING EITHER
WITHIN OR OUTSIDE OF
THE SCHOOL SITUATION

and/or

GERALD FINDS A WAY TO
PROVIDE SOME ATTENTION
FOR THIS MINORITY BY
RE-ARRANGING HIS PRIOR-
ITIES AND TIME WITH CO-
OPERATION FROM HIS
SUPERIORS

<u>Intentions</u>

PART V
RELATED READINGS

Note: In this section of the book, the reader is offered a series of readings written by the author on various aspects of ethics as related to sport and physical education commencing in the early 1970s. Some of these papers are metaethical in nature (e.g., Chapter 14), while others are strongly normative (e.g., Chapter 16). They are arranged chronologically as to the date of preparation and presentation, so the reader will be able to identify the progression of thought on the part of the author during this decade. However, the papers are not presented exactly as they were originally, because some of the material in them has been used in Chapters 1-11. Thus, where necessary to avoid needless repetition, they have been adapted for use here. (If the course outline recommended in Appendix A is used, the reader will note that they are assigned for outside reading at the rate of one per week starting with Week #4 and extending through Week #12.)

141

CHAPTER 12
LANGUAGE, MEANING, AND PHYSICAL EDUCATION

The field of physical education has most certainly been suffering from an "identity crisis" in North America for more than a decade.* The pressure starting in the early 1960s for a much stronger disciplinary orientation, albeit a most worthy and absolutely necessary development, has since become so intensified in one university that the term "physical education" has now become completely anathematized--its usage has been banned on any sign on the campus; the term itself is employed only disparagingly; and the top administrator has withdrawn his membership from the national professional association, and appears to be actually working so as to undermine that organization in favor of what often appears to be a Peters' "floating apex"-like disciplinary group. This unit will somehow "burst upon the world" with all sorts of new knowledge that will bring academic prestige hitherto undreamed of to all concerned. Of course, it may well be that the term "physical education" has indeed been far too heavily overworked, and some changes are necessary and/or advisable. Thus, a brief analysis of this situation is the main purpose of this paper. William Foote Whyte's earlier designation of another area of endeavor as a "field in search of a focus" may well apply to physical education at present. What follows is designed to explain what is meant when the term "physical education" is employed in the English language today.

Such difficulty with language is, of course, not confined to the field of physical education. Such problems are now national and international in scope, and they demand at least adequate attention. The field of philosophy--and others as well --have shown great concern, and "philosophy of language" describes a perhaps loosely, but most certainly related series of investigations about the nature of language. Linguistic questions arise constantly in any consideration of metaphysics, epistemology, logic, and axiology. Those concerned with the reform of language may be roughly grouped into two divisions-- those who attempt to explain how ordinary language has been

---

* A paper presented at the Annual Meeting of The American Academy of Physical Education, Atlantic City, New Jersey, March 12, 1975.

plagued with nonsensical deviations, and those who have sought to construct language free from defects. Obviously, neither group has succeeeded. Another group of philosophers--and such a grouping extends to physical education and sport philosophers as well--works diligently at what has been called "conceptual analysis"--an approach which hearkens at least as far back as the time when Socrates is purported to have asked for a definition of the term "justice."

Euphemisms and "Playing Games with Words"

The use of the English language on the North American continent in the 1970's could not be characterized typically as clear or correct or stylish--albeit it quite often frank, blunt, and explicit. Certainly four-letter words are more common than previously, and discussions about sexual topics are seemingly quite acceptable in most circles. However, our society is still plagued daily by the employment--or possibly "deployment"--of the euphemism (i.e., "telling it like it ain't"). As is readily understood, a recent political administration raised the euphemism to the level of an art in its nearly successful effort to "fool all of the people all of the time"--a feat which most of the populace felt was impossible since Abraham Lincoln stated so just over one hundred years ago. Even the drunk who believes he is lost on the corner of "walk" and "don't walk" is undoubtedly in a much better position fundamentally than are people who receive daily "barrages" via the multi-media which seem designed to befuddle and deceive. It may be that this "semantic aphasia" is necessary in these troubled times--that people are unwilling to confront head on the many psychological stresses that change and "future shock" add to their overburdened lives. George Orwell's "doublespeak" is now part of our way of life, and there are even games being played with euphemisms. "Liberating" a city really means to "capture by force." An "underachiever" could really be known as a "poor student." "Ecological destruction" somehow comes out quite often as "forest management." By this time, it should be obvious to us all that "the rose of physical education will smell just the same if the end result is a child who is physically unfit and poorly adjusted through a poor program offered by kinanthropologists or human kineticists." What games we do play! Maybe it helps to "fool ourselves most of the time," but one can play hope that the end result is not complete deception all of the time. As Norman Rosen said so pointedly, "We have only a handful of crucial words standing between light and darkness. To blur the meaning of even one is to hasten the darkness." (The New York Times, 3/29/71)

Meanings Ascribed to the Term "Physical Education"

Even though this writer has long been concerned with the multitude of objectives propounded for physical education by the normative philosophers of yesteryear, it was only in the later 1960s that he became aware of the four meanings ascribed to the term "education" by Frankena (1965, p. 6). This type of analysis of the term indicated that it could mean any one of four things: (1) the activity of educating carried on by teachers, etc.; (2) the process of being educated which takes place within the child; (3) the result, actual or intended; and (4) the discipline or field of enquiry that studies or reflects on education. The next logical step was to attempt to transpose this schema to the field of physical education, and in the process it became apparent that a fifth meaning had somehow been overlooked. This was envisioned as the profession of education, however defined, and presumably it was a totally encompassing term which in a sense embodied the disciplinary aspect of education.

Interestingly enough, somehow a sixth meaning of the term "physical education" emerged. It became quite obvious that "physical education" also meant the subject-matter (e.g., tennis, or some other physical educational involvement that was considered to be part of the total physical education program). At this point the writer began to sense what an investigator using experimental group method feels like—he had discovered something never before, to the best of his knowledge, reported in the history of the field. He then planned for just the right moment to call this "great discovery" to the attention of the unsuspecting world of physical education. Such an occasion presented itself quite soon when the speaker was requested to make the opening presentation at the First Canadian Symposium on the History of Sport and Physical Education at the University of Alberta, Edmonton, in 1971.

Initially, it was stated that, "As might be expected, there is great ambiguity to the term "physical education," and then it was explained that up to this moment it had been possible to identify some six different meanings as follows:

1.   The subject-matter, or a part of it (e.g., tennis, or some other sport or active game; some type of physical activity involving exercise such as jogging or push-ups, a type of dance movement or activity; physical recreational play; movement with purpose relating to these four types of activities);

2. The activity of physical education carried on by teachers, schools, parents, or even by oneself;

3. The process of being physically educated (or learning) which goes on in the pupil or child (or person of any age);

4. The result, actual or intended, of (2) and (3) taking place through the employment of that which comprises (1);

5. The discipline, or field of enquiry, in which people study and reflect on all aspects of (1), (2), (3), and (4) above; that which is taught (the "body-of-knowledge") in departments, schools, colleges and/or faculties of physical education; and

6. The profession whose members employ (1) above; practice it (2); try to observe (3) taking place; attempt to measure or evaluate whether (4) has taken place; and base their professional practice on the body-of-knowledge developed by those undertaking scholarly and research effort in the discipline (5).

    (Adapted from W. K. Frankena, 1965, p. 6; the reader should see also Zeigler and VanderZwaag, 1968, p. 8.)

(At this point I have a confession to make. I really did not expect thunderous applause for my "important discovery"--I needn't have worried about that reaction. Nevertheless, I must admit to a certain amount of chagrin because no one has ever mentioned what I considered to be a fairly important piece of language analysis--even to this very day! Therefore, it seems safe to say that, insofar as the field of physical education is concerned, the philosophy of language has not yet "arrived" in our domain!)

One further development should be reported. It revolves around the writer's subsequent realization that the term "physical education" might indeed be a "family resemblance" term according to an approach promulgated by Wittgenstein. This was a theory of meaning propounded for certain general terms such as "see," "know," "reason," and "free." Such terms have been used in many different ways--that is, the conditions for the accurate use of the word vary in different circumstances.

This approach is, of course, basically at variance with the traditional method of analyzing a term in which it is necessary to discover the specific conditions or characteristics which appear in all cases in which the term is employed. With the traditional approach it is possible to determine what might be considered to be the essential definition of the term under discussion.

However, with the "family resemblance approach" the idea of determining requisite properties for employment in the definition of a specific term is discarded. This is done because it has been shown that the term may be employed correctly in different situations even though no one essential property (or set of properties) appears each and every time that the term is used. But all of the uses do indeed bear a "family resemblance" to each other (i.e., to a certain extent elements of characteristics overlap so that every use has something "in common with every other use," even though "there is no property which it holds in common with all of these other uses" (Gochnauer, 1973, p. 216).

The question then is, "Can this 'family resemblance approach' be applied to the term 'physical education'?" The answer at present is not conclusive, although the answer must typically be in the negative. However, for certain groups within the profession an affirmative answer seems reasonable. This is so, because the adherents within these groups striving to turn the "thrust" of the field toward their positions view "physical education" as either sport, or physical activity, or human movement, or play, or what have you? If there were almost unanimous agreement that "human movement" or "human motor performance" is or should be the essential definition, then it would be possible to dispense with the "family resemblance term" idea. Obviously, those in the field are far from unanimity on this fundamental point.

Conclusion

On the basis of investigation reported more fully elsewhere (Zeigler, 1975), it may be stated quite conclusively that there is great confusion in connection with the use of the term "physical education." Further study is needed. In the meantime, if and when the term "physical education" is employed by those whose philosophical persuasion is not offended by such usage, its use should be qualified, and great care should be taken to employ ancillary, descriptive terms precisely on such occasions.

Bibliography and Selected References

Feigl, H. "Logical Empiricism," in H. Feigl and W. Sellars, Readings in Philosophical Analysis. New York: Appleton-Century-Crofts, 1949.

Frankena, W. K. Three Historical Philosophies of Education. Chicago, Illinois: Scott, Foresman and Company, 1965.

Gochnauer, M. L. "Analysis of Knowledge." Ph.D. dissertation. The University of Western Ontario, 1973.

Kaplan, A. The New World of Philosophy. New York: Random House, 1961.

Metheny, E. and Ellfeldt, L. E. "Movement and Meaning: Development of a General Theory." Research Quarterly, 29:264-273, October, 1958.

Osterhoudt, R. G. "A Descriptive Analysis of Research Concerning the Philosophy of Physical Education and Sport." Ph.D. dissertation, University of Illinois, Urbana, 1971.

Patrick, G. D. "Verifiability (Meaningfulness) of Selected Physical Education Objectives." Ph.D. dissertation, University of Illinois, Urbana, 1971.

Pearson, K. M. "Inquiry into Inquiry." An unpublished special project, Graduate Department of Physical Education, University of Illinois, Urbana, 1970.

_____. "A Structural and Functional Analysis of the Multi-Concept of Integration-Segregation (Male and/or Female in Physical Education Classes." Ph.D. dissertation, University of Illinois, Urbana, 1971.

Russell, B. The Autobiography of Bertrand Russell. New York: Bantam Books, Inc., Vol. 1, 1968.

Siedentop, Daryl. Physical Education: Introductory Analysis. Dubuque, Iowa: Wm. C. Brown Co., 1972.

Spencer-Kraus, P. "The Application of 'Linguistic Phenomenology' to Physical Education and Sport." M.S. thesis, University of Illinois, Urbana, 1969.

VanderZwaag, H. J. Toward a Philosophy of Sport. Reading, Mass.: Addison-Wesley Publishing Company, 1972.

Weitz, M. (Ed.). Twentieth Century Philosophy: The Analytic Tradition. New York: The Free Press, 1966.

White, M. G. The Age of Analysis. Boston: Houghton-Mifflin, 1955.

Zeigler, Earle F. Personalizing Physical Education and Sport Philosophy. Champaign, Illinois: Stipes Publishing Company, 1975.

Zeigler, Earle F. and VanderZwaag, H. J. Physical Education: Progressivism or Essentialism? Champaign, Illinois: Stipes Publishing Company, Revised Edition, 1968.

Questions for Discussion

1. To what extent are you aware that the field of physical education is suffering from an "identity crisis?" How might we emerge from this difficulty? Would a name change be of any help with this problem?

2. Are you aware of any euphemisms that may have slipped in-into your everyday language? Into others' speech patterns? Give some examples.

3. Do you use the term "physical education" ambiguously? If so, how can you correct such a deficiency?

4. Do you agree with the six meanings of the term "physical education" as explained in Chapter 12? Can you think of additional ways in which the term is used?

5. Explain what is meant by a "family resemblance" term? Give another example of such a term.

CHAPTER 13

A BRIEF ANALYSIS OF THE ORDINARY LANGUAGE EMPLOYED IN THE PROFESSIONAL PREPARATION OF SPORT COACHES AND TEACHERS

The analysis of concepts undoubtedly started before Socrates, but it wasn't until the twentieth century that there was such a sharp contrast drawn between analysis and other methods of philosophical endeavor.* Interestingly enough, it wasn't until the mid-1950's that educational philosophers became involved to a degree with so-called philosophical analysis, and then in the latter half of the next decade that philosophers of sport and physical education began to show any inclination to move in this direction as well. Whether this influence will be a lasting one remains to be seen.

Thus, despite the fact that various scholars of the Western world have been engaged in philosophical thought for more than 2,000 years, there is still disputation over the exact nature of philosophy. Early Greek philosophers thought that philosophy should serve a function not unlike that which we attribute to contemporary science. Today, we employ scientific method, of course, which involves reflective thought and hypothesis, long-term observation, and experimentation prior to subsequent generalization and theory-building. Unless today's philosophers engage in this sort of activity, there is serious doubt as to whether their investigation does result in knowledge after all. If not, what is the justification for philosophy?

In the twentieth century there have been three major developments, and several sub-developments, within philosophy that have sought to answer this question through the medium of what might be called language analysis: (1) logical antomism, which was preceded at the beginning of the twentieth century by the "realism analysis" of Russell, Moore, and Bradley; (2) logical positivism, which was followed by "therapeutic" positivism or "Neo-Wittgensteinianism"; and (3) ordinary language philosophy. The main idea behind these approaches -

---

* A paper presented at the Pre-Convention Session of the Philosophy of Sport and Physical Activity Committee, CAHPER Convention, Ottawa, Ontario, Canada, May 27-28, 1974.

those under categories #1 and #2 at least - is that philosophy's function is analysis. The last category (#3), ordinary language philosophy or linguistic analysis, or the related group of pursuits now known as "philosophy of language," assumes that the immediate goal of the philosopher is to explain the use, the function, or the actual workings of man's language. Within the this third major category, one faction argues that a philosopher should help man refrain from misuses of his ordinary language, while another group believes that they as philosophers should assist with the reconstruction of man's ordinary language.

It is this third approach that will be employed in this present investigation in an experimental fashion. The investigator is quick to use the word "experimental," mainly because he has not employed it previously, and also because he views this type of philosophizing as important but definitely as a "handmaiden" to philosophy as it engages in its major tasks.

The reader should keep in mind that it was during the period between 1930 and 1952 that Wittgenstein decided that it would not be possible to devise a language so perfect that the world would be accurately reflected. He came to believe that much of the confusion and disagreement over philosophy emanated from the misuse of language in several ways. He believed that it was necessary to decide what the basic philosophical terms were, and then it would be possible to use these terms correctly and clearly so that all might understand. With this approach it may be possible for the philosopher to solve some problems through clarification of the meaning of certain terms which have been used synonymously (albeit often incorrectly). In this way man may be able to truly achieve certain knowledge about the world. Philosophy practiced in this way becomes a sort of logico-linguistic analysis, and most certainly not a set of scientific truths or moral exhortations about "the good life."

Statement of the Problem. The main problem of this investigation was to apply the Austinian technique of analyzing ordinary language to the terms that are typically employed in the professional preparation of coaches and teachers. The basic assumption is that these words (e.g., knowledge, experience, skills, etc.) are typically employed loosely and often completely improperly.

In order that the basic problem posited may be answered in a reasonably comprehensive and satisfactory manner, the following sub-problems, phrased as questions, will be considered initially:

a. What particular area of the language will be con-
    sidered for study? (The terms that are typical-
    ly employed in the professional preparation of
    coaches and teachers.)

b. What terms will be recommended by a team using
    free association as a technique after the reading
    of relevant documents has been completed? (At
    this point use of a good dictionary is essential.)

c. How does the team or group decide whether the
    terms included are appropriate? (By describing
    circumstances and conducting dialogues.)

d. What results may be formulated that are correct
    and adequate in relation to the terms which have
    been chosen initially; have been described clearly
    and in reasonable detail; and which have been
    accepted eventually as correct in the circum-
    stances in which they are typically employed?
    (The terms selected are defined clearly, checked
    carefully on the basis of the experiences of the
    team members, and employed in a sequential
    fashion to describe accurately the total experi-
    ence under consideration.)

Need for the Study. The need for this particular study
became most apparent to the investigator while serving as a
member of an Experimental Undergraduate Physical Education
Committee in the 1963-64 academic year at the University of
Illinois, Champaign-Urbana under the chairmanship of Professors L. J. Huelster and C. O. Jackson. The group realized
very soon that their discussions were accomplishing very little
because of a "language problem." They were using the same
terms or words to describe the professional preparation experience of coaches and teachers of physical education, but they
were using these terms differently (i.e., with different meanings). It became obvious that certain basic or fundamental
terms would have to be selected, defined, used in descriptive
statements, re-defined (perhaps), and then related in a sequential narrative of some type.

Limitations and De-Limitations. Obviously, there is a
vary real possibility that the personal biases of the investigator and others involved in this early committee (team) may have
affected the way in which the terms were chosen, defined, and
employed. As a matter of fact, the group was not aware that
the Austinian technique was being employed to the "T," so to

speak; the steps of the techniques as described simply "made good sense," and they were adopted. Thus, there was inevitably a certain amount of subjectivity present in the analysis that was made, and the results that were adopted unanimously by the committee for further use. One definite de-limitation, of course, is that the terms to be collected were only those that are used commonly in the professional preparation of teachers and coaches.

Related Literature

In a brief presentation such as this, no effort will be made to document the related literature from the field of philosophy per se that might be otherwise included. Certainly philosophy is at present in the midst of an "Age of Analysis," although no one would claim for a moment that this approach should be classified as a homogeneous school of thought (White, 1955). This present study seems to be "hovering" at some point in a category that Weitz has defined as "Linguistic, Ordinary Language, or Conceptual Analysis" (1966, p. 1).

Those who concern themselves with the history of philosophy will endeavor to determine as accurately as possible Russell's influence on his student, Wittgenstein, but none can deny the originality of the latter's Tractatus Logico-Philosophicus, first published in 1921. The language of philosophical discourse must be phrased so that its propositions are meaningful and empirical in nature. If one hopes to understand and solve problems, language must be used correctly.

Since they were contemporaries and involved with the same "movement," one would think that Austin would almost of necessity be influenced by such a powerful and seminal thrust in philosophy as that engendered by Wittgenstein. It is true further that "Austin is sometimes counted among the group of philosophers vaguely labelled 'Wittgensteinians'" (Furberg, 1963, p. 62). Despite this, however, the burden of proof of any strong relationship still remains open for some future scholar. They were approaching philosophy in a very similar fashion, but their emphases do seem to have been different.

John Langshaw Austin was a classical scholar who turned to philosophy after taking a degree in classics at Oxford. He was undoubtedly influenced by Moore indirectly and more directly by Prichard (Hampshire, 1959-60, xii). "Doing" philosophy for Moore, however, was definitely in the direction of analysis, while for Austin the question of classifying distinctions within language was uppermost. In the process Austin was what might be called a "team man," since he believed in the necessity of working in groups to define distinctions among the language expressions employed by those whose language was being "purified."

Language Analysis Within the Field of Physical Education. There has been very little ordinary language philosophy or conceptual analysis within the field of physical education. In 1970 when Fraleigh presented his definitive account and analysis of types of philosophic research that had been carried out in the 1960's, he included "three types of research labeled as theory building, structural analysis, and phenomenology" (Fraleigh, 1971, pp. 29-30, in NCPEAM Proceedings). He did not exclude this methodology necessarily because of the lack of published material in physical education literature, but he might as well have taken such a stand. During that time James Keating of DePaul was beginning to make his case for the distinction between the terms "sport" and "athletics" in philosophical journals, but he has never agreed to classify himself as a philosopher of language (Keating, 1963, 201-210).

To the best of this writer's knowledge, the only physical education philosopher to consider the application of Austin's "linguistic phenomenology" to sport and physical education was the late Peter Spencer-Kraus, a student of this investigator at the University of Illinois in Champaign-Urbana (1970). (As a matter of fact, it should be stated parenthetically that one of the reasons for this paper is to give this interesting and valuable technique of investigation a bit more "mileage" in the hope that others will consider employing it further.)

Other approaches of this nature to the philosophy of language, generally speaking, were made by two other former graduate students working with the writer - George Patrick and Kathleen Pearson. The study by Patrick was entitled "Verifiability (Meaningfulness) of Selected Physical Education Objectives," and it is important to understand that the purpose of this investigation was not to show that any such objectives were justified. An analytic description in terms of form and function of the stated objectives was made, and the normative part of the study was based on the descriptive analysis of the objectives and the kind of knowledge provided by logic, ethics, philosophy of science, and philosophy of education. Positivism's "principle of verifiability" was subdivided into two forms: weak or logical possibility of confirmation, and strong or operationally testable. Objective statements were viewed as informative, expressive, directive, and performative. Three functions of objectives were stated (1) as a slogan, (2) as a guide to the educative process, and (3) as a test. It was found that objectives functioning as slogans were likely to be meaningless or verifiable in the second degree (weak); that objectives functioning as guides using informative-directive language were verifiable in the first or second degree; and that objectives functioning as a test must use the informative-directive mode of language before they could be considered verifiable in the first degree. Thus, "if physical educators wish to act responsibly, they should be able to state that for which they are accountable" (Patrick, 1971, p. 94).

Pearson's study was analytic in nature and certainly relted to conceptual analysis within what has been called "philosophy of language" by many. She examined (1) the structure of the multi-concept "integration-segregation" as it pertained to male and female participants in physical education classes, and (2) the functional aspects of this multi-concept in the intentional, purposive, and responsible actions of persons engaged in the professional endeavor called physical education (Pearson, 1971, p. 2). After extracting the various meanings attached to the concept and describing their extensional features in the "structural analysis" phase, Pearson proceeded to a "functional analysis" stage in which she delineated the reasons set forth for advocating the various "structures" or positions relative to the usage of the concept by writers in the available literature. She considered the assumptions implicit within each of the reasons and the empirical evidence available to support or case doubt on the validity of the hypotheses underlying these reasons. Lastly, the question was asked, "How might one be guided in making responsible decisions concerning the multi-concept in question?"

After carrying out the above steps, Pearson concluded specifically that physical educators attach many and varied meanings to the word "coeducation"; that the reasons set forth for this practice indicate a wide variety of objectives; that these claims or objectives have not been subjected to empirical research techniques; and that many contemporary physical educators still hold the dubious belief that jumping activities for girls and women cause injury to the pelvic organs. Generally speaking, she concluded that "the field is almost barren of empirical research to support or cast doubt on the advisability of integration-segregation of male and female participants in physical education classes" (pp. 213-214).

Methodology and Technique

J. L. Austin's technique was not spelled out in great length in innumerable papers as is sometimes the case with investigators, but the essence of it may be gleaned from his paper entitled, "A Plea for Excuses," as well as from his "Ifs and Cans" and from some notes called "Something About One Way of Possibly Doing One Part of Philosophy." (See Philosophical Papers published by The University Press in Oxford.) He himself coined the name "linguistic phenomenology" in connection with the technique (p. 130). In Austin's opinion there was hope in analyzing,

> . . . our common stock of words [which] embodies all the distinctions men have found worth drawing, and the connexions they have found worth marking, in the lifetimes of many generations: these surely are likely to be more numerous, more sound, since they have stood up to the long test of the survival of the fittest, and more subtle, at least in all ordinary and reasonably practical matters, than any that you or I are likely to think up in our arm-chairs of an afternoon--the most favoured alternative method. (Ibid., p. 130.)

Initially, the Committee at Illinois, after a series of meetings during which time it became apparent to all that they were not "talking the same language," decided which words and terms were relevant to the topic at hand--the professional preparation of teachers and coaches. Even though they employed common sense and their professional judgment, they found that it was necessary to read the available literature on professional preparation in both so-called general professional education and also in the specialized professional education area of physical education. Then through the process of free association, they were able to eliminate words and also to begin to delinate shades and nuances of meaning of the words that were left. When disagreements developed, or when fine distinctions were not known, the group referred to a dictionary.

Referral to a dictionary was not the final answer, because it was discovered that still other terms - synonyms - were typically available for consideration as well. Early corroboration of this type was most helpful since it provided a helpful cross-check. As a result of this "field work" stage, the Committee decided to employ a minimum of twelve words (terms) and accompanying definitions to be used in the final statement that was to be framed to explain the professional preparation process as carefully and as precisely as possible.

The Committee proceeded to the second stage by attempting to relate clear and detailed examples of instances or circumstances in which a particular term or word was preferred to another. Then, too, the members of the group made an effort to explain those times when the use of the word would not be appropriate. During this stage it is important that any and all theorizing be excluded. Achieving unanimity at this juncture may be somewhat difficult, but it is certainly less time-consuming if there are no unusual "personalities" in the group and if the members of the team are relatively inexperienced.

Finally, in the third stage, an effort is made to formulate the various terms under consideration into a coherent account that will stand close scrutiny. There will undoubtedly be changes and modifications in the preliminary account that is developed. The final account can be double-checked with some of the literature examined earlier to see to what extent changes have been made that will seemingly stand up under very close examination. After this was done in the Illinois situation, the final statements including the terms adopted were presented to a graduate seminar for the disinterested examination and evaluation that such a group of people would provide.

Findings

As a result of the "field work" stage, the Committee decided to employ the following words and definitions:

1. <u>Fact</u> – a real event, occurrence, quality, or relation based on evidence.

2. <u>Knowledge</u> – acquaintance with fact; hence, scope of information.

3. <u>Understanding</u> – comprehension of the meaning or interpretation of knowledge.

4. <u>Ability</u> – quality or state of being able; capability; aptitude.

5. <u>Competency</u> – sufficiency without excess; adequacy.

6. <u>Skill</u> - expertness in execution of performance; a "quality of expertness"; a developed ability.

7. <u>Appreciation</u> - a recognition of the worth of something.

8. <u>Attitude</u> - position assumed or studied to serve a purpose.

9. <u>Experience</u> - the actual living through an event(s) which may result in skill, understanding, ability, competency, appreciation, attitudes, etc.

10. <u>Problem</u> - a question proposed or difficult situation presented which may be met and/ or solved by experience(s).

11. <u>Resource Areas</u> - those subject-matters (disciplinary areas) referred to for facts.

12. <u>Functions</u> - the special duties or performances carried out by a person (or persons) in the course of assigned work.

The formulation of the various terms into a coherent account that describes what might actually occur in an experimental undergraduate curriculum for teachers and coaches resulted in the following statements:

A student is offered educational <u>experiences</u> in a classroom and/or laboratory setting. Through the employment of various types of educational methodology (lectures, discussions, problem-solving situations in theory and practice, etc.), he/she hears <u>facts</u>, increases the scope of information (<u>knowledge</u>), and learns to comprehend and interpret the material (<u>understanding</u>). Possessing various amounts of <u>ability</u> or <u>aptitude</u>, the student gradually develops <u>competency</u> and a certain degree or level of <u>skill</u>. It is hoped that certain <u>appreciations</u> about the worth of his/her profession <u>will be developed</u>, and that he/she will form certain <u>attitudes</u> about the work that lies ahead in his/her chosen field.

In summary, there are certain special duties or performances which the student preparing for the teach-
ing/coaching profession should fulfill (functions).
Through the professional curriculum, he or she is
exposed to both general and specific problems which
must be met successfully. Through planned experiences, with a wide variety of resource areas to serve
as "depositories" of facts, the professional students
develops competencies, skills, knowledge, under-
standings, appreciations, and attitudes which enable
him/her to be an effective physical educator-coach.

Conclusion and Discussion

Based on this limited experience with the Austinian technique applied to ordinary language--in this case some of the
terms employed typically in the professional preparation of
teachers and coaches--this investigator was able to conclude
that certain problems that have typically beset those concerned
with professional preparation are very definitely caused by linguistic confusion. This linguistic confusion is present because
of the equivocal use of many of the key words and terms.

This is not to say, however, that more detailed investigation of a similar nature would remove basic conflicts in educational philosophy that have plagued those concerned with the
transmission to others of the art and science of the teaching/
learning process. What constitutes education and teacher education ideally will not, in the opinion of this writer at least,
be resolved by the possible prevention of further ambiguous
usage of terms and idioms. These difficulties and differences
of opinion are far too deep-rooted and steeped in hoary tradition to vanish within the space of a few decades, if ever.

There is absolutely no doubt, however, but that highly
significant strides can be made in the near future if those
interested in sport and physical education philosophy will labor
to decrease the prevailing difficulties with language usage that
exist at the present time. The late Peter Spencer-Kraus was
preparing himself for this task, but his life was cut very short
in a tragic car accident. Patrick and Pearson have shown interest and ability along a similar, if not identical line, and
hopefully they will continue with this interest in the future.
Others are urged to experiment with Austin's approach as well.
It is relatively simple in design, but it may be difficult to bring
together a team of investigators to carry out similar studies in
the specialized area of sport and physical education. Such

investigation would appear to be a necessary cornerstone for any further study in the years immediately ahead.

Selected References

Austin, J. L. Philosophical Papers. London: Oxford University Press, 1961.

Fraleigh, W. P. "Theory and Design of Philosophic Research in Physical Education," Proceedings of the National College Physical Education Association for Men. Minneapolis, Minn. 55455, 1971.

Furberg, Mats. Locutionary and Illocutionary Acts. Stockholm: Almquist and Wiksell, 1963.

Hampshire, S. "J. L. Austin, 1911-1960," Proceedings of the Aristotlean Society, N.S. LX (1959-1960).

Keating, J. W. "Winning in Sport and Athletics," Thought, 38:201-210, Summer, 1963.

Patrick, G. D. "Verifiability (Meaningfulness) of Selected Physical Education Objectives." Ph.D. dissertation, University of Illinois, Urbana, 1971.

Pearson, K. M. "A Structural and Functional Analysis of the Multi-Concept of Integration-Segregation (Male and/or Female) in Physical Education Classes." Ph.D. dissertation, University of Illinois, Urbana, 1971.

Spencer-Kraus, P. "The Application of 'Linguistic Phenomenology' to the Philosophy of Physical Education and Sport." M.S. Thesis, University of Illinois, Urbana, 1969.

Weitz, M. (Ed.). Twentieth Century Philosophy: The Analytic Tradition. New York: The Free Press, 1966.

White, M. G. The Age of Analysis. Boston: Houghton-Mifflin, 1955.

Wittgenstein, L. Tractatus Logico-Philosophicus. London: Routledge and Kegan Paul, 1961.

Questions for Discussion

1. What are the steps to be followed in the use of the Austinian technique of analyzing ordinary language? Specifically, what was the problem of this investigation?

2. What was Patrick endeavoring to find out with his study concerning the verifiability of selected physical education objectives?

3. What conclusions did Pearson come to in her analysis of the underlying reasons for the pattern of "integration-segregation" that has developed within the field of physical education?

4. To what extent did you agree with the words and definitions that were chosen for the field work stage of the ordinary language analysis study?

5. Can you appreciate how using these terms correctly might be of use to you in the improvement of your ability to communicate more effectively when speaking about the professional preparation of sport coaches and teachers? Please explain your opinion.

CHAPTER 14
FREEDOM IN COMPETITIVE SPORT

A brief analysis of the concept of freedom within the framework of competitive sport is the major concern or problem of this paper.* The consideration of such a topic, and especially as it might relate to so-called educational sport, is absolutely vital at this time in North American sport and/or athletics. Some people might not immediately see the rationale for such a presentation, but the American Council on Education, the Carnegie Corporation, and the Ford Foundation would not have paid out "hard cash" for an exploratory study in this area of education if they had not been convinced that a searching look at the phenomenon of competitive sport was warranted at this time. It is hypothesized here that enough evidence and opinion can be marshalled to convince others that many, if not most, sports (or experiences in sports by individuals) may need to be modified by the injection of opportunities for the participants to make individual choices and decisions that would enhance the quality of life for all concerned.

Freedom is used here to describe the "condition of being able to choose and carry out purposes."(1: xiiii) This concept will be discussed much more fully below, but for now it will simply be stated that the problem of individual freedom in what has been identified as a transitional society (the twentieth century) cannot be safely placed aside for future reference. Even though much progress has been made in the achievement of civil rights for man on this continent in this century, there have been a number of developments recently in both Canada and the United States which force a reflective person to realize how precarious a commodity an individual's freedom really is.

If it is indeed true that the present society is in the midst of a great transition, and that now "we must learn to master ourselves as we are learning to master nature," then along the way it will be necessary to avoid certain traps. If man is not able to steer his course around these traps, it is quite possible that life as it is presently known on this planet will cease.(2: p. 24) If sport has become an important part of

---

* An abridged version of a paper presented at the Fourth Annual Meeting of the Philosophic Society for the Study of Sport. London, Ontario, Canada, November 16, 1974.

culture--a culture that is in jeopardy in the years immediately ahead--it should be employed as a "socially useful servant." Such a purpose for sport is certainly justifiable for "individual man" and for "social man," whether its place in the formal educational system is being considered or whether its role in society at large is in question.

The terms "sport" and "athletics" will be used here interchangeably, because that appears to be the accepted general practice on the continent. This is not to say that James Keating is not etymologically correct in his earlier distinction between these two terms. It is only that the public doesn't tend to recognize the former as the involvement of a "gentleman sportsman seeking to maximize the pleasure of the occasion for himself and his opponent" and the latter as the "prize-hunting athlete with a win-at-all-costs attitude."

The main problem of this analysis is, therefore, to posit a workable definition of the concept of "freedom" for an evolving democratic society today--one that may be adapted to the experience of men in competitive sport in such a way that they may live fuller lives while at the same time strengthening the position of representative democracy as a system of government. Obviously, this is a tall task that can be considered only in an exploratory way in this short paper. Further, this discussion will be limited to men's sport, although the problem is equally as important for women (and will be treated in a separate paper later).

The broad outline of this paper will, therefore, revolve around preliminary answers to the following questions: (1) how has the concept of freedom been viewed in philosophy; (2) what is the status of "freedom" in men's sport and/or athletics in North America; (3) what are some of the prospects for individual freedom in the future; and (4) what conclusions may reasonably be drawn about the need for, and the possibility of, introducing more freedom into competitive sport in North America in the near future?

Freedom in Philosophy

The situation appears as follows: times are exceedingly difficult, and man's freedom is being challenged and delimited. Keep in mind Muller's definition of freedom as "the condition of being able to choose and carry out purposes," but ponder over Richard Goodwin's qualifying clause also which states "to the outer limits fixed by the material conditions and capacity of the

time."(3: p. 24)   To this Goodwin adds further a "social dimension" that some might reject: "Not only does the free individual establish his own purposes, but they are consistent with
the purposes of his fellows.   He seeks his own wants, and further to cultivate his own faculties in a manner which is consistent with the well-being of others."(p. 28)   One can just see
Thoreau shaking his head vigorously because of the constraints
imposed by Mr. Goodwin.

Despite the many outcries that are heard about the loss
of, or the possible loss of--or even the denial of--certain individual freedoms in North America.   Walter Kaufmann has recently postulated that the large majority of people really "crave
a life without choice."   In fact, he has coined the name Decidophobia for the "malady" that seems to afflict most men--the fear
of autonomy or personal decision-making that affects a great
many people.   In his Without Guilt or Justice, he delineates ten
strategies by which modern man avoids making serious life decisions that would lift him from a decidophobic state to one of
personal autonomy.   These strategies are (1) allegiance to a
religion; (2) drifting by either adopting a stance of "status-
quoism" or by "dropping out"; (3) commitment or allegiance to
a movement; (4) allegiance to a school of thought (less politi-
cally active than #3); (5) exegetical thinking--a "text is God"
approach; (6) Manichaeism, or an elementary "good and evil"
battleground approach to the world; (7) moral rationalism, or a
position which assumes that correct reasoning alone can demonstrate what a person ought to do in all difficult or fateful situations; (8) pedantry, which involves continued concern with
minute or microscopic details "while Rome is burning"; (9) "rid-
ing the wave of the future," a shortsighted position or faith
assumed by some to give support to the acceptance of dogmatic
political ideologies (a belief often connected with a religious
faith or similar movement); and (10), interestingly enough, is
marriage--an extremely popular strategy for women in many societies that delimits very sharply thereafter their potential for
autonomous decisions in their lives (a fate that often befalls
men similarly!).   Of course, a number of these strategies can
be combined in any one life with perhaps even more devastating
effect on the possibility of a person leading an autonomous life.
A truly autonomous person would strive successfully to avoid
employing any of these ten strategies, or at the very most
adopt only one or two of these strategies to a limited extent
and with "conscious foresight."(4: Chap. 1)

Throughout the history of the discipline of philosophy,
the concept of freedom has typically been employed in such a
way that it has related to events that occur in the everyday

relations of men, or it has involved particular aspects or conditions of social life. Despite this delimitation, significant differences of usage are still available, more or less legitimate and convenient to a greater or lesser extent. For example, the traditional, liberal meaning of freedom relates to the absence of constraint or coercion. Thus, in Partridge's words--actually a position similar to that defined by J. S. Mills as "negative" freedom or "freedom from"--the following definition has been typically considered first in the Western world:

> A man is said to be free to the extent that he
> can choose his own goals or course of conduct,
> can choose between alternatives available to him,
> and is not compelled to act as he himself would
> not choose to act, or prevented from acting as
> he would otherwise choose to act, by the will of
> another man, of the state, or of any other au-
> thority.(5: p. 222)

Obviously, this is a carefully worded definition and is quite complete, but some wonder if it should be broadened still further. For example, there are often natural conditions that limit man's freedom by preventing him from achieving his personal goals. Others would carry the definition one step further by the insertion of a stipulation that a man is not truly free unless he has the wherewithal to achieve his life goals. This means that he should be provided with the capability or power to attain a freely selected objective. Partridge complains at this point that this is stretching the definition far too much, and that indeed the ordinary language of this assumption has been distorted. Being free in his opinion is most certainly not the same as possessing the ways and means to employ in the achievement of the goals that one has set for his life!

Proceeding from the above premises--that is, the opportunity for uncoerced action--any definition of the term "coercion" must take into consideration the matter of indirect control of an individual's life style, as well as those obstacles or hurdles which are overtly placed in his path. For example, a rich man might covertly employ gifts of money and other valued articles so as to deprive another an opportunity to be selected as a candidate for some private or public office. Such a tactic could be carried out in a most subtle manner--or perhaps even unconsciously in certain cases--by the person with the large amount of assets. Still further, a person might not know enough to select the best possible alternative action leading toward a more successful future for himself and his family, no matter whether direct or indirect methods of control or coercion had been employed to limit his freedom by another person or group of people. The only conclusion to be drawn here is that a high degree of education becomes increasingly important for each individual in a society steadily growing more complex if we wish to guarantee citizens what might be called "full" freedom.

Up to this point this discussion about freedom has been limited to the idea or concept of freedom from certain impositions or controls in life, but obviously it is vitally important that the concept of freedom for certain opportunities or alternative actions be introduced here as being more positive (as opposed to negative) aspects of freedom. Throughout the history of philosophy, for example, a number of different possibilities for, or approaches to, "the good life" have been postulated. Without becoming too specific at this point about what these approaches to the good life might be, certainly in political and social matters--or even so-called moral matters--the free person should look forward to a variety of freedoms of, to, in, and from as he moves through life. Here are being suggested such freedom as freedom of thought, speech, association; freedom to assemble, worship, move about; freedom in the use or sale of property, or the choice of occupation or employer; and freedom from want, fear, etc. Obviously, these ideas are tremendously important in education and, as is being contended in this paper, the ramifications of the concept of individual freedom have only been vaguely and occasionally been considered seriously in North American competitive sport. When some individuals and/or groups become too powerful, other people's freedom is often curtailed. This situation can and does occur in both a negative and positive way in the various types of political states. Granted that pluralistic philosophical positions or stances are permitted in evolving democratic societies, what then can and should the concept of freedom mean in education and in competitive sport (within education primarily, but also in professional circles)? The remainder of the paper will be devoted to a relatively brief description of, and the recommendation of a few possible answers to, this very thorny problem that exists here and throughout the world at the present.

Freedom in Competitive Sport

The present pattern operative in competitive sport will be described with specific reference to the situation in intercollegiate athletics in the United States. (Selected references to interscholastic athletics and professional sport will be introduced where deemed pertinent. The concept of freedom as

as described above will be brought into the discussion when-
ever necessary.) The underlying hypothesis is that coaches of
competitive sport in only very rare instances consider the concept of freedom to be an important aspect of the sport which
they coach, of the methodology which they employ to carry out
their duties, or, for that matter, of the total educational experience being provided to their charges within the university
or college concerned. The prevailing competitive sport situation in Canadian universities is quite different than that of
most universities in the United States, but no effort will be
made to prove both this and the previously mentioned hypothesis from the standpoint of established research methods and/or
techniques. The idea here is to explore the prevailing situation tentatively using a philosophical orientation in which the
concepts of freedom from (a negative approach) and freedom
of, to, and/or in are considered. The idea of direct or indirect methods of control will be kept in mind also, but the definition of the term "freedom" will not be stretched to include all
of the ways and means needed to realize all of one's life goals.
The concept of "education for personal significance" will be
kept in focus to determine whether competitive sport typically
provides a "personal encounter" resulting in a subsequent personal choice that eventually leads to the "affective curiosity"
that Tesconi and Morris also refer to as a "gut-level passion"
to know.(13)

U. S. Intercollegiate Athletics--Then and Now. In 1929
the Carnegie Report entitled American College Athletics explained that "the defects of American college athletics are two:
commercialism, and a negligent attitude toward the educational
opportunity for which the American college exists." Additionally, the Report stressed that the so-called amateur code was
violated continually; that recruiting and subsidizing was "the
darkest blot upon American college sport"; that athletic training and hygiene practices were deplorable and actually jeopardized health in many instances; that athletes are not poorer academically, but that hard training for long hours impaired scholastic standing; that athletics as conducted fail in many cases
"to utilize and strengthen such desirable social traits as honesty and the sense of fair play"; that few of the sports which
are most popular contributed to physical recreation after college; that many head coaches were receiving higher pay than
full professors, but that their positions were dependent upon
successful win-loss records; that the athletic conferences were
not abiding by the letter, much less the spirit of the established rules and regulations; and that athletes were not receiving
the opportunity to "mature under responsibility."(6)

In 1974, some forty-five years later, there is every indication that the only one of the above-mentioned areas of criticism showing improvement would be that of athletic training and hygiene practices! Even on this point a cynic would be quick to point out that improved athletic training could be expected because of the desire to keep expensive athletic talent healthy enough to "earn its keep." At any rate, in 1974 the American Council on Education discovered that "there's a moral problem in college athletics," and that "the pressure to win is enormous"--facts which have been known to cognoscenti in educational circles for decades.(7) For example, The New York Times commissioned a survey of some forty colleges and universities and subsequently reported in 1951 that the flagrant abuses of athletic subsidization in many colleges and universities "promoted the establishment of false values"; "are the bane of existence in American education"; "lower educational standards generally"; force educators "to lose out to politicians"; and "do further injury to democracy in edcuation."(8) Obviously it serves no purpose to enumerate such statements endlessly, because volumes could be filled with them before 1929 and up to the present. Thus, the emphasis in this paper will be placed on exactly how these various abuses impinge on the freedom of those who are often identified as "student-athletes."

Athletes Are "Caught Up With the System". The contention here is that in the United States the talented young athlete is "caught up with or by the system" which finally negates just about every aspect of the philosophical definition of "freedom from" as explained by Partridge earlier. The young athlete is pressured inordinately to accept the society's goals, and thereby his course of conduct is limited. The truly gifted athlete is so besieged by forceful, hypocritical recruiting that it is not possible for him typically to choose intelligently between alternatives available to him. In the final analysis he is compelled to act as "he himself would not choose to act" or, to continue with phrases taken from Partridge's definition, he "is prevented from acting as he would otherwise choose to act." Lastly, all of this typically takes place or is forced upon him by "the will of another man, of the state, or of any other authority."(5: p. 222) Translated to the realm of competitive sport in the U.S., this becomes the will of the coach or members of his staff, the president of the university or even the governor of the state, and "any other authority" that could be well intentioned, but basically extremely shortsighted, such as parents, alumni, secondary school coaches, or friends.

To place these assertions in better perspective through some documentation, recall the recent statement by Moses Malone, the outstanding high school basketball star drafted by the pros: "They dragged me to as many as twenty-four schools; sometimes they brought me in to meet the president of the university, who talked to me like he wanted to be my father . . . they fixed me up with dates.   Then when I got home those girls called me long distance and pretended they were in love with me."(9: p. 20)   If the above isn't bad enough, and it most certainly isn't atypical, Putnam reports that:

> Perhaps the strongest of these episodes occurred when Oral Roberts showed up at Malone's home in Petersburg, Virginia and offered to cure his mother of her bleeding ulcer.   Roberts left the Malones in no doubt but that his university would be a fine place for Moses to play basketball.   (Ibid.)

This sort of ridiculous situation will be supplemented by only one other comment, this by the former great basketball player and coach, Bob Cousy:

> You get a kid to come to your school nowadays by licking his boots.   It's an unhealthy situation.   Once you have committed yourself to be begging him to come, there can never be a player-coach relationship.   The kid is the boss. There are plenty of rules that govern recruiting, yet there are no rules because there is no one to really enforce them.(10)

In addition to the pressure exerted upon the prospective athlete to attend a particular institution, the freedom of the athlete to "choose between alternatives available to him," or not to be "compelled to act as he himself would not choose to act" is typified by a famous, former football great.   "If I was smart I would have been a doctor, but I ain't so they got me in P.E.!" The situation in cases is simply one of an endless string of infringements upon the individual's freedom of choice by coaches eager to--and undoubtedly pressured to--win at almost any cost.   The writer has experienced this problem first hand at three major U.S. universities to varying extents.   Once to his amazement while serving as the physical education department chairman at a large university that was desirous of status as a football power, he discovered that the athletic association was paying an undergraduate counselor in his department "under the table" to help delinquent "student-athletes" to substitute courses in a way typically contrary to regulations, and to perform other needed "services" to athletes who either arrived on

campus as dubious scholars, or who were in scholastic difficulty for a variety of reasons. The point of this present discussion in regard to the concept of freedom is that other people were invariabley "leading the student-athletes around as if
they had rings in their noses and rocks in their heads." The
"life decisions" are being made to a large extent by men whose
very positions depend upon keeping the athlete eligible in order
to win games and thereby to bring in higher gate receipts! As
Tee Moorman, 1960 Look All-American, said at the award cere-
monies: "After you find out the cold facts, that you're all just
there for the same reason, the fun wears off."(11)

It is extremely difficult, if not impossible, to separate
the various aspects of individual freedom from that of man as
a social animal in a social setting. Careful analysis appears to
verify the assertion that the situation has gradually and stead-
ly developed in such a way that the social influences now almost completely envelop the individual in the gate receipt
sports in the United States, and that the athlete has been confronted typically by competitive sport's own particular brand of
"Decidophobia" as postulated by Kaufmann.(4: Chap. 1) In
other words, the tendered (financially) student-athlete, largely
because of social influences that negate his opportunity for
self-autonomy and the making of all sorts of personal decisions,
is almost forced to choose one or more of the strategies described by Kaufmann (but which are specifically adapted to the
world of competitive sport).

The problem is not so acute in most of the sports that do
not have a direct gate receipt relationship to the rise or fall of
the intercollegiate athletics program; yet, there is no doubt but
that "the system" takes away the individual's autonomy at the
very time that the athlete is in the formative stages insofar as
the development of his personality and character is concerned.
A tendered athlete must never speak too much about social
and/or controversial issues. He should always be dressed neatly when he takes an away trip with the team. Certain specific
regulations apply in regard to hair length, beards, moustaches,
sideburns, etc. The athlete must be careful about the people
with whom he associates on campus. He must be especially
careful not to appear nonconformist in regard to relations with
members of the opposite sex of a difference race and/or ethnic
background. He should study very diligently--or at least give
that appearance--so as to remain eligible for competition. He
should take the courses that coaches recommend, and even

recommended majors and minors, because the coaches know which professors are "soft touches" and favorable to athletics across the length and breadth of the campus. This list of "commandments" could be lengthened further, but it will be best perhaps to conclude this aspect of the analysis by reference to the famous "ABC" professor of the Big Ten--A for athletes; B for boys; and C for coeds. Woe to that small, insignificant golf player on scholarship who didn't alert this professor about his status, and who found himself with a neat D at mid-term! Of course, such a difficulty could usually be rectified by a coach in one sport talking to a coach in another sport, both of whom were on the physical education department's roster part-time, and who happened to have this lad with excellent motor ability in their physical education activity classes.

Freedom Available to Some on the Continent. It is not the intention of the writer to convey the impression here that all college and university athletes in the United States are having their individual freedom denied to them any more than the general run of the population is facing such curtailment. Of course, many citizens are truly worried about the level of individual freedom available to all regardless of race, creed, and financial status. Kaufmann's theory about the prevailing Decidophobia with people choosing one or more strategies to avoid personal autonomy in their lives deserves careful study also. Additionally, Skinner's future-oriented, behavioristic approach implying a concept of "beyond freedom and dignity" has many wondering about what the future might hold in store for them and their descendents. But in the field of competitive sport there are some colleges and universities where wise leadership has somehow prevailed with resultant opportunity for athletes to be relatively free from undue coercion and able to make choices among alternatives courses of action regarding their individual lives. One has to go no further than the Little Three in New England, most Ivy League institutions, Wayne State University in Detroit, DePauw University, and Springfield College, to name just a few. There are a number of non-gate receipt sports, of course, where the amount of athletic scholarship help is relatively low (and is indeed declining) in the larger universities where revenues from football, basketball, hockey, etc. must be upheld to keep the entire program operational. Despite the hue and cry of many that educational progressivism has taken over the schools, competitive sport at both the university and high school levels is typically regarded as extracurricular. It must fend for itself largely because of this shortsighted educational philosophy, and thereby are planted the seeds for a great many of the serious ills that prevail.

There may still be some hope for a return to sanity in competitive sport. This statement is made despite what to many is the fact that the concept of individual freedom for the person holding an athletic scholarship in the United States today has been hopelessly destroyed. Those people who are vitally interested in the future of competitive sport in educational institutions must work their way out of the prevailing situation. The goal of a "free man living the good life in a free society" --an aim which in itself offers certain guarantees to the student-athlete--cannot be cast aside as hopelessly idealistic and impractical.

Freedom in the Future

What is the hope for individual freedom in the future in an overpopulated world? This is obviously an impossible question to answer here, and perhaps anywhere for that matter, but it is a query that has direct implications for the question of freedom in competitive sport in North America--and, of course, throughout the world eventually. Gallup, in The Miracle Ahead, addresses the question as to how civilization can be lifted to a new level. In suggesting "new ways to actualize our potential," he recommends a new educational philosophy of individual effort that embraces a plan covering man's entire life span. Secondly, he points out that society hasn't truly taken advantage of the great opportunity for collective effort. Further, he looks to the social sciences for assistance in the solution of social problems presently causing slow progress or institutional failure. Lastly, he explains that man must develop means whereby the new generation understands the concept of change and develops ways to overcome the various "resistances" to change. (12: p. 24) Approaching his subject from a quite different standpoint than Tesconi and Morris with their "anti-culture man," Gallup nevertheless sees a vital role for the education profession. He asks for an educational system that will arouse the intellectual curiosity of the students and that, in the final analysis, will cause them to become dedicated to the cause of self-education and subsequent informed political activity(p. 40).

What does this mean? It would seem to return to the fact that present-day education is not providing a sufficient quantity of humaneness or concern for fellow man--highlighting the true personal significance of the individual! "If an experience expands awareness and intensifies personal significance, it is educational."(13: p. 208) This is the plight of education in North America, and it is most certainly the plight of overly-organized sport in educational institutions. Is individual freedom a hopeless dream? The answer to this rhetorical question must be in the affirmative <u>unless</u> a re-ordering of educational priorities can somehow take <u>place</u>. Such a dream is difficult enough to envision for those aspects of the educational program that are typically deemed educational, but how far-fetched is it to hope for such a goal in competitive sport that is so often designated as <u>extracurricular</u>? One needs at least to make the squad, before <u>he will</u> be allowed to play the educational game!

The intent here is not to spread "gloom and doom," even though many aspects of the present situation could quite easily drive a concerned person to despair. This assertion is made despite Etzioni's recent statement that social scientists are beginning to re-examine their core assumption "that man can be taught almost anything and quite readily." He states further that, "We are now confronting an uncomfortable possibility that human beings are not very easily changed after all."(14: p. 45)

As mentioned earlier, there are indeed a number of colleges and universities in the United States where programs of competitive sport have been kept in educational perspective with a resultant modicum of individual freedom for the athlete. Further, this condition of "educational sport" does actually still exist generally throughout Canadian higher education. Still further, there are many so-called individual sports functioning reasonably well even in those universities where the "Big Business" approach to competitive sport has taken control out of the hands of the educators. Thus, there are indeed many athletes today who still <u>believe</u> that they are "self-posturing" individuals--and this <u>ranges</u> from the body-builders seeking perfectly developed physiques, to the long distance runner who trains himself, to the skier, the mountain climber, the surfer, the parachutist--and, of course, the tough-minded athlete who despite the outcome still makes many key decisions for himself. All are to be commended!

Not to be forgotten in this discussion is the intelligent, sensitive, hard-working coach who appreciates this problem of freedom in competitive sport, and who makes every effort to encourage the athletes on his teams to think for themselves to plan their efforts, to pursue their self-chosen curricula successfully, and to feel that "joy of effort" that comes from a truly fine individual or team experience in competitive sport. These athletes can be called "self-posturing" individuals. These people have made "an assessment of their own feelings and attitudes" and also compared them "with the feelings and attitudes of others." As a result they have made a personal choice that is a wholesome blending of a "personal contract"

with a "social contract." Finally, these lucky, and unfortunately all too rare, athletes have acquired a "gut-level passion"
or "affective curiosity" to know more about themselves and their
sport; a desire to achieve a "personification" of knowledge; and
an opportunity to receive guidance along the path toward the
establishment of a personal identity with a significant amount
of self-esteem.(13: p. 208 et ff.)

Conclusion

With this statement immediately above, the writer has
spelled out for himself the only acceptable, workable definition
in which a concept of individual freedom can be carried out for
athletes in competitive sport situations in education within an
evolving democracy. This is the only way that competitive
sport can assist athletes to live full, rich lives while at the same
time strengthening the fabric and position of democracy as possibly the best underlying theory of government.

Campbell has called to our attention that there hasn't yet
developed an adequately functioning mythology for today's world
in which man has acquired what he feels to be a sufficient explanation of the mysterious universe and man's place in such a
vast enterprise. As a result Campbell claims that people haven't
been receiving the necessary guidance that was available in the
past to assuage the psychological crises that inevitably appear
during the life cycle. If it is indeed true that men need new
myths, perhaps even more individualized and small-group oriented myths(15), then it seems logical that sport--which must
be recognized as a vital force in culture today--needs to contribute positively to the creation of a new myth in the Western
world. To this end a new myth is being recommended--that of
free man molding the future in competitive sport according to
his personal values, but in keeping with the values and norms
of an evolving, democratic society. This can, and indeed must,
be the new myth promulgated by those guiding competitive sport
in education. There can be no compromise if competitive sport
is to serve as a "socially useful" force leading to a democratic
educational ideal.

References

1. Muller, Herbert J. Freedom in the Ancient World. New York: Harper & Row Publishers, 1961.

2. Boulding, Kenneth E. The Meaning of the Twentieth Century. New York: Harper & Row Publishers, 1964.

3. Goodwin, Richard N. The American Condition. Garden City, N. Y.: Doubleday & Co., Inc., 1974.

4. Kaufmann, Walter. Without Guilt and Justice. New York: Peter H. Wyden, Inc., 1973.

5. Partridge, P. H. "Freedom," in Encyclopedia of Philosophy (Paul Edwards, Editor). New York: The Macmillan Company & The Free Press, 1967, Vol. 3, pp. 221-225.

6. Carnegie Foundation for the Advancement of Teaching, The. American College Athletics (edited by Howard J. Savage et al.). New York: The Foundation, Bulletin #23, 1929.

7. Cady, Steve. "Educators Prepare for First Major Study of Sports in 55 Years," The New York Times, March 10, 1974.

8. Grutzner, Charles. "The Impact of Athletics on Education." Washington, D. C.: Babe Ruth Sportsmanship Awards Committee, 1951. (This pamphlet was reprinted with the permission of The New York Times.)

9. Putnam, Pat. "Don't Send My Boy to Harvard . . ." Sports Illustrated, Nov. 4, 1974, 20-21.

10. Goldaper, Sam. "N.I.T. Rings Down Curtain for Cousy," The New York Times, March 9, 1969, S3.

11. Tuckner, Howard M. "All-Americans Stalwarts Still Love Football, But . . .," The New York Times, Dec. 11, 1960.

12. Gallup, George. The Miracle Ahead. New York: Harper & Row Publishers, 1964.

13. Tesconi, Charles A., Jr. and Morris, Van Cleve. The Anti-Man Culture. Urbana, Ill.: University of Illinois Press, 1972.

14. Etzioni, Amitai. "Human Beings Are Not Very Easy to Change After All," <u>Saturday Review</u>, June 3, 1972, 45-47.

15. Clarke, Gerald. "The Need for New Myths," <u>Time</u> Essay, Jan. 17, 1972.

Questions for Discussion

1. To what extent do you agree with the definition of the term "freedom" used here?

2. Explain the problem that was investigated in Chapter 14.

3. Discuss the "strategies" Kaufmann claims we employ in our everyday lives to avoid making decisions? To what extent do any or all of these characterize your own way of life?

4. Do you agree that many college and university athletes in the United States are "caught up in the system?" Why is "freedom" available to some and not to others?

5. As affairs are moving currently, do you see an possibility of a new myth developing--that of "free man and woman molding the future in competitive sport?" Explain your answer in some detail.

CHAPTER 15
THE EDUCATION OF "ECOLOGICAL MAN": IMPLICATIONS FOR SPORT AND PHYSICAL EDUCATION

The influence of ecology has only been felt in a recognizable and significant way for the past five or ten years by north American society; so, it is not unusual that very little attention has been paid to the environmental crisis by those related to sport and physical education.* Our field cannot be especially criticized for this failing; as a matter of fact, the large majority of people conduct their lives in a manner which quite clearly indicates that they still don't appreciate the gravity of man's situation on Planet Earth. Very recently the writer has come to realize that this topic can also be considered a persistent problem to the field in the same way as the other five social forces of values, politics, nationalism, economics, and religion. Granted that it has not been with man over the centuries in similar fashion, the influence of ecology is now with man on a seemingly indefinite basis. No longer as it has been almost always possible in the past when natural resources were depleted, can man simply move elsewhere to locate another abundant supply of game to hunt, water to drink, or--for that matter--mineral resources to exploit for his purposes.

Ecology is usually defined as the field of study which treats the relationships and interactions of man and other living organisms with each other and with the natural (or physical) environment in which they reside. Until very recently very few scientists were known as ecologists; they were identified either as biologists or zoologists. Now many of these scientists are being asked to consider man's situation (plight?) in relation to his environment in a much broader perspective than that in which an experimental scientist typically functions. His outlook must of necessity become macroscopic rather than microscopic-- and very few people are prepared to make this transition in such a relatively short span of time.

---

* A paper presented at the Annual Meeting of the Canadian Association of Sport Sciences, Ottawa, Ontario, Sept. 29 - Oct. 1, 1975.

For a variety of reasons man can no longer proceed on the assumption that his responsibility is to "multiply and replenish the earth." In the past he has been exhorted to both increase the population and to develop an economy to cope with the various demands. Now there are close to four thousand million people on earth, and approximately four babies are being born somewhere in the world every second! It has also be become starkly obvious to reflective people that strong attitudes favoring population control must be developed, or it is quite possible that some version of Malthusian Law will soon be operative on a massive scale. (Although there are some who disagree with such a statement today, the reader will recall that Thomas R. Malthus theorized in 1798 that the population tends to increase more rapidly than the food supply--a question of geometric progression as opposed to arithmetical progression. This idea still seems valid today with the only possible checks being war, disease, natural catastrophes, famine, and birth control.)

Moving more directly into the realm of economics, it has been pointed out strongly that the United States--as opposed to Canada--for example, has some extremely difficult choices to make in the next few decades; in fact, a number of these choices may necessarily be made because of the severe crises that the nation will encounter. Those who look ahead optimistically seem willing to allow a continuous-growth economic system, while those who will undoubtedly be classified as pessimists by many argue for the wisdom of a no-growth economic system (Murray, 1972, p. 38). It is imperative for us all to understand that the forecasting models developed by economists and ecologists quite typically differ sharply--that is, the consequences of their recommendations, respectively, are so completely different. Certainly all are aware of contradictory economic theories that appear in the daily press, but it is also obvious that very few people, relatively speaking, are aware of the "collision course" seemingly being taken if the ecologic models have any validity at all. In an article entitled "The Ecologist at Bay," Grahame Smith explains that "The decline in quality of this planet and the precarious aspect of continued existence of life on Earth are largely the results of this comfortable shell of consumer technology with which each American is surrounded" (1971, p. 69). Thus, the ecologist finds himself in a situation where he comprehends fully the dangerous position in which some people on Earth--a relatively few million as a matter of fact--are ensconced. However, for the ecologist to cry out in alarm to the general populace in the favored countries any more vigorously, and to have them truly understand the reality of the precarious approach being followed generally, is to risk being ridiculed and being branded as a pessimist and doomsayer. Nevertheless, the problem is most definitely here, and it cannot be escaped by closing one's eyes. As Pogo, the cartoon possum, has stated--and it is a remark which we must accept ruefully--"we have met the enemy, and he is us!"

In an effort to consider this problem more carefully and in the process to place it in some perspective for all educators --and specifically those involved with sport and physical education--the writer will (1) offer a few definitions; (2) present a brief historical background; (3) highlight the problem as it is faced in modern society; (4) analyze it from a particular philosophical perspective with implications for education generally and for sport and physical education specifically; and (5) offer a concluding statement.

Definitions

As a result of the development of ecology and what has been called "environmental science," many new words and phrases have been added to everyone's vocabulary. Ecology itself "is the science of the mutual relations of organisms with their environment and with one another" (Huxley, 1963, p. 6). Or, to be somewhat more precise, Murray states that "ecologists study competition between individuals and between populations for resources, the growth of populations and the movement of materials (e.g., water and minerals) in ecological systems (eco-systems)" (1972, p. 36). It is not possible or pertinent to define even the most common terms usually employed in this area of study here, but it should be understood that man has polluted the earth--and is doing so now and may continue to do so in the future--in both the biosphere (the zone of life) and in the remainder of the atmosphere. This includes that area from 35,000 feet up to perhaps 600 miles above the earth. The term "biosphere" explains "that envelope made up of the Earth's waters, land crust, and atmosphere where all organisms, including man, live" (Kunz, 1971, p. 67). An eco-system is "an integrated unit or 'system' in nature, sufficient unto itself, to be studied as a separate entity--e.g., a rotting log in the forest, a coral atoll, a continent, or the Earth with all its biota" (Ibid.). Fortunately, many of these common terms are already recognizable at least, and hopefully their continued use in the various communications media will make them part of one's everyday vocabulary. A few such terms are as follows: allowable release level, biodegradable, biota, carcinogen, coliform bacteria, compost, decibel, demography, effluent, energy cycle, green revolution, greenhouse effect, herbicide, atmospheric inversion, non-renewable resources, recycling, smog, sonic boom, symbiosis, thermal pollution, etc. (Ibid.).

Brief Historical Background

As was reported above, there are now approximately four thousand million (four billion!) people on earth. At the beginning of the so-called Christian era that figure was only (!) two hundred and fifty million. By the time America was settled by Europeans, that total had been doubled to about five hundred million--in a period of only sixteen hundred years. Then by 1830 the figure had increased twofold again to one thousand million people in somewhat less than two hundred years. Next in one hundred years the amount doubled again to two billion, and now, in about only fifty years, the total number of men, women, and children on Earth is approaching four thousand million or four billion. As Huxley says, "By the year 2000, unless something appalling bad or miraculously good should happen in the interval, six thousand millions of us will be sitting down to breakfast every morning" (1963, p. 2). And to make matters still worse--if such could be the case--it is in the underdeveloped countries (e.g., India) where the rate of increase is so much higher than the average. It will presumably not be possible for such nations to move ahead to full industrialization because of the inevitable drain upon its basic resources by such rapid growth.

In another realm--that of poor husbandry insofar as land and animal abuse are concerned--man's careless and ignorant abuse of the planet probably goes as far back as 8,000 years ago when he first began to farm the land. There are today innumerable archeological sites that were once thriving civilizations. For a variety of reasons, including poor use of the land certainly, most of these locations are now dusty and desolate ruins. An example of such an area is North Africa that was once exploited extensively by the powerful Romans. The valuable topsoil here was undoubtedly eroded by poor farming techniques, incorrect grazing by livestock, and flagrant abuse of timberland.

One can go back somewhat further to Ancient Greece to find another example of once fertile land with an abundant supply of water and forested hills. Now much of the area seems blighted by rocky hills and barren lowlands denuded of their former topsoil. Wild life is almost extinct as well.

Much the same story can be related about early Turkey. Early port cities, such as Ephesus and Tarsus, offer no evidence today of their early history as valuable trading ports. The former "fertile crescent" of Biblical times has long since gone, and the "land between the rivers" (the Tigris and the Euphrates) shows almost no evidence of its former luxuriant state. Thus, turn where one will, to the areas desolated by fifteen century sheep-raisers in Spain, to the pre-Columbian American civilization on Monte Alban in Mexico, or to many other, formerly highly desirable locations in the world, one is apt to find further examples of poor management and land and forest degradation. Obviously, there are some examples of wise endeavor by the people of different nations. The Netherlands (Holland) and Japan are two such countries, and such "shining examples stand out like beacons" in an otherwise often seriously ravaged landscape. The discussion that follows will describe concisely why the coming century will need to be characterized by a concern for this vital problem that has never been shown before.

The Problem in Modern Society

What then is the extent of the environmental crisis in modern society? Very simply, man has achieved a certain mastery over the world because of his scientific achievements and subsequent technological advancements. We are told that he "is at the top of the food chain" (Mergen, 1970, p. 36) by his mastery of much of the earth's flora and fauna. Because of the exponential (geometric) explosion of the human population, increasingly greater "pressures will be placed on our lands to provide shelter, food, recreation, and waste disposal areas. This will cause a greater pollution of the atmosphere, the rivers, the lakes, the land, and the oceans" (Ibid.).

All of this has been explained most graphically by the National Geographic Society in a chart entitled "How Man Pollutes His World" (1970). Here the earth is "divided" into air, land, and sea, although it is now vital to understand that this satellite is self-sustaining, is possessed only of a finite quantity of oxygen water, and land, and has no means of reconstituting itself with further natural resources once the present supply is exhausted. This means that man must give immediate attention as to what the effect of supersonic jet aircraft is on the atmosphere at various levels; what increasing urbanization will mean insofar as strain on the physical environment is concerned; how significant the stripping of vegetation is to the earth's soil supply and to its ability to produce oxygen; how

dangerous the effects of the mercury waste, the harmful pesti-
cides, the chemical fertilizers, and the trash and sewage disposal are to the natural environment; and what the oil spills
and dumping at sea will mean to the earth's great bodies of
water and their ability to sustain fish, bird, and bottom life.
We need to ask ourselves questions about the extent to which
nature's self-renewing cycles are being disturbed.   To reiterate a point made earlier, what sort of a world will the more
than six billion people of the year 2000 inherit?

Thus, in the United States alone, many rivers, lakes,
and streams are being used as sewers; the air in some cities
is so polluted that one might as well be smoking a pack or so
of cigarettes daily; New York City alone is estimated to have
as many rats as it has people (more than eight million); three
and a half billion tons of garbage are produced each year;
more than four-fifths of the original forests have been convert-
ed for other purposes, as has 280 million acres of crop and
range land; at least 3,000 acres a day is covered with concrete
and other black top substances; and various other types of
"parasitic action" are taken by man.   And, of course, many
other nations in the world are following the same path, not to
mention the underdeveloped nations who are "standing in the
wings" waiting their opportunity for "the good life."   Further,
if all of this may sound a bit melodramatic, as these words are
being written there are news stories in the press explaining
how "a global network of international agricultural research
centers, none of them more than twenty years old, is facing an
'explosion' of demands from individual nations for help in increasing food production to meet rapid increases in population"
(The New York Times, Aug. 3, 1975, p. 20).   And still further, "air pollution plagued several large and populous areas
along the Eastern seaboard today, causing serious potential
hazards for people with respiratory or other health problems
and at least some discomfort for countless others" (Ibid., p. 37).

This diatribe could be continued, but hopefully the point
has been made.   Generally the gravity of the prevailing pattern
of life is recognized by many, but such recognition must become
knowledge to a great many more people who are in a position to
fashion positive action in the immediate future.   Interestingly
enough, "a group of Protestant theologians asserted . . . that
Christianity had played its part in provoking the current environmental crisis and that any solution to it would require major modification of current social and religious values" (The
New York Times, May 1, 1970).   Attending a conference whose
theme was the "theology of survival," it was stressed that typical Christian attitudes "toward nature had given sanction to

exploitation of the environment by science and technology and thus contributed to air and water pollution, overpopulation, and other ecological threats" (Ibid.). The participants agreed that the desirable changes would have to be brought about by local, regional, national, and international political action, but such improvements would never be realized without prior radical alterations in man's fundamental attitudes (values) toward nature and all of the flora and fauna therein. All of these thoughts and ideas are encouraging, of course, and one can only hope that positive, concerted action will be forthcoming. However, when an ecologist decries the "fragmented approach that we tend to take in seeking solutions" (G. J. C. Smith, 1971, p. 69), and when noted scientists like Paul Ehrlich asserts that The President's Council on Environmental Quality is "dodging the crisis" through its inability to make available the best scientific advice to the President (Saturday Review, Nov. 7, 1970, p. 73), one cannot be criticized for shaking his head somberly and wringing his hands in silent despair. Hopefully, the reader at this point will realize the necessity for all of us to be responsible, enlightened citizens ready to take our places in groups promoting desirable political action.

Philosophical Analysis

How does one approach a question such as the influence of ecology or the "environmental crisis" philosophically? Presumably no one philosophical position or stance would actually include any tenets designed to bring about the end to life on the Planet Earth as it has been known. Of course, some particularistic approaches might be so despairing and pessimistic about the future that the inevitability of man consciously or unconsciously destroying himself and his fellows is a distinct possibility.

In a highly interesting article, however, Holmes Rolston has asked what to many might seem like a contradiction--"Is There an Ecological Ethic?" (Ethics, Jan., 1975, pp. 93-109). He inquires whether an environmental ethic--the values that men hold about their environment--is simply based on a specific ethical approach (within a philosophical position) or whether there is actually a built-in naturalistic ethic in the universe. Commencing from the position that the dividing line between science and ethics is definite if one but accepts the philosophical categories of descriptive law and prescriptive law as being separate and distinct, Rolston explains that descriptive law, presented in the indicative mood, is employed in science and history. Prescriptive law, on the other hand, is used in ethics, and the imperative mood is involved implicitly or explicitly.

Thus, in moral philosophy the quickest way to be accused of committing a naturalistic fallacy is to blithely assume an "ought" from an "is"--at least in the eyes of philosophers with a scientific orientation. Transposed to the discussion of so-called "ecological ethics," environmental <u>science</u> should tell us what man thinks he knows through observation, experimentation, and generalization about the environment. Environmental <u>ethics</u>, on the other hand, means presumably that man has applied one or another set of ethical values to his understanding of and relationship to the environment.

Interestingly enough, those who argue for the concept of 'ecological morality' have differences in opinion that take adherents in one or the other direction: (1) those who equate homeostasis with morality, and (2) those who appear to go even further by arguing that there is "a moral ought inherent in recognition of the holistic character of the ecosystem"--which results in an ecological ethic (Rolston, 1975, p. 94). In treating #1 above first, Rolston seeks a "moral translation" from the paramount law in ecological theory--that of homeostasis (i.e., a closed planetary ecosystem, recycling transformations, energy balance, etc.). Paul Sears is quoted to the effect that "probably men will always differ as to what constitutes the good life. They need not differ as to what is necessary for the long survival of man on earth . . . As living beings we must come to terms with the environment about us, learning to get along with the liberal budget at our disposal . . . we must seek to attain what I have called a steady state" (Sears in Shepard and McKinley, 1969, p. 401).

Here the argument appears to be as follows: if you wish to preserve human life--and you ought to do so--the ecological law (that the life-supporting eco-system must recycle or all will perish) indicates that technically you ought not to disturb the eco-system's capability to recycle itself--and according to moral law (which equals natural law) you ought to assist such recycling wherever possible. With this approach (logic) the values are not strictly inherent in the make-up of the world; they are ascribed to it by man attempting to employ careful husbandry with what he has assumed to be his possession (the earth). Rolston argues that we can call the balance of nature (and the ends which we seek that are presumably compatible with an ecosystemic balance) "ultimate values if we wish, but the ultimacy is instrumental, not intrinsic" (p. 98).

The other major claim, referred to above, allows one to employ the term "ecological ethic" without the use of quotation marks, because the assumption is "that morality is a derivative

of the holistic character of the ecosystem" (p. 98). Rolston
recognizes that this is a radical idea that will not receive ready
acceptance. It endows nature and its integral ecosystem with
value. This is obviously a proposal for the broadening of the
concept of value--nature in and of itself would have value
whether man was here to appreciate it and employ it for his purposes or not! The leap is made from "is" to "ought" because
"the values seem to be there as the facts are fully in" (p. 101).

Because of past philosophical and religious speculation,
not to mention so-called philosophy of science, it is extremely
difficult to find a logical place for a primary ecological ethic in
which man's long-standing "classical ought has been transformed, stretched, coextensively with an ecosystemic ought" (p. 104).
Are intelligent human beings ready to agree that "egoism should
be transformed into ecoism" (Ibid.)? Thus, the self would be
identified with Nature as one of its components, as part of the
ecosystem. It would not be man and nature; it would be man
in nature with such a transformation of outlook. Then man
would have a much stronger obligation to preserve nature's balance, because he is truly a part of the world--and the world is
a part of his body!

With such an outlook, man would create what might be
called Ecological Man, and he might be able to postulate an authentic naturalistic ethic:

> Man, an insider, is not spared environmental pres-
> sures, yet in the full ecosystemic context, his
> integrity is supported by and rises from transac-
> tion with his world and therefore requires a cor-
> responding dignity in his world partner. Of late,
> the world has ceased to threaten, save as we
> violate it. How starkly this gainsays the alien-
> ation that characterizes modern literature, seeing
> nature as basically rudderless, antipathetical, in
> need of monitoring and repair. More typically
> modern man, for all his technological prowess, has
> found himself distanced from nature, increasingly
> competent and decreasingly confident, at once dis-
> tinguished and aggrandized, yet afloat on and
> adrift in an indifferent, if not a hostile universe.
> His world is at best a huge filling station, at worst
> a prison or "nothingness." Not so for ecological
> man; confronting his world with deference to a
> community of value in which he shares, he is at
> home again (pp. 107-108).

Implications for Education

Even though the difficulty of moving from an "is" to an "ought" has been recognized above in the realm of science and ethics, there is quite obviously a number of scientific findings classified as environmental science which should be made available to the citizenry of all ages whether these children, young people, or adults are enrolled in educational institutions or are part of the everyday world. Simply making the facts available will, of course, not be any guarantee that strong and positive attitudes will develop on the subject. It is a well-established fact, however, that the passing of legislation in difficult and sensitive areas must take place through responsible political leadership, and that attitude changes often follow behind--albeit at what may seem to be a snail's pace. The field of education must play a vital role in the development of what might be called an "ecological awareness." This is much more than the former approach which was usually called the Conservation Movement within forestry and closely related fields that were bent on the preservation of this or that feature of nature. Now ecology (or environmental science) places all of these individual entities in a total context in which the interrelationship of all parts must be thoroughly understood.

Sound educational planning should take place at all levels --from early childhood education through free tuition courses that are now being offered to many elderly citizens by certain universities. As Mergen states, "the knowledge that has been accumulated is vast, and ecological principles should be made part of the educational menu for economics, city planners, arc architects, engineers, the medical profession, the legal profession, religious groups, and all people concerned with the public and private management of natural resources, as well as politicans and governmental employees" (1970, p. 37). Obviously, those concerned professionally with physical education and sport, health and safety education, and recreation and park administration from the standpoint of professional education have a most important stake in this total educational process equally as much as all of those mentioned in Mergen's listing. As a matter of fact, these latter three professions are more concerned than most with man himself and with his interrelationship to his total environment whether natural or manmade.

Presumably the usual educational struggle will prevail among those who will want to introduce a new subject in the curriculum; those who will demand that environmental science be taught incidentally as part of existing subjects within the

educational program; and those who will see no need for the
study of environmental interrelationships to be in the basic
curriculum anyhow. Further, some will want the subject-matter
taught as facts and knowledge in subject-centered curriculum
based on a logical progression from the simple to the complex,
whereas other will stress that interest on the part of the learner should dictate if and how the subject should be introduced
--because this is the way people learn best. The urgency of
the ecological crisis would seem to warrant an approach which
"veers neither to the right or left or center." The point would
seem to be that a literally devastating problem is upon us, and
that we should "move ahead rapidly and soundly" to see that
some of the basics of environmental science are made available
somehow to all. These other issues have been on hand for so
many centuries that they will not be solved "tomorrow" no matter how the crisis is resolved--or how we attempt to resolve it.

It is difficult to state that certain information and attitudes should be taught to the population of a pluralistic society
--and then to look forward confidently to the effective execution of such a pronouncement throughout the land. This is
simply not the way that things happen in countries like the
United States and Canada, for example, where educational autonomy prevails in the many states and provinces, respectively.
All that can be hoped is that knowledge about the several positions regarding economic growth will be made available fairly to
the people as a controversial issue. Above it was mentioned
that certain ecological theories and economic theories indicate
quite clearly that following recommended courses of action as
promulgated by these theorists, respectively, will presumably
result in a seemingly impossible position in the near future.

B. G. Murray, an ecologist, makes it quite clear that
Americans (U. S. citizens, not necessarily Canadians) are definitely being placed in a position where a decision will have to
be made between a continuous-growth economic policy or a no-
growth one. This does not appear to be an "either-or" matter
in the eyes of the adherents of each of these theories about
which direction should be taken (1972, p. 38). Immediately it
is apparent that citizens typically are not even aware that some
scholars are recommending such a thing as a no-growth policy.
Is this not the land of capitalism and democracy where a steadily increasing Gross National Product is a quite certain indicator
of economic prosperity? One wonders whether it is a case of
the optimists saying, "full speed ahead, if we ever hope to re-
duce poverty in the United States," and the pessimists responding with the idea that "population and economic growth
must certainly strive for steady-state by the next century (if

that is not too late)."   Who ever heard of such nonsense as a steady-state situation?   This is the most difficult task that educators are facing as they attempt to carry forward the various forecasting models developed by scholars in both the natural sciences and the social sciences.

In a comparison of these conflicting models between ecology and economics, Murray examines the concepts of 'growth," 'movement of materials,' and 'competition.' First, in regard to growth, he explains that all types of biological growth follow a characteristic pattern which in time reaches a steady-state or equilibrium in which as many organisms are dying as young are being born into the system.   In United States business, however, the high standard of material living has been reached by continuously increasing growth in GNP to meet the needs and demands of a continuously increasing population.   Question: how long can this growth curve be maintained--and at what cost to all (including the rest of the world)?   It is explained further there by Murray that "such continuous growth curves are not unknown in biological and physical systems" (Ibid.).   However, the result typically leads to a disastrous result--death of the host organism as when uncontrolled cell growth takes place in cancer, or even when the chain reaction of fissioning uranium-235 nuclei result in the "inefficient use of energy in nuclear explosions" (p. 39).   The rule of the ecologist here implies that a system will eventually collapse unless it stops growing at some point and <u>recycles</u>.

The second concept discussed is the 'movement of materials,' and here reference is being made to the bio-geochemical cycles operative within nature--"the movement within ecosystems of minerals, water, oxygen, carbon dioxide, and other nutrients essential for life" (Ibid.).   One example of this process, of course, is that which carbon dioxide follows on its cyclic path between the earth's atmosphere and the many organisms that inhabit this planet.   Interestingly enough, the recycling that takes place is not completely efficient, with a result that the process known as "succession" results in a somewhat different make-up based on the ecosystem's chemical composition. The serious difficulty created by man is that both his food requirements and the demands of his vast technological progress are simply not recycled in such a way as to sustain even a steady-state situation indefinitely.   In other words, the "movement of materials" (as implied in Murray's concept of 'movement of materials') is all in one direction--for the temporary service of the earth's expanding population (that is increasing in number exponentially)!

Thirdly, and lastly, the other fundamental rule of ecology is discussed--sooner or later competition excludes some of the competing species. Practically this means that, if two organisms are competing for an exhaustible resource (and which one isn't in a closed system?), one of the competitors will be dispensed with by its rival "either by being forced out of the ecosystem or by being forced to use some other resource" (Ibid., p. 64). Thus, there exists a basic contradiction between the economic theory that states "competiton is supposed to maintain diversity and stability systems," and the theory based on the ecological model described above which has been tested in both natural and laboratory situations.

By now it should be readily apparent to all that this issue of conflicting models and resultant theories should have an overriding priority for inclusion "somewhere, somehow, and very soon" in the educational system. We need to know what all of this means to the cherished concepts of 'increasing growth,' 'competiton,' 'capitalism,' 'advancing technological revolution,' and other such terms. The merging of tenable principles of environmental science with altered values and norms into acceptable and highly desirable educational theory and practice represents an immediate challenge for all educators in programs that have either a disciplinary or professional education orientation.

Implications for Physical Education and Sport
(including health & safety education and recreation and park administration)

If the field of education have a very definite responsibility and strong obligation to present the various issues revolving about what has rapidly become a persistent problem (or social force) in North American society (and especially so in the United States), this duty obviously includes the teaching professionals at all educational levels who are specialists in all of the subject-matter areas taught in the curriculum. The primary concern in this context is, of course, with those who teach in physical education and sport (and/or some combination of health and safety education and recreation and park administration). (The reader will appreciate immediately that these three fields are now designated as allied professions, even though many physical educators and coaches get involved typically with certain duties that often are carried out by the professional practitioners in one or both of the other two allied fields. The same can be said, of course, for personal functioning in each of the two allied fields.)

The physical educator and sport coach, as do those practicing in the other two allied professional fields, quite naturally has a certain general education responsibility to all participants in their classes or their community recreation programs. Thus, he is directly concerned with man's relationship with himself, his fellow man, other living organisms, and also the physical environment and the remainder of the biological environment. A responsible citizen and educator will have an understanding of world-wide population growth and what problems such growth is going to present to man. Granted that there are conflicting views on this matter, the student should at least be able to expect that his instructor will have a reasoned position about this controversial issue. The physical educator and coach should also understand how continuous-growth economic theories contradict basic ecological theory. There can be no argument about the fact that both population growth and advancing technology--the latter with the capability to improve the material living standard of all to the extent possible--seem to be leading Earth's population to a position where some fundamental changes in attitudes and practices will probably necessarily result (or ought to change, at any rate). Although attitudes toward improved international relations have waxed and waned over the decades, the responsible physical educator and coach will realize that the quality of life cannot be steadily improved in some countries on earth without due consideration being given to improving the conditions of all people everywhere. Lastly, the informed citizen and educator will be aware of the urgent need to take care of the manifold ecosystems on this "closed" planet and will do all in his power to assist with the necessary recycling so that a "reconstituted" earth will be transmitted to future generations.

Now we must consider whether there are any specific implications for the physical educator and coach as he faces his own professional task. As matters stand now, he is confronted daily with the fact that for a variety of reasons modern, urbanized, technologically advanced life in North America has created a population with a very low level of physical fitness with a resultant decrease in overall total fitness. What makes matters so extremely difficult is that the large majority of the population has been lulled into a false sense of complacency by what Herbert Spencer over a century ago called a "seared physical conscience" that is unable to "monitor" the body properly and accurately (1949, p. 197). As a result of this presumed sense of complacency, there is an unwillingness to lead a life similar to that of their forebearers that may indeed be characterized as "physically vigorous." What we have created,

therefore, is a ridiculous situation in which people on this continent are to a large extent overfed and poorly exercised, whereas a multitude of people on many other continents on earth are
"underfed" and often quite strenuously exercised! All of this
adds up to a world situation that may well bring disaster to us
all before Planet Earth is barely into the twenty-first century.

Although many professions will undoubtedly be "focusing
in" on this dilemma soon, it is the profession of physical education and sport that is uniquely responsible for the exercise
programs that will enable "man (and woman) to be a rugged animal fit to withstand the excessive wear and tear that life's informal and formal activities may demand" (Zeigler, 1964, p. 55).
Additionally, it is this same physical educator who gets involved with health education courses in which nutritional practices
and habits are discussed. Once again, as Spencer indicated
earlier, "generally, we think, the history of the world shows
that the well-fed races have been the energetic and dominant
races." He explained further that animals can work harder
when they are fed more nutritiously. The point he wishes to
make is that a sound diet is necessary for both energy and
growth (1949, p. 191). What this adds up to is that the physical educator/coach is typically also in a situation where he
teaches about nutrition at least indirectly in daily practice--and
quite often directly in classroom situations. Thus, he can to
some extent advise his students about the correct food to eat
so that he may lead a physically vigorous life, as well as which
amounts of what food will enable him to receive adequate nutrition to maintain normal health--not to mention advice about how
to keep from being overweight or underweight.

These factors of a vigorous exercise program and correct
nutritional instruction relate quite directly to the two aspects
of the ecological crisis discussed earlier--that is, the pollution
of the earth and its atmosphere, and adequate nutrition for the
children born on this earth. Without getting involved in the
moral question of birth control, the physical educator/coach
should do all in his power to curtail pollution because it will in
a short time--in a variety of ways--make it increasingly difficult for man to exercise vigorously and to maintain so-called
physical fitness (implying a mind-body dichotomy). When the
air we breathe and the water we drink become increasingly im-
pure, how then will we maintain the fitness of all?

Secondly, there is the matter of adequate nutrition for
the rapidly increasing population in the countries least able to
feed their offspring. Although some may believe that the Malthusian principle should be allowed to take effect (can it be

stopped?) and that the favored nations should take care of their own needs, it would seem to be more humane to keep the world's hungry people as adequately supplied with staples as possible--but at the same time we in physical education should redouble our efforts to make certain that young people learn correct eating habits to guarantee relatively lean and fat-free bodies that are nevertheless quite capable of vigorous exercise to ensure physical fitness. There is so much food wasted on this continent that our moral sense should be affronted. For example, how many people could be kept alive with our garbage? Or to view the question in another way, is it quite so necessary that millions upon millions of dogs and cats be sustained when human beings are dying of malnutrition? Perhaps so; however, we might make an effort to cut down the breeding of the canine and feline population somewhat, while we are exporting human birth control to the rest of the world's undeveloped nations.

In addition, people at all stages of life show evidence of a variety of remediable physical defects, but there is typically an unwillingness on the part of the public to make exercise therapy programs readily available through both public and private agencies. Reference here is not directed at the many physiotherapy programs available briefly after operations or accidents. Such assistance is typically most helpful and fills an important need. The concern is with the unavailability of exercise therapy programs in the schools and certain private agencies under the supervision of qualified physical educators upon exercise prescription by a physician.

Keeping in mind the ecological principle that "competition kills competitors," it would appear to be the direct responsibility of the physical educator/coach to involve all young people. male and female, normal or with remediable or permanent defect, in that type of vigorous program of physical activity--human movement in sport, dance, and exercise--that can be characterized as interesting, joyful, and exuberant. In this way it is quite possible that interest will be maintained throughout life. If such were to be the case, the society could possibly then be characterized as a "nation of good animals" able to again meet the criterion of a necessary "first condition" for the maintenance of independence and prosperity--a population characterized by a quality of physical fitness within a concept of total fitness (Spencer, 1949, p. 177). (In the process we should presumably direct young people away from such sporting activities as the use of snowmobiles, auto racing, and speedboats which pollute the environment, tend to destroy the ecosystemic

balance, and provide a mechanical means for propelling the
body from one point to another!)

It should be further appreciated that physical education
and sport can play an important role in the social and psychological development of the individual. As important as the element of competition may have been in the past--and may continue to be in the future--it is now time to place at least equal
emphasis on the benefits to be derived from cooperation in the
various aspects of sport competition. Most certainly the future
of life on this planet will present all sorts of opportunities for
cooperative effort both at home and abroad. A wholesome balance between competition and cooperation in a child's education
can develop highly desirable personality traits, while at the
same time offering numerous occasions for the release of overly
aggressive tendencies seemingly present in so many individuals.

As indicated earlier, those teaching physical education
and sport skills often get involved directly or indirectly with
health and safety education and/or recreation education. These
instructors have some contact with practically every student in
the school. Thus, they have great potential for conveying
knowledge and assisting in the formation of correct attitudes
about all three of these allied fields through effective teaching.
Additionally, the physical educator/coach can set an example
personally for all young people to follow. For example, the
area of health and safety education provides innumerable ways
to demonstrate safety practices, personal hygiene, and attitudes
(and practice) toward the use of alcohol, tobacco, marijuana,
and what presumably are the more harmful drugs. Wholesome
attitudes and practice in the area of sex and sex education are
also extremely important--the whole area of family life education
for that matter should be taught well both by "precept and
practice."

Similarly, the area of recreation education offers many
opportunities for the education of man in ways that will promote improved ecological understanding. In the first place, a
change in leisure values--at least as they have been established by many--should take place. Through recreation education
it should be possible to promote an understanding of and respect for the world's flora and fauna, not to mention the whole
concept of ecosystemic balance. Even though so-called post-
industrial society is not reducing working hours for many at
the rate predicted by some earlier, and many in leadership
roles are putting in even longer hours, there is still an urgent
need to promote the concept of 'creative leisure.' We need a
return to what used to be considered by many as the "simple

recreational pleasures"--perhaps with a few variations to satisfy the young. The physical educator/coach should promote the concept of 'physical recreation' for all, of course, but by precept and example the idea of the young person getting involved with aesthetic and creative activities and hobbies (involving "learning" recreational interests) should be fostered as well.

Concluding Statement

Everything considered, the writer has concluded that the influence of ecology is now such that it must be included as a persistent problem along with the other social forms of values, politics, nationalism, economics, and religion. Although it was recognized that there is a dividing line between science and ethics, it is recommended that perhaps morality should now be viewed as being derived from the fundamental, all-encompassing nature of the ecosystem. This plea for the broadening of the concept of value--perhaps a truly naturalistic ethic--would have both direct and indirect implications for education to play a highly important role in the development of an "ecological awareness." The physical educator/coach, and those in the allied professions, have a unique function in helping man to develop and maintain physical fitness within a concept of 'total fitness' based on a goal of international understanding and brotherhood.

References and Bibliography

Selected References

Berg, Alan. "The Trouble with Triage." The New York Times Magazine, June 15, 1975, 26, 28, 30-31, 35.

Burch, William R., Jr. "Recreation and Leisure Time in an Expanding Industrial Society." Yale Alumni Magazine, Vol. XXXIII, No. 8, May 1970, 67, 69-72.

Colwell, Thomas B., Jr. "The Balance of Nature: A Ground for Human Values." Main Currents in Modern Thought, Vol. 26, 1969, 50.

Darwin, Charles. The Descent of Man (new edition). New York: D. Appleton & Co., 1895. See pages 124-125 for his comments about man's standard of morality and its possible application to all creatures on earth.

Dasmann, Raymond. A Different Kind of Country. New York: The Macmillan Company, 1968.

DeBell, Garrett. The Environmental Handbook. New York: Ballantine, 1970.

Disch, Robert (Ed.). The Ecological Conscience: Values for Survival. Englewood Cliffs, N. J.: Prentice-Hall, Inc., 1970.

Dubos, René. A God Within. New York: Charles Scribner's Sons, 1972, pp. 166-167.

Graham, Frank. Since Silent Spring. Boston: Houghton-Mifflin Company, 1970. Graham likens Rachel Carson's Silent Spring, published in 1963, to Uncle Tom's Cabin insofar as societal impact is concerned.

Helfrich, Harold W., Jr. (Ed.). The Environmental Crisis: Man's Struggle to Live With Himself. New Haven, Conn.: Yale University Press, 1970.

Leopold, Aldo. "The Land Ethic," in A Sand County Almanac. New York: Oxford University Press, 1949, pp. 201-226.

Marsh, George Perkins. Man and Nature: Or Physical Geography as Modified by Human Action. Boston: Harvard University Press, 1965. This is a new edition, edited by David Lowenthal, of Marsh's 1864 classic work on the subject.

Nicholson, Max. The Environmental Revolution: A Guide for the New Masters of the World. London: Hodder and Stoughton, 1970.

Revelle, Roger and Landsberg, Hans H. (Ed.). America's Changing Environment. Boston: The Beacon Press, 1970.

Bibliography

Christophers, The. "God's Good Earth--and Ours." A pamphlet published by The Christophers, 12 East 48th Street New York, N. Y. 10017. n.d.

Ehrlich, Paul R. and Holdren, John P. "Dodging the Crisis," Saturday Review, November 7, 1970, 73.

Huxley, Aldous. "The Politics of Ecology." A pamphlet published in 1963 by the Center for the Study of Democratic
Institutions, Santa Barbara, California. 6 p.

Kunz, Robert F. "An Environmental Glossary," Saturday Review, Jan. 2, 1971, 67.

Mergen, François. "Man and His Environment." Yale Alumni
Magazine, Vol. XXXIII, No. 8, May 1970, 36-37.

Murray, Bertram G., Jr. "What the Ecologists Can Teach the
Economists." The New York Times Magazine, Dec. 10,
1972, 38-39, 64-65, 70, 72.

National Geographic Society, The. "How Man Pollutes His
World." A detailed map of the earth and its atmosphere,
with accompanying narrative, published by The National
Geographic Society, Washington, D. C., 1970.

New York Times, The. "Nations Demand Agricultural Aid,"
August 3, 1975. An article written by Victor K. McElheny.

_____. "Foul Air Poses Health Threat to East,"
August 3, 1975. An article written by Lesley Oelsner.

_____. "Christianity Linked to Pollution," May 1,
1970. An article written by Edward B. Fiske.

Rolston, Holmes III. "Is There an Ecological Ethic?" Ethics,
Vol. 85, No. 2, January 1975, 93-109.

Sears, Paul. "The Steady State: Physical Law and Moral
Choice," in P. Shepard and D. McKinley (Eds.). The
Subjective Science. Boston: Houghton-Mifflin Company,
1969, p. 401.

Smith, Grahame J. C. "The Ecologist at Bay." Saturday Review, Jan. 2, 1971, 68-69.

Spencer, Herbert. Education: Intellectual, Moral, and Physical. London: C. A. Watts & Co., Ltd., 1949. Originally published in 1861.

Zeigler, Earle F. Philosophical Foundations for Physical,
Health, and Recreation Education. Englewood Cliffs,
N. J.: Prentice-Hall, Inc., 1964.

Questions for Discussion

1. When do you first become aware of the world's "ecological problem?" Do you agree that it should be listed as one of the six basic "social forces" discussed by the author in Chapter 19?

2. Do you agree with Rolston that there is such a thing as an "ecological ethic?" If so, how do you get an "ought" from an "is?" In other words, on what basis is it possible to postulate an authentic naturalistic ethic?

3. What are some of the ways in which the field of education can help to develop an "ecological awareness?"

4. How does Murray seek to explain his thesis in regard to the dilemma that is being faced--i.e., do we have a continuous-growth economic policy or a no-growth one? What might having a steady-state situation in this realm do for us ecologically?

5. Everything considered, in what ways should those of us in the allied professions (health education, sport and physical education, safety education, recreation and leisure studies, dance) become involved so as to help develop the required consciousness to help in the resolution of this global problem?

CHAPTER 16

A METAETHICAL ANALYSIS OF 'WORK' AND 'PLAY' AS RELATED TO NORTH AMERICAN SPORT

The main problem of this paper is to analyze critically - from a so-called metaethical standpoint - the concepts of 'work' and 'play' and to relate such distinctions to the current scene in sport and/or athletics as we know them typically in North America.* It was during my early college days about forty years ago that I realized the amount of confusion in people's minds about the uses of these two everyday terms. Or perhaps it would be more accurate to say that I sensed the presence of confusion when the topic was discussed in more than a superficial manner. But I suppose for the large majority of people there really was no problem at all: work was what you did in life to earn a living or to take care of your basic needs; thus, both my grandparents and parents viewed it as a serious matter, and a significant amount of such arduous endeavor was included as part of my normal upbringing. Play, conversely, was what you were free to do after you had carried out your work responsibilities. Whereas work was serious, play was supposed to be fun and re-creative - and trifling or trivial as opposed to being earnest and weighty.

It was while studying philosophy of education at Yale with John S. Brubacher in the mid-1940s that he called to my attention the many limitations inherent in the typical usage of the two terms by laymen and educators alike. This led to preliminary analysis which indicated that some people "worked at play," whereas certain others "played at their work." Further, it became apparent that there was considerable educational value - however that might be defined - in many structured or semi-structured activities that were typically designated as play. And so, for the first time, I became aware of what has been designated as a scientific (Deweyan) ethical analysis technique - with the remainder of the triumvirate being called an authoritarian approach or a relativistic technique. As explained by Fromm,

---

* A paper presented at the Sixth Annual Meeting of the Philosophic Society for the Study of Sport, Hartford, Connecticut, October 21-23, 1976.

> The most significant contemporary proponent of a
> scientific ethics is John Dewey, whose views are
> opposed both to authoritarianism and to relativism
> in ethics. As to the former, he states that the
> common feature of appeal to revelation, divinely
> ordained rulers, commands of the state, conven-
> tion, tradition, and so on, 'is that there is some
> voice so authoritative as to preclude the need of
> inquiry' (J. Dewey and J. H. Tufts, Ethics.
> N. Y.: H. Holt & Co. Rev. ed., 1932, p. 364).
> As to the latter, he holds that the fact that some-
> thing is enjoyed is not in itself 'a judgment of the
> value of what is enjoyed' (Dewey, Problems of Men.
> N. Y.: H. Holt & Co., 1946, p. 254). The en-
> joyment is a basic datum, but it has to be 'verifi-
> ed by evidential facts' (Ibid., p. 260). (Fromm,
> 1967, p. 37).

But even though I had evidently understood the possible educational implications of play based on pragmatic theory, I recall myself writing for Ontario's developing recreation profession in the 1950s that "play" was for children! This was
followed by a statement that "recreation" was for mature adults.
Looking back upon that "profound" statement some twenty-five
years later, I can't comprehend why no one present challenged
such pedantic dictum. Can't you just imagine telling people
today that adults should never play - just recreate!

    Then in the 1960s James Keating offered us his distinc-
tion between the concepts of 'sport' and 'athletics.' When you
analyzed this idea - which was basically sound albeit highly
impractical in a world where the public often ignores etymological distinctions - it turned out that the terms or concepts may
be likened fundamentally to 'play' and 'work' respectively.
Thus, however rational Keating's distinction may have been
(Keating, 1963, pp. 149, 201-210), the words "sport" and "athletics" are currently being used interchangeably on the North
American continent, although in England and on the European
continent - and perhaps in the rest of the world - there seems
to be an identification of the word "athletics" more directly
with track and field events only.

    However, the concepts of 'work' and 'play' are still
strongly dichotomized just about everywhere. There seems to
be no trend whatsoever toward clarifying that which is obviously imprecise and actually muddled in typical usage, even
though many educators holding various educational philosophical
stances would affirm that "play" under certain "educational"

conditions contributes to a child's educational experience and growth. And nowhere is the confusion more evident that when we are discussing to what extent the nomenclature of "work" and "play" may be applied when referring to various levels of participation in sport and/or athletics on the North American scene.

To repeat, therefore, the main problem of this paper is to analyze critically (or metaethically) the concepts of 'work' and 'play' as they are currently employed in North America, and to relate such distinctions to sport and/or athletics as we know them typically in society at large or within the educational setting specifically. The following sub-problems of the topic, phrased as questions, will be discussed in this order: (1) how may some of the fundamental terms being employed be defined initially? (2) what is the status of sport and/or athletics in North America? (3) does such status have a possible relationship to the prevailing social forces at work in North America? (4) would altered concepts of 'work' and 'play' – in a democratic culture where individual freedom is valued highly – possibly exert an influence on the prevailing pattern in sport/athletics? and (5) how may this question be summarized and what reasonable conclusion(s) may be drawn from this analysis?

Definition of Terms

Work. The term "work" can be used as a noun in a number of different ways (e.g., "something that is or was done; "something to do or be done"; "a person's action of a particular kind"; "an action involving effort or exertion directed to a definite end" - i.e., "one's regular occupation or employment"; "a particular piece or act of labour"; "a task, job"; and "exercise or practice in a sport or game"; also, "exertion or movement proper to a particular sport, game, or exercise" (The Oxford Universal Dictionary, 1955, p. 2449). Used in a second sense as a noun, the term "work" is "the product of the operation or labour of a person or other agent" (Ibid.)

The term "work" is used also as both a transitive and intransitive verb and, of course, such usage has a close relationship to its use as a noun. Some twenty different usages are listed for its employment as a transitive verb (e.g., "to do a deed"; "to effect something or some action"; "to move something into position," etc.). The intransitive verb is used in approximately fourteen ways, some of which have direct application to our purposes here (e.g., "to do something or to do things generally"; "to pursue a regular occupation"; "to perform the work proper or incidental to one's business or avocation" (Ibid., p. 2449).

Synonyms for the word "work" are achievement, business, drudgery, effort, employment, labor, occupation, opus, performance, production, task, toil, and travail. Antonyms for "work" are ease, leisure, play, recreation, vacation (The Living Webster Encyclopedic Dictionary of the English Language, 1975, p. BT-34).

Play. The term "play" can be used as a noun in many ways (e.g., "exercise, free movement or action"; "exercise or action by way of recreation, amusement, or sport"; and "mimic action" (The Oxford Universal Dictionary, 1955, p. 1920).

The term "play" is used as a verb in five general ways, and such usage - as was the case with the term "work" - has a close relationship to its use as a noun. These usages are as follows: (1) "to exercise oneself, act or move energetically"; (2) "to exercise oneself in the way of diversion or amusement"; (3) "to engage in a game, etc."; (4) "to perform instrumental music"; and (5) "to perform dramatically, etc." (Ibid., p. 1521).

Synonyms for the word "play" used as a noun are listed under the word "recreation." They are as follows: amusement, diversion, entertainment, fun, game, pastime, and sport. Antonyms for "play" are boredom, labor, toil, and work (listed also under "recreation") (The Living Webster Encyclopedic Dictionary of the English Language, 1975, p. BT-26).

Freedom. The term "freedom" is used here to describe the "condition of being able to choose and to carry out purposes" (Muller, 1961, xiii). Or to be more precise, keeping in mind that the traditional, liberal meaning of freedom relates to the absence of constraint or coercion, the following definition appears to describe the term more adequately:

> A man is said to be free to the extent that he can choose his own goals or course of conduct, can choose between alternatives available to him, and is not compelled to act as he himself would not choose to act, or prevented from acting as he would otherwise choose to act, by the will of another man, of the state, or of any other authority (Partridge, 1967, Vol. 3, p. 222).

Synonyms for the word "freedom" are exemption, familiarity, immunity, independence, liberation, liberty, ridiculous, senseless, silly, and simple. Antonyms are bondage, compulsion, constraint, necessity, and servitude (The Living Webster, etc., p. BT-14).

Amateur. An amateur is "one who cultivates any art or pursuit for the enjoyment of it, instead of professionally or for gain, sometimes implying desultory action or crude results; a devotee" (The Living Webster, etc., p. 32).

Synonyms for the term "amateur" are apprentice, beginner, dabbler, dilettante, learner, neophyte, and novice. Antonyms are adept, authority, expert, master, and professional (Ibid., p. BT-2).

Semipro. A semipro (Colloq., a semiprofessional) is one who engages in some sport or other activity for pay but only as a part-time occupation (Ibid., p. 876). The person resembles a professional, but his/her performance demands less skill, knowledge, and the like.

Professional. A professional is a member of any profession, but more often applied, in opposition to amateur, to persons who make their living by arts or sports in which others engage as a pastime (Ibid., p. 761).

Sport. A sport is a "diversion, amusement, or recreation; a pleasant pastime; a pastime pursued in the open air or having an athletic character, as hunting, fishing, baseball, bowling, or wrestling, etc. (Ibid., p. 942). Further meanings are listed which are not applicable to the present discussion.

Synonyms for the term "sport" are listed under "games" as amusement, contest, diversion, fun, match, merriment, pastime, play, and recreation. Antonyms mentioned are business, drudgery, hardship, labor, and work (Ibid., pp. BT 14 and 15).

Athletics. Athletics is a plural noun that is acceptable in usage as either singular or plural in construction. It (they) may be described as "athletic exercises: sports such as tennis, rowing, boxing, etc." (Ibid., p. 63). (Note that track and field are not mentioned as typical or prototype examples, although they are undoubtedly considered part of the sports included under the term "athletics" in North America.)

In a preliminary, inspectional way, therefore, it is possible to construct a diagram based on the more or less traditional definitions of the terms "play," "work," "freedom," "constraint," "sport," "athletics," "amateur," and "professional." With each pair of terms there is a sharp dichotomization in normal usage except with the terms "sport and "athletics." Nevertheless, in this diagram they are shown as being dichotomized because of Keating's recommendation. Despite what has just been said, and which is diagrammed in Figure 1 below, subsequent consideration of a more careful nature gives rise to the idea that the concepts of 'play' and 'work' could truly be placed on a continuum as opposed to a discontinuum as shown at the top of the figure. In this instance the continuum would extend from 'frivolity' on the left through 'play' to the concept of 'work' and finally to 'drudgery' on the far right.

A PLAY/WORK DEFINITIONAL DIAGRAM RELATING TO THE
CONCEPTS OF 'SPORT,' 'FREEDOM', AND 'AMATEURISM'

Note: A sharp dichotomization is typically implied when the concepts are considered initially and typically employed in common parlance. Even the dictionary definitions - including both synonyms and antonyms - appear as a discontinuum.

Play---------------------------------(as typically used)---------------------------- Work

Freedom--------------------------(as typically used)------------------------- Constraint

Amateur--------------------------(as typically used)-----------------------Professional

Sport----------------------------------(Keating's etymological)------------------------- Athletics
                          analysis stresses dichotomization, but
                          the two terms are typically used syn-
                          onymously in this culture.

Note: The terms "play" and "work," along with "frivolity" and "drudgery," are placed on a continuum below - as opposed to the discontinuum shown above.

Presumably the same approach could be employed with the other terms indicated as the several continua are extended to their extremities. As J. S. Brubacher indicates in correspondence dated September 27, 1976, "work and play tend to overlap toward the middle of the continuum when work can be pleasant and play can be toilsome . . . Similarly, at the drudgery end, it is all constraint, and at the frivolity end of the continuum the freedom becomes license."

A Continuum Approach

Frivolity -------------------Play----------------------Work--------------------Drudgery

Figure 1.

The Status of Sport/Athletics

The comments made, and the opinions offered, about the status of amateur, semiprofessional, and professional sport are based upon a half century of personal experience and observation as a performer, as a coach of performers, as a teacher of coaches, as a professor writing about the professional preparation of coaches, and as a person writing about sport within society from a disciplinary standpoint. After my first ten years of coaching experience in three different sports in two major universities in the United States and Canada and in a Y.M.C.A., I began to write about sport in a normative, hortatory, and common sense fashion. This type of article was superseded to a large extent in the 1960s by an effort to draw implications from the various educational philosophical stances extant at the time. However, realizing the uncertainty and imprecision of normative ethics and ethical relativism, I maintained a continuous flow of material down to the present time in which I have espoused what might be called a Deweyan scientific ethic based upon a merging of the historic value-facts controversy (Zeigler, 1960, 1962, 1964, 1965, 1968, 1969, 1971, 1972, 1973, 1974, 1975, etc.). More recently I have been following a more eclectic philosophical methodology involving several techniques, including metaethical or critical analysis of sport and physical activity - hence this present effort to delineate somewhat more carefully problems that arise typically in the use of such terms as "work," "play," "freedom," "constraint," "sport," "athletics," "amateur," "semipro," and "professional" when discussing sport and its myriad problems and contentious issues.

Writing in 1967 (Zeigler, pp. 47-49), for purposes of discussion about "leading a good life," I noted that:

> it is not necessary to delineate the various meanings of play too carefully; so, we will accept the definition that play is an instinctive form of self-expression through pleasurable activity which seems to be aimless in nature . . .

In discussing work at the same time, it was pointed out that:

> Many people are now choosing leisure instead of more work, because they wanted to "enjoy life."

Speaking at the Athletics in America Symposium at Oregon State University in 1971, the point was made that "North Americans must ponder the term 'freedom' deeply today as they face an uncertain future. Here freedom is defined as 'the condition of being able to choose and carry out purposes" (p. 79). Subsequently the statement was made that "the field of athletics and sport seems to be at least as poorly prepared as any in the educational system to help young people to get ready for the future."

For many years also I have been attempting the "philosophical analysis" of one of the most persistent problems facing higher education - that of so-called amateur, semiprofessional, and professional sport and its relationship to our educational system, as well as our entire culture (in Flath, 1964). I have argued the necessity for reevaluation of our treasured, basic assumptions about the amateur code in sport. Further, I have decried the materialistic image of today's professional in sport, the argument being that he is being professional only in the limited sense of the word - that it brought money to him quickly for athletic performance at a high level, without his commitment as a true professional whose primary aim in life is to serve his fellow-man through his varied contributions to his own sport in particular and to all sport in general. Thus, I have argued that the amateur should be regarded as the beginner - not as the Olympic performer who somehow refrained from taking cash but who received all kinds of invaluable support along the way. I have presented the idea of a logical, bonafide, and desirable progression - if the person wished to progress and was capable - through the ranks of the amateur athlete to that of the semipro, and finally to that of the highly trained, proficient athletic performer - a professional!

I would not wish to create the impression that this has been a solitary effort - far from it. As far back as 1929, the Carnegie Report entitled American College Athletics explained that "the defects of American college athletics are two: commercialism, and a negligent attitude toward the educational opportunity for which the American college exists." Additionally, the Report stressed that the prevailing amateur code was violated continually; that recruiting and subsidizing was "the darkest blot upon American college sport"; that athletic training and hygiene practices were deplorable and actually jeopardized health in many instances; that athletes are not poorer academically, but that hard training for long hours impaired scholastic standing; that athletics as conducted fail in many cases "to utilize and strengthen such desirable social traits as honesty and the sense of fair play"; that few of the sports which are most popular contributed to physical recreation after college; that many head coaches were receiving higher pay than full professor, but that their positions were dependent upon successful win-loss records; that the athletic conferences were

not abiding by the letter, much less the spirit of the established rules and regulations; and that athletes were not receiving
the opportunity to "mature under responsibility."

In 1974, some forty-five years later, there seems to be
every indication that the only one of the above-mentioned areas
of criticism showing improvement would be that of athletic training and hygiene practices! Even on this point a cynic would
be quick to point out that improved athletic training could be
expected because of the desire to keep expensive athletic talent
healthy enough to "earn its keep." At any rate, in the year
1974 the American Council on Education was perceptive enough
to discover that "there's a moral problem in college athletics,"
and that "the pressure to win is enormous" (Cady, The New
York Times, March 10, 1974) – facts which have been known
to cognoscenti in educational circles for decades. For example,
The New York Times commissioned a survey of some forty colleges and universities and reported in 1951 that the flagrant
abuse of athletic subsidization in many colleges and universities "promoted the establishment of false values"; "are the bane
of existence in American education"; "lower educational standards generally"; force educators "to lose out to politicians";
and "do further injury to democracy in education" (Grutzner,
1951). Obviously, it serves no good purpose to enumerate
such statements endlessly, because volumes could be filled with
them before 1929 and up to the present.

Even though this paper is not designed so that it will
prove logically that the status of athletics or sport in United
States' education is unsound according to the so-called educational standards or principles upon which most colleges and
universities are based, it is essential to justify the conclusion
that many colleges and universities are conducting intercollegiate athletics in such a manner that many questions have been
raised over the years about their educational value – and the
situation seems to be as bad today as it ever was! This is the
reason for inclusion of the section on the status of such programs. It is important to keep in mind further that not all
colleges and universities are conducting their intercollegiate
athletic programs so as to warrant such severe criticism. One
has to go no further than the Little Three in New England,
most Ivy League institutions, a large university like Wayne
State in Detroit, and also Springfield College in Massachusetts,
to name just a few. Further, Canada has been most fortunate
in the realm of university competitive sport, and the prevailing
"amateur spirit" there has definitely influenced the secondary
school outlook as well. This is not to say that there aren't
warning signs on the horizon, but a recent survey carried out

by the Association of Universities and Colleges of Canada reported that intercollegiate athletics has been able to maintain what was called its amateur spirit and educational balance, generally speaking. As reported by Matthews,

> Canadian universities appear to be in a position to strive for a very high level of athletic and recreational development in international comparison. University athletic programs must be seen as a need of the people - of individuals, of groups, and of the entire university community . . .
>   (Matthews, 1974, p. 3)

Relationship of Status to Prevailing Social Forces

Keeping in mind that our objective is to analyze the concepts of 'work' and 'play' as currently employed, and to relate such distinctions to sport and athletics in a more precise way, it is important to reiterate at this point (see pp. 201 and 202 above) that both terms ("work" and "play") may be used correctly in a number of ways. Such correct usage ranges from "something that is done" to "exercise or practice in a sport or game" for the concept of 'work.' Similarly the term "play" ranges all the way from "exercise or action by way of recreation, amusement, or sport" to so-called "mimic action" in a dramatic performance in the theater. Highly important, therefore, and crucial to the argument being presented here, is the fact that in each case these terms ("work" and "play") have assumed so-called typical meanings in the language and thought of people - "effort" or "labor," for example, for "work," and "amusement" or "fun" for the term "play." Furthermore, it is argued that the sharp dichotomization of these two concepts in everyday usage, when they actually have almost identical, strongly overlapping meanings in a dictionary, has often caused confusion when sport and athletics were being considered as part of the cultural configuration of North American society.

It seems to be impossible to state precisely why such a sharp dichotomization of the two concepts of 'work' and 'play' have persisted in everyday usage, but such a distinction undoubtedly has some relationship to the influence of the pivotal social forces on our culture (e.g., values, type of political state, nationalism, economics, religion, and now ecology). It was obvious to people in earlier centuries that work had a so-called survival value - and presumably much more of this quality than play. Indeed it took so very long for the average man on this continent to earn and use leisure. There have been so many wars, and nothing is more devastating to an

economy. We can't escape the fact that a surplus economy is
absolutely necessary if people are to have a high standard of
education and leisure (Brubacher, 1966, p. 76 et ff.). Secondly, the truism that times change slowly must be mentioned.
It is extremely difficult to change the traditions and mores of .
a civilization. The existing political system continued to prevail, and it took a revolution, a civil war, and other conflicts
of varying magnitude before the concept of 'political democracy'
had an opportunity to grow (Zeigler, 1975, p. 457).

Thirdly, the power of the church - almost absolute at
times - had to be weakened before the concept of 'church and
state separation' could become a reality - and all of us appreciate the several basic reasons why the church affirmed the
concept of 'work' and accordingly denigrated the concept of
'play,' or those of 'leisure' and 'recreation.' Fourthly, the
many implications of the natural sciences had to be consolidated
into very real gains before advanced technology could be realized and could lead men into an industrial revolution, the out-
comes of which we possibly still cannot foresee, and which -
on this continent at least - have lowered many men's working
hours down to the point where the idea of play and leisure
could loom more importantly in their purview than heretofore.

Consequently, one could argue that the prevailing social
forces have most definitely influenced the status of sport and
athletics (if defined identically or even similarly). If the United States, for example, can become "Number #1" in the world
through a unique, but probably not reproducible, set of circumstances in which the concept of 'work' was exalted by all
of the pivotal social forces - and the idea of 'play' was viewed
typically as "frivolous refreshment from worthwhile toil and
labor" - it is not difficult to understand why such a sharp
dichotomy developed between these two terms. Accordingly, it
is only a short step to the position that playing games or
sports is really not very important, is extracurricular, and
must come after effort has resulted in achievement at any rate.
This would seem to be the rationale, therefore, for the sharp
dichotomization - and differentiation in value - of the two
terms of everyday usage.

Possible Relationship of Altered Concepts to Sport

What we are perceiving here, of course, is a relationship
or "proposition seemingly self-contradictory or absurd, and yet
explicable as expressing a truth" - in other words, a paradox.
A paradox is typically incredible, and (as Brubacher explains)
we have created a situation in which our language - or choice

of words - actually downgrades that which we seem to be seeking in the so-called good life:

> The oldest and perhaps most persistent position
> regards work or labor principally as the means
> whereby leisure used in our culture as a word
> synonymous with recreation and play is pur-
> chased to devote to education. Stated succinct-
> ly, the good life depends on labor but consists
> in leisure (Brubacher, 1969, p. 34).

The assumption here is that leisure (play) is actually superior to labor (work) in this culture. People must work in order to stay alive or live, but they have completely free rein when it comes to the use of their leisure. Leisure (play) is worthwhile on its own account! Further, any educational theory which does not encourage wise use of leisure for so-called educational purposes might soon run into difficulty. But if the student, for example, felt an obligation to pursue education diligently, we are then back to the position where education could be regarded as work again! Interestingly enough, what all of this leads to is a position where work becomes subservient to leisure, and this is just fine for an aristocratic society: one social class works so that another class can be free to enjoy leisure. If this situation is reversed and the place of work dominates educational policy, we have a Marxian type of society in which economic theory looms very large in the educational system. Presumably in between these two extremes would be the position in this regard of the evolving democratic society - one in which work is a continuing opportunity for man to follow an evolutionary pattern onward and "upward" (whatever that may mean). "Work finds its educational significance in its humanization of man," and a "child"s active occupation" in school is not regarded as tedious, laborious schoolwork. Work, play, and art all relate to the "active occupation" of the boy or girl, and no significant difference can be made as to the educational significance of any of the three aspects. Art, for example, is "work permeated with the play attitude" (p. 36).

Such a theoretical approach contradicts the dualistic or dichotomous theory of work and play upon which we have been focusing. Now they are viewed as possessing overlapping and not separate entities or categories. Thus - and isn't this the way it really happens? - some people take their play very seriously, while others seem to play at being professional in their work. In fact, it all becomes most confusing when an effort is made to analyze the situation as to where play leaves off and becomes work (and vice versa). All of which has led me to conceive of a "play-work definitional continuum" in quite different terms than was explained above (see Figure 1, p. 204).

This newer conception has been called "aspects of a person's 'active occupation'" (see Figure 2 below) - a situation in which so-called work, play, and art have epistemological and

ASPECTS OF A PERSON'S "ACTIVE OCCUPATION"

(1. Play ------- 2. Art ------- 3. Work)*

Freedom-Constraint Continuum	Freedom ------------------ Limited Freedom -------------- Constraint (No Freedom)
Level IV	

Amateur-Professional Continuum	Amateur ------------------ Semipro --------------------- Professional
Level III	

Goals Continuum	Short Range ------------- Middle Range ---------------- Long Range
Level II	

Categories of Interest	The Unified Organism	1. Physical education-recreation interests 2. Social education-recreation interests 3. "Learning" education-recreation interests 4. Aesthetic education-recreation interests 5. Communicative education-recreation interests
Level I		

* John Dewey reasoned that "work finds its educational significance in its humanization of man." He believed further that a "child's active occupation" in school is not regarded as tedious, laborious schoolwork. Work, play, and art all relate to the "active occupation" of the boy or girl, and no significant difference can be made as to the educational significance of any of the aspects. Art, for example, is "work permeated with the play attitude." (J. S. Brubacher, 1969.)

Figure 2.

ethical significance in the realization of the person's humanity in a social environment. First, on Level I, we have the person - conceived as a "unified organism" - with his/her educational and/or recreational interests of varying nature that will presumably be present throughout the individual's life. Second, on Level II, is the so-called goals continuum of short range, middle range, and long range goals. It is at this point that such a differentiation in approach is being recommended from the prevailing sharply dichotomized definitions of the terms "work" and "play." Presumably - and it is not being proposed that it is possible or desirable to reverse people's language habits markedly in any direction - an effort could be made to use the term "work" for <u>educational</u> purposes primarily when the purposes or goals are middle or long range in nature, and to use the term "play" when the goals are short to middle range. Thus, if a boy plays baseball after school, his goals are short range and therefore conceived as 'play.' If this boy continues with his interest in high school and college, and were to receive an athletic scholarship, play would quite often take on the aspect of work. Further, at this point he could then be considered a semipro, and this would be so because of the time being spent, the middle range goals attendant to his athletic activity, and the level of ability or performance he had achieved - <u>as well as</u> the fact that he was being paid a certain amount of money for performing the baseball skills he had mastered. Such consideration brings us to the third subdivision of Figure 2, Level III. Now if this young man were to be selected in the draft by the major leagues, he would then be forced to make a decision on Level III, the Goals Continuum. If he did well in his tryouts and was granted a substantive contract, baseball would then be related to this person's long range goals, and he would be considered a professional in sport

This brings us to a brief consideration of Level IV, the Freedom-Constraint Continuum. Gradually, but steadily as this young man moves up through the various stages of organized baseball, the status of his freedom or independence changes. This is true in most people's regular lives in a social environment as well, but such an alteration is particularly true in this instance where the relationship between a young man and organized baseball is being discussed. Of course, many other similar examples come to mind relative to all phases of people's lives.

Altering these concepts of 'work' and 'play' - not to mention those of 'amateur' and 'professional' - would in my opinion have a positive influence on the prevailing pattern in North American sport and athletics. For more than thirty years I have been speaking and writing to help to bring about a change in the United States Amateur Athletic Union rules for those who participate locally, state-wide, regionally, nationally, and internationally under their auspices. This organization had a noble ideal once in the late 1800s, but changing times and increasing role differentiation in society has brought us to the point today where the situation is absolutely ridiculous! Writing in 1964, in an effort to urge others to distinguish more carefully between the ways that we used the various terms being considered, I stated:

We will have to re-evaluate some of our treasured,
basic assumptions about the amateur code in sport.
What are the reasons today for the continuation of
such a sharp distinction between the amateur and
the professional? History tells us where the ideal
originated, but it tells us also that the conditions
which brought it about do not exist in America
today . . . And what is so wrong with a young
sportsman being classified as a semiprofessional?
Do we brand the musician, the artist, or the actor
in our society who develops his talent sufficiently
to receive some remuneration for his efforts as being a "dirty pro"? Why must this idea persist in
sport - a legitimate phase of our culture? . . .
We cannot agree wither with the cynic who says
that there are no more amateurs in sport. This is
not true. There are, and ever will be, amateurs
in the only logical sense of the words today. The
amateur is the beginner, the dabbler, the dilettante . . .

(Zeigler, in Flath, 1964,
Introd. Chapter)

In my opinion, therefore, careful consideration of this matter,
including conceptual analysis of the ordinary language employed, could well have a significant influence of a positive nature
on the prevailing pattern in North American sport and athletics
today.

Summary and Conclusion

To summarize, then, after introducing the topic and
placing it in philosophical perspective in regard to the major
approaches to ethical analysis extant, the main problem of the
paper was indicated as a metaethical or critical analysis of the
concepts of 'work' and 'play' as currently employed in North
America. The second phase of the main problem was to relate
the various definitions of the terms reviewed to sport and athletics as we know them typically in society at large and within
the educational setting specifically.

The following sub-problems were analyzed in sequence to
serve as data to assist with the analysis of the main problem:

    1.   Definitions of the following words, along with
        appropriate synonyms and antonyms, were enu-
        merated: work, play, freedom, amateur, semi-
        pro, professional, sport, and athletics.

These terms were placed in a "traditional" play-work definitional diagram as applied to sport and athletics.

2. The status, along with some brief historical data, sport/athletics in the United States and Canada was reviewed (with particular emphasis on the college and university level).

3. The possible relationship between the prevailing, pivotal social forces, and the status of sport was discussed. It was explained why the terms "work" and "play" had become so sharply dichotomized.

4. Prior to the recommendation of altered concepts of work and play as being more appropriate for an evolving democratic society, the relationship of these concepts within communism and aristocracy was described. A model entitled "Aspects of a Person's 'Active Occupation'" was constructed with play, art, and work (Dewey) included as the three appropriate aspects. These terms were related from the standpoint of the "unified organism" and that person's varied educational-recreational interests (Level I) to the Goals Continuum (Level II), the Amateur-Professional Continuum (Level III), and the Freedom-Constraint Continuum (Level IV).

Finally, it was pointed out that modifying these various concepts - notably "work," "play," "amateur," and "professional" would in all probability have a positive influence on the prevailing pattern in North American sport and athletics.

One final conclusion seems justifiable if this argument has merit: the concepts of 'work' and 'play' should be modified - especially in the educational setting - so that a continuum between them and the concept of 'art' is recognized rather than the sharp dichotomization that exists currently. A similar spectrum should be applied to the terms "amateur" and "professional" with the term "semipro" in the middle. Such changes would in all probability exert a positive influence and help to clarify the "language ailment" that afflicts sport and athletics in North America. Once the "disease" is identified, treatment and prognosis may be possible. The time to apply such a remedy is long overdue.

General Bibliography

Baker, Russell. "Good Bad Sports." The New York Times, February 1, 1976.

Bloy, Myron B., Jr. "Second Edition/The Christian Norm." The Center Magazine, Vol. 8 (1975), No. 6: 71-74.

Brandt, Richard B. Ethical Theory. Englewood Cliffs, N. J.: Prentice-Hall, Inc., 1959.

Brubacher, John S. A History of the Problems of Education. New York: McGraw-Hill Book Company, 1966.

_____. Modern Philosophies of Education. 4th edition. New York: McGraw-Hill Book Company, 1969.

Carnegie Foundation for the Advancement of Teaching, The. American College Athletics (Howard J. Savage et al., Eds.). New York: The Foundation, Bulletin #23, 1929.

Dewey, John. Problems of Men. New York: H. Holt & Co., 1946.

_____ and Tufts, J. H. Ethics. New York: H. Holt & Co., Revised Edition, 1932.

Flath, Arnold W. A History of the Relations Between the N.C.A.A. and the A.A.U. Champaign, IL.: Stipes Publishing Company, 1964.

Frankena, William K. Ethics. Englewood Cliffs, N. J.: Prentice-Hall, Inc., 1963.

Fromm, Erich. Man for Himself. New York: Fawcett World Library, 1967. (Published originally by Holt, Rinehart & Winston, Inc., in 1947).

Grutzner, Charles. "The Impact of Athletics on Education." Washington, D. C.: Babe Ruth Sportsmanship Awards Committee, 1951. (Reprinted as pamphlet with permission of The New York Times).

Harrison, Geoffrey, "Relativism and Tolerance," Ethics, Vol. 86 (January 1976), No. 2: 122-135.

Henry, Jules. Culture Against Man. New York: Random House, 1963.

Keating, James W. "Winning in Sport and Athletics," Thought (Fordham University Quarterly), Vol. XXXVIII, No. 149: 201-210 (Summer 1963).

Ladd, John (Ed.). Ethical Relativism. Belmont, Calif.: Wadsworth Publishing Company, Inc., 1973.

Ladenson, Robert F. "A Theory of Personal Autonomy." Ethics, Vol. 86 (October 1975), No. 1: 30-48.

Living Webster Encyclopedic Dictionary of the English Language, The. Chicago, Ill.: The English Language Institute of America, 1975.

Lyons, David. "Ethical Relativism and the Problem of Incoherence." Ethics, Vol. 86 (January 1976), No. 2: 107-121.

Maeroff, Gene I. "West Point Cheaters Have a Lot of Company." The New York Times, June 20, 1976.

Martens, Rainer. "Kid Sports: A Den of Iniquity or Land of Promise." An address given at the National College Physical Education Association for Men, Hot Springs, Arkansas, Jan. 8-11, 1976.

Matthews, A. W. Athletics in Canadian Universities. Ottawa: Association of Universities and Colleges of Canada, 1974.

McDermott, John J. (Ed.). The Philosophy of John Dewey (Volume II - The Lived Experience). New York: G. P. Putnam's Sons, 1973.

Muller, Herbert J. Freedom in the Ancient World. New York: Harper & Row Publishers, 1961.

Oxford Universal Dictionary, The (C. T. Onions, Ed.). London: Oxford University Press, Third Edition, 1955.

Partridge, P. H. "Freedom," in Encyclopedia of Philosophy (Paul Edwards, Ed.). New York: The Macmillan Company and The Free Press, 1967, Vol. 3, pp. 221-225.

Richardson, Deane E. "Ethical Conduct in Sport Situations," in Proceedings of the 66th Annual Meeting of the National College Physical Education Association for Men, 1963, pp. 98-104.

Sahakian, William S. Ethics: An Introduction to Theories and Problems. New York: Barnes & Noble Books, 1974.

Salmon, Wesley C. Logic. Englewood Cliffs, N. J.: Prentice-Hall, Inc., 1963.

Taylor, Paul W. Problems of Moral Philosophy. Belmont, Calif.: Dickenson Publishing Company, Inc., 1967.

Zeigler, Earle F. "A True Professional Needs a Consistent Philosophy." Australian Journal of Physical Education, No. 18: 15-16 (Feb.-March 1960).

_____. "Naturalism in Physical, Health, and Recreation Education," The University of Michigan School of Education Bulletin, Vol. 34, No. 2: 42-46 (December 1962).

_____. "A Philosophical Analysis of Amateurism in Competitive Athletics," School Activities, Vol. XXXV, No. 7: 199-203 (March 1964).

_____. "A Philosophical Analysis of Recreation and Leisure," Quest, Monograph V: 8-17 (December 1965).

_____. "A Riddle for Tomorrow's World: How to Lead a Good Life," Parks and Recreation, Vol. 11, No. 9: 28, 47-49 (September 1967).

_____. Problems in the History and Philosophy of Physical Education and Sport. Englewood Cliffs, N. J.: Prentice-Hall, Inc., 1968.

_____. "Vigorous Physical Education and Sport as Essential Ingredients in America's Pattern of Physical Education," The Physical Educator, Vol. 26, No. 1: 14-17 (March 1969).

_____. "The Rationale for Philosophical Analysis with Implications for Physical Education and Sport," Illinois Journal of Health, Physical Education, and Recreation, 1: 17-18 (Winter 1970).

_____. "A Comparative Analysis of Educational Values in Selected Countries: Their Implications for Sport and Physical Education," in Proceedings of the National College Physical Education Association for Men, Minneapolis, Minn., 1971, pp. 169-174.

_____. "The Black Athlete's Non-Athletic Problems," _Educational Theory_, Vol. 22, No. 4: 421-426 (1972).

_____. "The Pragmatic (Experimentalistic) Ethic as It Relates to Sport and Physical Education." A paper presented at the 2nd Annual Meeting of the Philosophic Society for the Study of Sport, SUNY, College at Brockport, New York, October 26-28, 1972.

_____. "Putting the Greek Ideal in Perspective in North American Athletics Today," in _Athletics in America_ (A. W. Flath, Ed.). Corvallis, Oregon: Oregon State University Bookstore, 1972.

_____. "Intramurals: Profession, Discipline, or Part Thereof? in _Proceedings_ of the National College Physical Education Association for Men, Minneapolis, Minn,, 1973, pp. 85-90.

_____. "Freedom in Competitive Sport." A paper presented at the 4th Annual Meeting of the Philosophic Society for the Study of Sport, The University of Western Ontario, London, Canada, November 16, 1974. (Published subsequently in Zeigler's 1975 book listed below).

_____. _Personalizing Physical Education and Sport Philosophy_. Champaign, Ill.: Stipes Publishing Company, 1975.

Questions for Discussion

1. Explain what is meant when it is stated that the work/play definitions in any dictionary always appear as discontinua? Why do you imagine that this sharp dichotomy has persisted historically down to the present?

2. Explain Brubacher's continuum approach in this connection? To what extent do you agree with it?

3. Explain the revised theoretical approach being explained by Zeigler that contradicts the dualistic or dichotomous theory of work and play.

4. What is John Dewey's definition of art? Can you see how this definition can be combined with those of "work" and "play" to permit thereby a different approach to the subject under discussion? Do these terms include all of the "Aspects of a Person's 'Active Occupation'?"

5. If this "spectrum approach" were applied to the terms "amateur" and "professional," would that help us out of our present dilemma? Explain your answer.

CHAPTER 17
SOME EXPRESSED VALUES WITHIN
THE OLYMPIC EXPERIENCE

Note: In the earlier version of this paper, the following were included: (a) a review of the "good" and "bad" in historical perspective; (2) some consideration of social forces as value determinants; and (3) a glimpse of axiology (the study of values) as a subdivision of the discipline of philosophy. This material has been omitted here because it now appears in Chapter 2.

Really what is "the Olympic experience" all about?* Whom is it intended for--the athlete, the officials, the country where the Games are held, the actual spectators, those who follow it through the various media, the community of man throughout the world? We could well argue that the Olympic experience is held to provide a fine experience for all of those entities just mentioned. My fear is, however, that we talk blithely about it all and have made practically no attempts to analyze the experience in an even reasonably careful manner. In this brief presentation I will consider some of the attitudes and opinions held by (1) people who have been involved in the Olympic Games in the past; (2) people who will be involved in the 1976 Montreal Games; and (3) people who are training for the Games, but who for some reason may not qualify.

Prior to the discussion of the responses from those named above, the question of intrinsic and extrinsic values will be reviewed briefly. It ties in with the qualitative aspects of the question of values. Some things in life are desired by the individual, whereas others may be desirable mainly because society has indicated its approval of them. A continuous appraisal of values occurs. The value existing in and for itself is said to have an intrinsic value. One that serves as a means to an end, however, has become known as an extrinsic or instrumental value. When intense emotion and appreciation are involved, this gradation of value is called esthetic. High level Olympic sport competition presumably offers many opportunities

---

* A paper adapted from a presentation made to the Philosophy Section of the Humanities Division of The International Congress of Physical Activity Sciences, Quebec City, July 11-16, 1976.

to realize such esthetic values. In many of the world's cultures, it is unfortunately true that such high level sporting competition is regarded far too narrowly. Thus, many confine esthetic values to experiences in the established fine arts and literature.

Responses from a Sampling of Olympic Athletes

It must be understood that this was a biased sampling of Olympic athletes - actually two-thirds of some thirty athletes answered from among one university's participants in the Games - responded to an open-ended questionnaire about the values that he/she found within competitive sport at the high level of participation in the Olympic games and trials. Despite the inherent limitations of this approach, the results obtained were very interesting. The responses have not been tabulated on a percentage basis, nor has the question of statistical significance been considered. Further, it must be kept in mind that the respondents might well give the types of responses that would be expected of Canadians in an evolving democratic society where there would be no opportunities for careers as professional athletes in the particular sports represented within this preliminary survey (i.e., no hockey players were included in the sample).

Basically, then, the intrinsic values of the Olympic experience were listed much more frequently and much more importantly by these men and women athletes whose activities ranged over the past twenty-five years. A number of those responding indicated the importance of "striving for a set goal in life - a really tough one to achieve." They felt that the experience had "made them better persons" by giving them the opportunity to impose the severest kind of "self-discipline" upon themselves. (The words in quotation marks here are actual quotations from the responses.) The Olympic experience had provided them with a chance for "personal fulfillment," an opportunity to "live life most fully." Here was a ready made "chance to prove yourself," and I "felt the need to do so." Actually, the largest number stated literally as individuals that "I was proud that I was involved." It - the experience - gave me an "added sense of personal worth."

Of the some twenty respondents, only a couple of people mentioned the idea of "developing loyalties to people and institutions" and the opportunity to work "cooperatively" with others in the possible achievement of a common goal (victory). One indicated that he felt there was a "carry-over value" into later life, and that he has experienced a "continued desire for excellence." Three participants mentioned that they felt a keen "awareness of country" because of the actual experience. Only one spoke specifically of the training experience leading up to the competition, although a number of others implied the value of such training with their various comments. Two respondents mentioned that they had "gained knowledge of people from other cultures," and only one mentioned that he felt a "sense of humility" being with the world's greatest athletes.

Insofar as the so-called extrinsic values are concerned, it is a bit unusual that more were not listed. Two respondents said that the extrinsic values were definitely "secondary" to their way of thinking. One stated that they were "important, but were greatly outweighed by the other aspects of the experience." Several mentioned that their Olympic experience gave them "greater status in society," and one stated that in Canadian society the fact that he won a gold medal seemed "more important" to his relatives, friends, and colleagues. Three mentioned that the travel itself had been important to them, while one indicated that "the lasting friendships" made would undoubtedly mean much to him in the years ahead.

Interestingly enough, only three or four people mentioned aspects of the experience that could be identified as dis-values. One stated that the disvalues were undoubtedly increasing over the years. Another cited examples of individual behavior that were distasteful to him and others. Three people were quite concerned by all of the "politics" evident on the part of officials from their own and other countries. Two men mentioned the over-emphasis on nationalism and the keeping of team scores and medal counts by representatives of the media. One person went so far as to say that the Olympic experience had actually been a detriment to his career because of the time, money, and energy spent.

Concluding Statement and Discussion

A preliminary analysis was made of "some expressed values within the Olympic experience" based on the responses from a stratified population of Canadian men and women Olympic athletes over a period of twenty-five years with an affiliation with one university. After placing the concepts of 'good' and 'bad' in historical perspective, the importance of social forces as value determinants was discussed. Values, or the study of axiology, was explained briefly as a highly important and (to some) culminating subdivision of the discipline of philosophy.

Responses from the athletes themselves were tabulated in regard to the values or disvalues of "the Olympic experience." The large majority of the respondents directed a preponderance of their statements to what they felt were the intrinsic values resulting from the experience. Extrinsic values were indicated, but they were considered to be largely secondary in nature. The greatest importance of the experience was obviously that which related to the achievement of personal goals, the opportunity to prove oneself, and pride along with an added sense of personal worth because of the involvement.

Discussion. On the assumption that the fundamental values of social systems have a strong influence on the individual values held by most citizens in a country, a preliminary comparison might be made between the value system of Canada and the values mentioned prominently by the Canadians who have been involved in "the Olympic sporting experience." Lipset, basing his study on pattern variables established by Parsons as the means for classifying the fundamental values of social systems (e.g., self-orientation - collectivity orientation or how separate needs are perceived in relation to the defined interests of the larger group), stated that there now seems to be consistent movement in Canada toward the twin values of equalitarianism and achievement (values which have been paramount in American life all along). He found further that Canadians were quite achievement oriented, universalistic, equalitarian, and self-oriented, but were exceeded in these characteristics by Americans to a degree (Lipset, 1973, p. 6). An important point to consider here is that there has been reluctance on the part "of Canadians to be overoptimistic, assertive, or experimentally inclined" (Ibid., p. 9).

In this preliminary investigation we are dealing with a select group of athletes, of course, but it is true that they attached the greatest importance of their athletic experience to the achievement of personal goals. It is quite possible, of course, that the attitudes of Canada and Canadians are changing. In the area of national and international sport, we are now witnessing a strong effort on the part of the federal government to become optimistic, assertive, and experimentally inclined. Further, now many Canadians are showing an attitudinal change in the direction of regarding the United States as "the leading defender of traditional social forms." It is not possible to make a definitive statement on the basis of this preliminary analysis, of course, but there does seem to be some movement away from an earlier quite consistent "middle ground position" between the United States and England on the part of

Canada. This area does seem to offer opportunities for further investigation by sport historians, philosophers, and sociologists.

References

Encyclopedia of Philosophy, The. (Paul Edwards, Ed.). New York: The Macmillan Company and The Free Press, 8 vols., 1967.

Brubacher, John S. Modern Philosophies of Education (4th Edition). New York: McGraw-Hill, 1969.

Johnson, Harry M. "The Relevance of the Theory of Action to Historians." Social Science Quarterly, June, 1969, 46-58.

Lipset, Seymour. "National Character," in Readings in Social Psychology: Focus on Canada (D. Koulack and D. Perlman, Eds.). Toronto: Wiley Publishers of Canada, Ltd., 1973.

Zeigler, Earle F. Personalizing Physical Education and Sport Philosophy. Champaign, Ill.: Stipes Publishing Co., 1975.

_____. Physical Education and Sport Philosophy. Englewood Cliffs, N. J.: Prentice-Hall, Inc., 1977.

Questions for Discussion

1. Explain the difference between a so-called intrinsic value and what has been termed an extrinsic value? Which of these is presumably "instrumental" in nature? How does this approach "square" with the argument presented in Chapter 14?

2. What did the investigator find after tabulating responses from the athletes in regard to the values or disvalues of "the Olympic experience?"

3. Were the intrinsic values of the experience rated more highly than the extrinsic ones? Attempt to explain your answer.

4. Where did they feel that the "greatest importance of the experience" lay?

5. What comparison is made between the value systems of Canada and the United States? Did the athletes' responses seem consistent with the presumed value system of the country?

CHAPTER 18

APPLICATION OF A SCIENTIFIC ETHICS
APPROACH TO SPORT DECISIONS

Note: When this paper was prepared originally, the introductory and background material included the following: (1) evidence that others see the need for study in ethics; (2) a brief discussion of the history of ethics; (3) an explanation of how a person develops his or her implicit "sense of life"; and (4) an analysis of the major ethical routes presently available for use in the Western world. This material has been included in earlier chapters, and thus will not be repeated here.

Having considered the various approaches to ethical decision-making that are extant in the Western world, I have come to the conclusion that the application of scientific method to ethical analysis should be carried out to the greatest possible extent right now.* I believe such an approach is required because all of us are discovering that there is indeed a "crisis of human values" in existence, and the confidence that we had previously in religion and philosophy has been seriously undermined. This crisis mentality is heightened by the communications revolution that has thrust the world's people closer together still holding the often-conflicting values systems of the eleven to thirteen great world religions. Daily we hear on the one hand that onrushing science and technology are our great benefactors. Then in the next moment we learn that science and technology may actually destroy life on our planet permanently--at least in the sense that we have known it to this point (Saturday Review, 1977, p. 13).

Further, we have learned that the 20th century is a transitional one--that the old order has most definitely been replaced by the new! But what is not generally appreciated is that the rate of change in society is gradually accelerating, and that this acceleration will continue to increase. All of this has

---

* This chapter has been adapted from a paper presented originally as "Bridging the Gap from One's Sense of Life to Ethical Sport Decisions" at the 6th Annual Meeting of the Philosophic Society for the Study of Sport, Ft. Worth, Texas, October 6, 1978.

led me to conclude that in the Western world we must eliminate the persisting dualism that has separated investigation about the physical world from the study of human behavior in relation to moral values and virtues. In an evolving democratic society, I cannot personally find a strong rationale for any authoritarian or legalistic doctrine governing ethical behavior-- one in which ironclad conformity is required because of the presence of absolute good and rightness in the world. Such an assumption is a personal one on my part, of course. If is fortunate for me that our society guarantees individual freedom in such matters as long as the laws of the land are not abrogated.

I have considered the antinomial, relativistic position as well. As pleasant as it may be on occasion to rebel against society in a radical manner, antinomianism appears to be so far to the left on an authoritarian-anarchistic freedom spectrum as to be fundamentally "out of key" in a democracy. Despite the appeal of the emotivist approach and the logic of the language analyst, it is my position that society's present plight requires more than the application of this technique alone to life's many ethical problems. I believe that our failure to employ scientific method in the realm of so-called moral goods, as well as in the realm of so-called natural goods, keeps our world in a position where changes in values have come about accidentally or arbitrarily. Social theory has warned us continually about the powerful, controlling influence of societal values and norms. If in the near future we are only able to obliterate the idea that there is a difference in kind between what we have called "human nature" and what we have identified as the "physical world," we will then be able to bring the forces of science to bear more effectively on all human behavior. What we need, therefore,

> . . . is intelligent examination of the consequences that are actually effected by inherited institutions and customs, in order that there may be intelligent consideration of the ways in which they are to be intentionally modified in behalf of generation of different consequences (Dewey, 1929, pp. 272-273).

We need a faith that (a) science can indeed bring about complete agreement on factual belief about human behavior; (b) such agreement in factual belief will soon result in agreement in attitudes held by people; and (c) resultantly a continuous adaptation of values to the culture's changing needs will eventually effect the directed reconstruction of all social institutions (Dewey, 1948, p. xxiii).

I wish to explain further that placing our faith in scientific method in no way negates the work of the analytic philosopher who subscribes to the language analysis phase of the emotivist approach. Such analytic endeavor is actually scientific and can assist science in a vital way by dispensing with fallacious premises and non-sense terms so that hypotheses will be stated correctly and understood as completely as possible. However, it is at this point that a wholly scientific approach to ethics parts company with emotivism, because the problematic factual statements are not automatically referred to the social scientist. Indeed, the distinction between the so-called factual statements and the so-called value statements is not made in the scientific ethics approach--it is explicitly rejected!

With this approach the scientific method itself is brought to bear in problem-solving. Reflective thinking begets the ideas that function as tentative solutions for concrete problems of all kinds. In the process a rapidly changing culture confronts the person who, as a problem-solving organism, must be prepared to make adjustments. Habitual and/or impulsive responses will often not be effective--and assuredly not as effective as reflective thinking that employs both the experience of the past and the introduction of creative ideas. Thus, as explained by Albert, Denise & Peterfreund, the "criterion of truth is directly related to the outcome of the reflective process. Those ideas which are successful in resolving problematic situations are true, whereas those which do not lead to satisfactory adjustments are false" (1975, p. 282). Viewed in this manner, we can appreciate what James called the "cash value" of an idea --the import that certain knowledge, having served as an instrument for verification for people, has for the fulfillment of human purpose.

An Application of Scientific Method to Ethical Analysis

At present when we encounter ethical problems in our lives, be they personal problems, work problems, or in situations relating to competitive sport--and assuming that we recrecognize that a problem is an ethical problem--we seem to be resolving any such issue on the basis of either authoritarianism, relativism, or perhaps on the basis of what might be called "common sense, cultural utilitarianism." One would feel somewhat more secure if only Fletcher's situationism embodying the principle of "God's love" were employed. How much better would it be, however, if we would avail ourselves of the opportunity to expand the mind's potential toward its true capability by using the experimental method for the solving of problems? Based on such a theory of knowledge--where the mind serves to form knowledge or truth by undergoing experience--we would have an approach that could be regularly employed with a much better chance of success.

Let us now follow this postulation with a series of theoretical steps that would be involved in the application of this approach to one persistent, truly vexing problem in competitive sport--the amateur-professional controversy. The steps followed in this experimental approach would be as follows:

> Theory - Step 1--the smoothness of life's movement or flow is interrupted by an obstacle. This obstacle creates a problem, and the resultant tension must be resolved to allow further movement (progress?) to take place.
>
> Here we are faced with the problem (obstacle) that the concepts of 'work' and 'play' are typically strongly dichotomized in North America, and their usage is imprecise and muddled. Nowhere is the confusion (tension) more evident that when we are determining to what extent the nomenclature of "work" and "play" may be applied when dealing with the various levels of sport participation. This describes what may be called the "amateur-professional controversy"--a problem or obstacle that has been with mankind since ancient times.
>
> Theory - Step 2--humankind marshals all available and presumably pertinent facts to help with the solution of this problem. Data gathered tends to fall into one or more patterns. Subsequent analysis offers the possibility of various alternatives for action, one of which should be chosen as a working hypothesis.
>
> The basic terms or concepts were defined carefully and then placed in a traditional play-work definitional diagram as applied to sport and physical activity. Differentiation was made among synthetic, analytic, and pseudo-statements. Second, the status and a brief background of sport/athletics in North America were reviewed (with emphasis on the university level).
>
> Third, the possible relationship among the prevailing, pivotal social forces and the status of sport

was considered. The differences in the interpretation of the various concepts in the three leading
types of political state--democracy, communism, and
aristocracy--were explained. It was explained further why and how the terms "work" and "play"
have become so sharply dichotomized. Still further,
it became apparent that a need exists for re-evalu-
ation of some of our basic assumptions about the
amateur code in sport. It was pointed out that the
so-called professional in sport today is being professional in only a very limited sense of the word.
There is typically no commitment as a true professional whose primary aim in life is to serve one's
fellow man through lifelong service. The argument
was made that the amateur should be regarded as
the beginner--not as the Olympic performer who
somehow refrained from taking cash (but who has
somehow received all kinds of comparable support
along the way).

Fourth, as a result of the investigation described
above, one alternative (hypothesis) was selected
from the various course of action open on the basis
of the type of political state being considered (a
democracy). Proceeding from this hypothesis, a
model was recommended was consideration and possible implementation--one in which the concepts of
'work' and 'play' are altered, and one in which in-
surmountable problems do not arise in an evolving
democracy. The model was entitled "Aspects of a
Person's Active Occupation," with work, play and
art included as the three appropriate aspects.
These terms were related from the standpoint of a
concept of the 'unified organism.' (See Figure 1
on top of next page).

Theory - Step 3--the hypothesis must be tested
through the application of the model developed to
test its suitability. If one hypothesis does not
solve the problem for our society, then another
should be tried. A hypothesis that works--in the
sense that it gradually achieves recognition as being fair and equitable--thereby turns out to be
true. If offers a framework for organizing facts,
and this will result subsequently in a central
meaning that may then be called knowledge.

ASPECTS OF A PERSON'S "ACTIVE OCCUPATION"

(1. Play ------- 2. Art ------ 3. Work)

Freedom-Constraint Continuum Level IV	Freedom ----------------- Limited Freedom ------------- Constraint (No Freedom)
Amateur-Professional Continuum Level III	Amateur ----------------- Semipro --------------------- Professional
Goals Continuum Level II	Short Range ------------ Middle Range ---------------- Long Range

Categories of Interest Level I	The Unified Organism	1. Physical education-recreation interests 2. Social education-recreation interests 3. "Learning" education-recreation interests 4. Aesthetic education-recreation interests 5. Communicative education-recreation interests

Figure 1.

Theory - Step 4--the final step in this scientific approach to the resolution of sport decisions that are ethical in nature relates to acceptance of the working hypothesis as evidenced by changing attitudes on the part of the general public. The assumption is that determination of knowledge based on agreement in factual belief that is communicated to citizens in an evolving democracy should soon result in agreement in attitude.

Admittedly, sociological progress is never a "straight-line affair," but continuous adaptation of values to the culture's changing needs should effect the directed reconstruction of all social institutions.

It is at this point that experimentalistic theory of knowledge acquisition merges with the value theory of scientific ethics. Knowledge acquired frees all people to initiate subsequent action furthering the process of movement and change indefinitely into the future (as adapted from Zeigler, 1964, pp. 72-74).

I believe that there is logic in a bonafide progression--
if the person wishes to progress and is sufficiently capable--
through the ranks of the amateur athlete to that of the semipro, and finally to that of the highly trained, proficient athletic performer. Such a person becomes a professional in at
least one sense of the term. Based on the model employed, if
a boy plays baseball after school (for example), his goals are
short range and therefore conceived as 'play.' If he continues
with his interest in high school and college, and were to receive an athletic scholarship to attend college, play might soon
take on many of the aspects of what we now call "work." Thus
when the young man (and now it might be a young woman too)
goes away to college on an athletic scholarship, he may then
be considered a semipro. This is logical because of the time
being spent, because of the middle range goals attached to his
athletic activity, and because of the level of performance he
has achieved--as well as the fact that he was being paid an
amount of money for performing the baseball skills he has mastered. If the young man is then chosen in a draft by the major leagues, he will then be forced to make a decision on Level
II, the Goals Continuum, about moving on to the far right of
the continuums at Levels II, III, and IV. Further, as shown
at Level I (Categories of Interest), the same approach would
hold for all aspects of a person's "active occupation."

Concluding Statement

We can all grant that these seem to be truly unusual
times; that a world transformation is taking place; and that it
is occurring rapidly because the tempo of civilization appears
to be increasing exponentially. We are told that the "dialogue
of freedom" may go on indefinitely, but the "solutions to our
problems are not primarily ideological but structural. . . .
They constitute a new political direction in the world--not left
or right as in the past--but human and forward" (Platt, 1972,
pp. 21-22). It is this type of reasoning that has rekindled
my interest in the abolition of the longstanding, but probably
unwise, distinction between what we in the past have called
moral and natural goods.

We are exhorted further to prepare for a continuing
technological thrust, and also told that "the only indispensable
human component is the mind component for design, redesign,
complex evaluation, and control" (p. 26). If these predictions
have any validity, then as Platt states, "Yet millions of the
older generation, alternately disgusted and terrified by these
developments, will have to learn new values and a new language. . . ." (p. 26).

In this same vein, Callahan writes about searching for an ethic in a new culture that is on its way here, but that still does not yet exist (Callahan, 1972, p. 4 et ff.). My general conclusion is that the scientific ethics approach, embodying also careful application of language analysis at all appropriate points, offers the best and ultimately the most humane approach to the problematic situation our culture is now facing --that of new and continually changing values that will bring about a new and continually changing culture. Whether we are facing ethical decisions in our home life, our professional endeavor, or even in our competitive sport pursuits whether they be amateur, semiprofessional, or professional, this approach offers everyone not a philosophy _of_ life, but an explicit approach to philosophical understanding--a philosophy _for_ the living of life today and tomorrow.

References

Abelson, R. and Friquegnon, M. Ethics for modern life. New York: St. Martin Press, 1975.

Albert, E. M., Denise, T. C. and Peterfreund, S. P. Great traditions in ethics. (3rd edition). New York: D. van Nostrand, 1975.

American Assocaition of University Professors. Statement on professional ethics, American Association of University Professors Bulletin, 55(1), March, 1969, 96-87.

Ayer, A. J. Language, truth and logic. New York: Dover Publications, 1946. (Rev. edition).

Baier, Kurt. The moral point of view. Ithaca, New York: Cornell University Press, 1958.

Baker, Russell. Good bad sport. The New York Times Magazine, Feb. 1, 1976.

Barrett, W. Irrational man: a study in existentialism philosophy. Garden City, New York: Doubleday, 1958.

de Beauvoir, Simone. The ethics of ambiguity. New York: The Citadel Press, 1964.

Blumenthal, W. Michael. Business morality has not deterior-
ated--society has changed. The New York Times, Jan.
9, 1977.

Bok, Derek C. Can ethics be taught? Change 8(9), October,
1976, 26-30.

Brandt, R. B. Ethical theory. Englewood Cliffs, N. J.:
Prentice-Hall, 1959.

Burtt, E. A. In search of philosophical understanding. New
York: The New American Library, 1965.

Callahan, D. Search for an ethic: living with new biology.
The Center Magazine V(4), July/August, 1972, 4-12.

Chace, James. How "moral" can we get? The New York Times
Magazine, May 22, 1977.

Committee on Professional Ethics. Suggested code of ethics for
teachers of physical education. Journal of Health, Physical Education, and Recreation 21(6), June, 1950, 323-
324, 366.

Crawford, Melvin M. Critical incidents in intercollegiate athletics and derived standards of professional ethics. Doctoral dissertation, University of Texas, Austin, 1957.

Dennis, Ann B. A code of ethics for sociologists and anthropologists? Social Sciences in Canada 3(1-2), 1975, 14-16.

Dewey, John. The quest for certainty. New York: Minton,
Balch & Co., 1929.

Dewey, John and Tufts, James H. Ethics. New York: Holt,
Rinehart and Winston, 1921. (Rev. edition).

Dewey, John. Reconstruction in philosophy. (Enl. and upd.
edition). Boston: The Beacon Press, 1948.

Etzioni, Amitai. Do as I say, not as I do. The New York
Times Magazine, Sept. 26, 1976.

Fairlie, H. The seven deadly sins today. Washington, D. C.:
New Republic Books, 1978.

Fletcher, J. Situation ethics: the new morality. Philadelphia:
The Westminster Press, 1966.

Fox, M. (Ed.). Modern Jewish ethics. Columbus, Ohio: Ohio State University Press, 1976.

Fraleigh, W. P. Ethics in professional life. Keynote address, Working Conference on Ethics, American Association for Health, Physical Education, and Recreation, Minneapolis, Minn., 1973.

Frankena, W. K. Ethics. Englewood Cliffs, N. J.: Prentice-Hall, 1963.

Fromm, E. Man for himself. New York: Fawcett World Library, 1967.

Gordis, H. Politics and ethics. Santa Barbara, Cal.: Center for the Study of Democratic Institutions, 1961.

Gouinlock, J. Dewey's theory of moral deliberation. Ethics 88(3), April, 1978, 218-228.

Harrison, J. Ethical objectivism. The Encyclopedia of Philosophy (P. Edwards, Ed.). New York: The Macmillan Co. and The Free Press, 1967, 3, 71-75.

Hazard, G. C., Jr. Capitalist ethics. Yale Alumni Magazine and Journal, XLI (8), April, 1978, 50-51.

Hechinger, F. M. Whatever became of sin? Saturday Review/World, Sept. 24, 1974.

Hospers, J. An introduction to philosophical analysis. Englewood Cliffs, N. J.: Prentice-Hall, 1953.

Johnson, A. H. Modes of value. New York: Philosophical Library, 1978.

Kanin, G. It takes a long time to become young. Garden City, N. Y.: Doubleday & Co., 1978.

Kaplan, A. The new world of philosophy. New York: Random House, 1961.

Keenan, F. W. A delineation of Deweyan progressivism for physical education. Ph.D. dissertation, University of Illinois, Urbana, 1971.

Kretchmar, S. Ethics: teacher and student. A paper pre-
    sented at Working Conference on Ethics, AAHPER, Minne-
    apolis, Minn., 1973.

Kurtz, P. Moral problems in contemporary society. Englewood
    Cliffs, N. J.: Prentice-Hall, 1969.

Ladd, J. The issue of relativism. Ethical Relativism (J. Ladd,
    Ed.). Belmont, CA: Wadsworth, 1973.

Laughter, R. J. Socio-psychological aspects of the develop-
    ment of athletic practices and sport ethics. Ph.D. dis-
    sertation, The Ohio State University, 1963.

Lyons, D. Ethical relativism and the problem of incoherence.
    Ethics 86(2), Jan., 1976, 107-121.

Maeroff, G. I. West Point cheaters have a lot of company.
    The New York Times, June 20, 1976.

Martens, R. Kid sports: a den of iniquity or land or promise.
    Proceedings of the 79th Annual Meeting, NCPEAM,
    L. L. Gedvilas. Chicago, Ill., 1976.

Mills, C. W. Sociology and pragmatism. New York: Oxford
    University Press, 1966.

Moore, G. E. Principia ethica. New York: Cambridge Univer-
    sity Press, 1948.

Morland, R. B. A philosophical interpretation of the educa-
    tional views held by leaders in American physical educa-
    tion. Ph.D. dissertation, New York University, 1958.

New York Times, The. The growing dishonesty in sports: is
    it just a reflection of our American society" Nov. 7,
    1976.

New York Times, The. The ethical imperative. News of the
    Week in Review, Feb. 26, 1978.

Noel-Smith, P. H. Ethics. Baltimore: Penguin Books, 1954.

Olafsen, F. A. Ethics and twentieth century thought. Engle-
    wood Cliffs, N. J.: Prentice-Hall, 1973.

Patrick, G. Verifiability of physical education objectives.
    Ph.D. dissertation, University of Illinois, Urbana, 1971.

Platt, J. What's ahead for 1990? The Center Magazine V(4),
    July/August, 1972, 21-28.

Rand, Ayn. The romantic manifesto. New York and Cleve-
    land: The World Publishing Co., 1960.

Rawls, J. A theory of justice. Cambridge, Mass.: Harvard
    University Press, 1971.

Richardson, D. E. Ethical conduct in sport situations. Pro-
    ceedings of 66th Annual Meeting, NCPEAM, Washington,
    D. C., 1963.

Ross, Saul. An investigation into the Jewish concept of ethics
    regarding its application to sport. Proceedings of the
    2nd International Seminar on Physical Education and
    Sport, Wingate Institute, Israel, July 5-8, 1977.

Rucker, D. Dewey's ethics (Part Two). Guide to the Works
    of John Dewey (J. A. Boydston, Ed.). Carbondale and
    Edwardsville: So. Illinois University Press, 1970, 112-
    130.

Sahakian, W. S. Ethics: An introduction to theories and
    problems. New York: Barnes & Noble, 1974.

Saturday Review Special Report. Watergating on Main Street,
    3(3), Nov. 1, 1975, 10-28.

Saturday Review Special Report. God and science--new allies
    in the search for values, Dec. 10, 1977.

Scott, H. A. Preliminary report of the Committee on Profes-
    sional Ethics. Journal of Health, Physical Education,
    and Recreation, 1(11), Nov. 1930, 19.

Seebohm, C. Nonfiction in brief. The New York Times Book
    Review, Spring, 1978.

Shea, E. J. Ethical decisions in physical education and sport.
    Springfield, Ill.: C. C. Thomas, 1978.

Sidgwick, Henry. Outline of the history of ethics. London:
    Macmillan, 1960. (Published originally in 1886).

Skousen, Cleon. Human ethics in human conduct. The Academy Papers (No. 7) (M. G. Scott, Ed). Iowa City, Iowa: The American Academy of Physical Education, 1973, 62-75.

Stevenson, C. L. The nature of ethical disagreement. Sigma, 1-2, 8-9, 1947-48.

Taylor, P. W. Problems of moral philosophy. Belmont, CA: Dickenson, 1967.

Titus, H. H. and Keeton, M. Ethics for today. (5th Edition). New York: D. Van Nostrand, 1973.

Urmson, J. O. The emotive theory of ethics. London: Hutchinson University Library, 1968.

Warnock, Mary. Ethics since 1900. New York: Oxford University Press, 1966.

Zeigler, E. F. Philosophical foundations for physical, health, and recreation education. Englewood Cliffs, N. J.: Prentice-Hall, 1964.

Zeigler, E. F. Freedom in competitive sport, in Personalizing physical education and sport philosophy. Champaign, Ill.: Stipes, 1975.

Zeigler, E. F. Basic considerations about a philosophy of sport (and its possible relationship with success in competitive sport). Canadian Journal of Applied Sport Sciences 3(1), March, 1978, 35-42.

Questions for Discussion

1. Now that we appreciate that there are a number of so-called ethical routes available from which you may choose your own approach to ethical decision-making, which one appeals to you personally? Explain your position concisely with any possible justification that you can muster.

2. In what direction were you "inclined" implicitly as a result of your background and upbringing? In which ways, if any, has your approach changed as a result of formal educational experience? Of informal, life experience?

3. Are you inclined to agree or disagree with the scientific ethics approach that the author states that we need for the future? Explain the fundamental basis of your agreement or disagreement.

4. Explain the "facts vs. values" dualism that confronts us in connection with this choice that we must make. Where do you stand in this connection?

5. In this chapter the author tries his approach out on the amateur, semiprofessional, professional persistent problem faced in sport. Does this scientific ethics approach appear to have potential for the eventual resolution of this problem? Explain your response.

CHAPTER 19
COACH AND ATHLETE--IN
EACH OTHER'S POWER

Walt Kelley's Pogo said, "We have faults which we have hardly used yet."* This wise creature seems to be describing the situation in the United States in which "a typical roll call of contemporary villains: shoplifters, trashers, time-clock cheaters, expense-account padders, tax evaders, political bribe takers, perjurers, economic exploiters . . . and those responsible for violent crime" affect the quality of life both directly and indirectly (Marty, 1975). With such a situation prevailing, one could hardly expect that competitive sport would be free from society's influences or that, in turn, the growing influence of sport would not affect societal practices.

Problems such as this take us into the realm of ethics and morality, a topic that is receiving a greater amount of attention in professional preparation in many fields today. We are discovering, however, that the entire matter is quite thoroughly tangled; we are tied into knots from which we are only feebly seeking to extricate ourselves. Nowhere do we seem to find weaker efforts to escape from our ethical dilemma than in the realm of highly competitive sport. We hope that the "good guys" will win, but we are haunted by the slogan that "nice guys finish last"--and who wants to be a "good loser?"

Part of our problem stems from the fact "we have reached a stage in our civilization where many different strands of ethical tradition have been woven together," and this has resulted in our society being faced with a variety of distinctive ethical patterns from which to choose--actually an almost impossible task (Miller, 1960). Thus, we have been influenced by (1) the Hebraic culture based on the Ten Commandments; (2) the Christian system based on the Beatitudes; (3) the Medieval way of life based on penance; (4) the Renaissance culture based on individual development along with freedom; (5) the Industrial Revolution based on the application of science to technology; and (6) the scientific approach based on

---

* A paper presented to the First Annual Meeting of the National Association for Physical Education in Higher Education, Milwaukee, Wisconsin, June 2, 1979.

empirical method and its influence on the determination of truth (Ibid.). Our dilemma today, rather than continuing along seemingly hopelessly mired in the sludge that characterizes the welter of conflicting value systems with which we are confronted, is to seek to make sense out of a situation that demands serious attention as we approach the twenty-first century.

Concomitants of the Demand for Improved Levels of Performance

One of the aspects of highly competitive sport where we need to make sense is in that area where stimulants, painkillers, and/or body-building agents are being employed by the athlete, often through the advice and encouragement of the coach and/or athletic therapist, to improve the level of performance required for success in an increasingly competitive environment. This question has a direct relationship to what has been identified as "the need for ethics in a sports world of cheating and violence." Jean Borotra, of France and a former world class tennis player, spoke out as chairman of the International Fair Play Committee in an article which decried the ever-increasing departure from the true "sporting spirit" (as reported in The New York Times, 1975).

This appeal for "fair play" has been expanded and clarified in Peter McIntosh's excellent new volume Fair Play in which he speaks of the "industrial transformation of sport" because "the level of performance necessary for success" has been causing an upgrading that "has recently been accelerating curvilinearly" (McIntosh, 1979, p. 136). As a result the highly intensive training required for success in competition today "has led to the adoption of methods which may permanently injure the athlete, such as the taking of anabolic steroids to increase muscular bulk" (Ibid.).

The entire problem of drugs and performance is one which demands continuing investigation. This is only part of a still greater societal issue--the use of marijuana, LSD, heroin, alcohol, tobacco, and the variety of related major and minor drugs being used. It is true, of course, that many different natural and synthetic chemical substances and preparations have been used since ancient times in efforts to improve both physical performance and endurance. At the present time, for example, the International Olympic Committee has declared the following doping substances to be unacceptable and cause for disqualification from further participation--when their use can be detected: (1) stimulants used to increase performance and ward off fatigue (such as the psychomotor stimulants--e.g., amphetamines, and sympathomimetic amines--e.g., ephedrine and related compounds); (2) painkillers employed to help the athlete continue with top performance despite sprain and injury with varying levels of pain (such as the narcotic and synthetic narcotic analgesics--e.g., morphine and novacaine); and (3) so-called body-builders used to promote growth and weight gain (such as anabolic steroids). As we have learned, the large majority of the drugs in the stimulant and painkilling groups are addictive in nature. Further, when they are used to disguise fatigue, the overexertion and heat build-up may effect circulatory failure. The body-building agents have been shown to have damaging side- and after-effects.

Even though many of us are parents, and all of us consider ourselves professionals in the field of sport and physical education, we may know little more than the average parent about drugs. The average pusher would probably regard the large majority of us as being "out of it" in regard to overall knowledge of the subject of drugs. We may know generally that drugs are classified typically as opiates, stimulants, psychedelics, and depressants. For example, did you know that heroin is prepared from morphine, which is extracted from opium? Further, did you know that a stimulant like amphetamine is not physically addictive like an opiate, but that it does produce a psychological dependence? Still further, did you known that mescaline is a drug derived from the peyote cactus; that it is stronger than peyote itself and produces more vivid visual impressions than the cactus from which it is derived? Finally, moving from the psychedelic category to the depressants, did you know that more people die in the United States from an overdose of barbiturates (addictives taken in capsule form) than of any other single substance? (I'll omit the inhalants such as glue-sniffers from our present discussion.)

Level of Consumption Is Not Known

Just how many people of all ages have been, and are presently, involved with the consumption of some type of stimulants, painkillers, and body-builders as part of their efforts toward winning and high-level achievement in competitive sport? Who knows? One can't help but believe, however, that what we see, hear, and read on the subject represents merely the tip of the iceberg--that this problem has assumed large proportions, and that its severity is increasing almost daily.

We can get some indications about the matter from Shinnick's "Testimony to the U. S. Senate Subcommittee on Juvenile

Delinquency" in 1973 in which he discussed his earlier experiences and observations in the 1960s. He concluded that "there seems to be evidence that drug usage is on the rise, especially among highly specialized competitive teams with management structures that insulate them from close interaction with the team members" (p. 20). In a study completed about the same time, O'Shea states, "while there seems to be no serious side effects associated with short term treatment (3 to 6 weeks) of anabolic steroids, long term usage must be viewed with extreme caution" (p. 13). Of course, who is there to control the individual who experiments with such body-building agents?

The number of articles on this topic seems to be increasing. Just recently, for example, Renate Neufeld, the former East German female sprinter claimed that she was forced to take performance-enhancing drugs in the form of hormone tablets (Maclean's, 1979, p. 31). This was followed by Steve Riddick's innocuous admission that he was taking pills made of bees' pollen and enriched with Vitamin E as an essential part of his diet (The London Free Press, Canada, Feb. 21, 1979). Then a few weeks later, we learned that Kenny Stabler, the football quarterback, was still under investigation in an incident in which a cocaine plant was evidently made on the car of a California sportswriter--although he denies any connection with the incident (The New York Times, Raines, March 4, 1979). During the same month Janice Kaplan stated her belief that drugtaking by women to turn them "into men or keep them in suspended childhood" is really not as widespread as the gossip would lead us to believe. Her concern is that we eliminate the idea that the "nymphet syndrome" is desirable for women because it leads them to greater success in any sport (The New York Times, Kaplan, March 4, 1979).

It is apparent that we are going to hear more, rather than less, about this perplexing problem in the months and years ahead. We will undoubtedly end up with ever more stringent regulations and accompanying testing to determine rule infractions. Of course, we will typically face the question of whether coaches and athletes are living up to the letter and/or the spirit of the various rules and regulations. One of the latest practices to plague us is blood doping (Webb, 1978, p. 189). Even though Webb states that "reported research is inconclusive and inconsistent regarding the benefits to be expected," a recent Canadian Association of Sports Sciences' Newsletter explains that "British Army tests over the past year have shown conclusively that blood doping can improve athletic performance substantially (December, 1978, p. 4). Question: Can we tell the athlete and his/her coach that he can't use

his/her own blood in this manner? Further, how can we detect
it by testing if such a practice is routinely followed?

Coach and Athlete--In Each Other's Power

The scenario has now been outlined. We now have a hypothesized chain of events in which one person may be exploited or used by another. I suppose it could be argued that it
usually is the coach who exploits the athlete, but I can also
imagine situations in which the opposite is the case. (In this
paper we will avoid largely discussion of the extent to which
the athlete is presumably exploiting himself or herself for benefits that are considered to be more important than the possible
harm imposed upon self, relatives, and close friends by the improper use of stimulants, painkillers, and body-building agents.

Let us consider first, then, the situation in which the
athlete may be exploited by the coach. We are all familiar with
the situation in California very recently in which a number of
athletes sued the coach and a university because they had presumably been used. They had been brought to the university
with the lure of athletic scholarships, university degrees, and
perhaps an opportunity to receive a contract to play "pro ball."
However, in the final analysis it is being argued that certain
academic programs were recommended so that continuing eligibility would be maintained, and that in the final analysis a trust
may have been broken because the desired educational knowledge, competency, and skill was not acquired. In some cases
not even the academic degree was obtained either, and the athlete was "cast adrift" because eligibility was used up after four
years of play. Finally, to make our case even stronger, let us
imagine that during the time of active participation the athletes
were often encouraged to take certain stimulants, painkillers,
and/or body-building agents. Certainly this last stipulation is
well within the realm of possibility and is probably occurring
regularly in the case of many athletes within a variety of sports
in the United States.

We are now very definitely faced with a philosophical
question to which we may seek appropriate and just answers.
Fortunately, there have been several attempts to look at some
of these questions recently in the philosophical literature, although the treatments are not based on problems of this nature
that arise in highly competitive sport. For example, Flemming
has asked the question, "Are we morally forbidden to treat a
man entirely as a means to some other end?" (Ethics, 1978,
p. 283). The "greatest good for the greatest number" argument of the utilitarians does seemingly give us the opportunity

to use a person to some extent for the good of the whole. Further, Nozick has argued that a Kantian must pursue the greatest good while only viewing the welfare of an individual involved as a "side constraint" to be considered while in active pursuit of a higher goal or greater good (Nozick, 1974, p. 32).

Blum approaches the subject from a different standpoint. He argues that it can be wrong to use a person even though the individual involved doesn't believe that he has been wronged and, in fact, is not the least bit unhappy about his involvement (Blum in Montefiore, Ed., 1973). He sees deception as using a person, and deception is wrong any way one looks at it. Secondly, he argues that people often know they are being used, and thus the fact that deception is being used is indeed separate from the wrong use of a person.

One of the most helpful philosophical treatments of this topic has been made available by Wilson in which he carries on with Blum's example of the love relationship between man and woman (Wilson, 1978, pp. 299-315). Obviously, we will need to transpose some of the questions raised into the realm of competitive sport and the relationship that may exist between coach and athlete (and vice versa). Wilson refers initially to the terms "entrapment" and "exploitation" while seeking to define them as accurately as possible. Entrapment is defined as actions that lure another into danger, difficulty, or self-incrimination. Exploitation, which usually accompanies entrapment, is the utilization of another for selfish purposes. (The latter, Wilson believes, can be active or passive in nature--passive when no deception is involved or necessary.)

Wilson argues further that entrapment "is thus a form of treachery, an abuse of trust, very akin, as the metaphors suggest, to the treachery of the solider who abuses the conventions for instituting a truce" (p. 303). Further, "if entrapment is the treacherous acquisition of power over a person, exploitation is the exercise of such power for selfish ends" (Ibid.). Obviously, there are general questions of a moral nature that arise when any form of unofficial or official power is used either for selfish or benevolent ends. Why is this so? It is true because "any source of power provides a kind of lever with which one person can move another, a means of influencing the other to act or to refrain from acting in a certain way, a means neither rational nor straightforwardly coercive" (p. 304). It has now become obvious to us as teachers and coaches what a tremendous ethical responsibility we have in our everyday dealings with student-athletes--a responsibility that often appears to be assumed in an almost unbelievably light manner!

The Sources of This Interpersonal Power

Power is defined as "the ability or official capacity to exercise control or influence over others." Politicians have such power or influence; bureaucrats have it; parents have it; and coaches most certainly have such power to influence their eager charges. Here we will not attempt to draw fine distinctions among the concepts 'power,' 'authority,' 'influence,' 'control,' etc. Our basic concern in this context will be the power that the coach exerts--i.e., the leverage that he/she can apply in regard to whether the athlete takes stimulants, painkillers, or body-building agents regularly in order to improve performance and thereby achieve success in sport performance. What are the elements or sources of interpersonal power, then, which the coach can bring to bear on his/her aspiring athletes --elements that must be employed very carefully and with foresight because of the great impact that they may have on young athletes striving for achievement and success.

First, Wilson introduces the concept of 'love' as perhaps the major one of a number of such feelings that one person might have for another. Other terms to describe such a feeling are affection, friendship, sympathy, trust, respect, awe, and admiration. If an athlete has any or all of these feelings for his/her coach, then the coach is continually faced with an assessment of what constitutes a reasonable request that might be made of the athlete, and what might actually be an imposition. If the coach were to make too great a demand of the athlete based on the amount of love or similar emotion felt, the reaping of excess benefit from such an excessive demand could well constitute exploitation to a greater or lesser extent. Also, in the case of the athlete, other feelings that might accompany those indicated above would be gratitude, indebtedness, obligation, and desire for approval. (See Wilson, pp. 304-307.)

Secondly, a frequent source of power over another that is held by the coach is that of fear--fear that can be overt, subtle, and is often irrational. A coach has a lever here that can be used if and when he deems it necessary to employ it in dealing with the athlete. The athlete may be afraid of losing his/her scholarship, education, place on the team, status as an athlete (and possible future employment), and even his status as a person.

A third source of interpersonal power that could well place the coach in too strong a position vis à vis the athlete is that the athlete may have too strong a desire, or too pressing a need, to make the grade athletically. If this were to be the case, the coach would not have to be exceptionally bright to realize this, and to be tempted occasionally to use such a desire or need for his own end--even if such use were against the best interests of the athlete concerned. Many athletes come from so-called lower middle and lower economic classes, and there may well be an urgent need, and therefore a stronger desire, to "make it" both financially and socially in our society.

A fourth way that is open to an unscrupulous or selfish person in our society whereby he may take advantage of another person is through the exploitation of that individual's virtues or qualities of character. In the case of the athlete, such qualities as goodness of nature, tolerance, good manners, gentleness, unselfishness, and sense of responsibility can often be exploited by the ill-natured, greedy coach.

Turning the "virtue coin" over, we can immediately find a fifth mechanism--that of character defects--which may be employed by person A to gain power over person B. The athlete may be gullible, susceptible to flattery, foolhardy, vain, or indeed may be subject to feelings of dislike and hatred of a rival university or particular opponent ("I'd die for dear old Yale if it meant we could beat those Harvard bastards!"). Such emotions are often very easily triggered by an unthinking or possibly unethical coach.

Flipping our virtue-vice coin back on the other side again, down through the ages youth has been especially prone to idealistic, unselfish commitments to causes. Such willingness to pledge allegiance may take the form of love of, or pride in, or concern for another. This sixth mechanism that might be used by the coach appeals to such elements as loyalty, idealism, patriotism, etc. For the athlete this involves a commitment, often irrational, to someone or something outside of himself-herself.

A seventh mechanism often exercised to gain power over another person is that of knowledge. How often have you heard the phrase "knowledge is power" in recent years? We are told almost daily that the ignorant, naive, and inexperienced person is practically powerless in our society in relation to those people who have the facts and know how to put them

to work. In the case of the athlete, the coach and his associates both individually and collectively usually know a great
deal more than the young athlete. In fact, typically a disap-
portionate mystique is built up around such knowledge that is
most often lacking in a scientific base. Nevertheless, the
young athlete will usually put his or her trust in the coach and
will typically follow their directions in just about all matters.
The coach should ask himself/herself just what responsibilities
go along with the holding of such knowledge and resultant
power.

An eighth consideration for the coach, or any person in
society relating to another for that matter, is the situation in
which A finds B rendered relatively powerless because of some
sort of temporary or permanent handicap or incapacity. Such
a condition may be exploited by the coach who is presumably
in possession of all of his faculties. (In fact, the coach could
be more intelligent, more facile in thought and verbal capacity,
and more self-confident.) Thus, the athlete could well be
dominated in this regard by a coach who was either unscrupulous or thoughtless because he/she might be injured, might
be worried about status as a student, or might even lack confidence in himself or herself for one of a variety of reasons.

Finally, then, we can agree that there will always be
opportunities to exert power over others in a society, because
we will probably always find greater or lesser dependency
existing in human relationships in any society which can be
conceived. This will be true with the status of the child, the
aged, the infirm, the poor, the ignorant, the mentally handi-
capped, etc. In the case of the athlete, we find typically a
strong dependency on the coach and the establishment in the
United States especially in the Western world - because of the
athletic scholarship system that has developed. This dependency is present until graduation, until eligibility is used up,
or until a pro contract becomes available. (I should state
parenthetically that I am in favor of the practice of striving
for excellent in intercollegiate sport, and I see no problem--
except the question of how long we can afford it--in the granting of financial assistance to bonafide student-athletes where
there is proven need.)

Summary and Conclusion

We began by stating that there is some evidence pointing
toward a conclusion that an increasing number of men and women in various countries in the world are consuming stimulants,

painkillers, and body-building agents in increasing amounts as part of their efforts toward winning and high-level achievement in competitive sport. We know further through the media that the International Olympic Committee has declared these substances to be unacceptable and cause for disqualification from further participation--if discovered. Still further, evidence is accumulating that great care should be exercised in the use of these materials because of temporary and/or permanent damage that may result in the human organism. Thus, we have a situation where the athlete, and his/her coach, are faced with ethical decisions in regard to both the letter and the spirit of the rules in this regard.

Then we discussed the question of being in another person's power, and this question was applied specifically to the relationship between the coach and the athlete. We explained nine different ways in which the coach may have both official and unofficial power over the athlete. This fact undoubtedly gives rise to certain general ethical or moral questions. The coach is therefore continually faced with ethical decisions as to when it is right to exercise certain levels of power over an athlete. If we join these two problems together, we can readily see that the athlete may well need guidance as to when and if he/she should consider taking stimulants, painkillers, and/or body-building agents.

Power over another may be exercised for one or more different reasons: for one's own benefit; for the benefit of the other; for the shared benefit of oneself and the other, etc. ad infinitum. We are forced to the conclusion that the coach truly faces an awesome responsibility in the world today in this regard. A coach may well rationalize using his power over an athlete for the coach's benefit by arguing that it is all right so long as the other is not hurt or made unhappy thereby. One final question: where in our programs of professional preparation for coaching do we help the prospective coach learn what's right?

Bibliography

1. Blum, L., "Deceiving, Hurting and Using," in Philosophy and Personal Relations (A. Montefiore, Ed.). London: Routledge & Kegan Paul, 1973.

2. Borotra, Jean. "The Need for Ethics in a Sports World of Cheating and Violence." The New York Times, Oct. 26, 1975.

3. Canadian Association of Sports Sciences Newsletter, Vol. X, No. 4 (December, 1978), 4.

4. Flemming, Arthur. "Using a Man as a Mean," Ethics, Vol. 88, No. 4 (July, 1978), 283-298.

5. Kaplan, Janice. "Women Athletes Are Women Too," The New York Times, March 4, 1979.

6. London Free Press, The. "Sprinter Credits Pill With Giving Him Pep." February 21, 1979.

7. Maclean's (Canada). "It's Not Nice to Fool Mother Nature." January 8, 1979.

8. Marty, Martin E. "Vice and Virtue: Our Moral Condition." Time, October 27, 1975, 64-66.

9. McIntosh, Peter. Fair Play. London: Heinemann, 1979.

10. Miller, Samuel H. "The Tangle of Ethics," in Ethics for Executive Series. (Reprints from Harvard Business Review), n.d., 51-54.

11. Nozick, Robert. Anarchy, State and Utopia. New York: Basic Books, 1974.

12. O'Shea, J. P. "The Effects of Anabolic Steroid on Blood Chemistry Profile, Oxygen Uptake, Static Strength and Performance in Competitive Swimmers." Doctoral dissertation, University of Utah, 1970.

13. Raines, Howell. "Drug Case Continues to Trouble Stabler." The New York Times, March 4, 1979.

14. Shinnick, Phillip K. "Testimony to U. S. Senate Subcommittee on Juvenile Delinquency." Unpublished statement obtained from the author, 1973.

15. Webb, James L. "Blood Doping: Help or Hindrance." The Physical Educator, Vol. 35, No. 4 (December, 1978), 187-190.

16. Wilson, John R. S. "In One Another's Power." Ethics, Vol. 88, No. 4 (July, 1978), 299-315.

Questions for Discussion

1. Discuss what you consider to be some of the most trouble-some concomitants of the demand for improved levels of performance in highly competitive sport.

2. Do you personally view the consumption of some type of stimulants, painkillers, and body-builders as being a very serious problem in competitive sport? Is this problem better or worse than we think? Explain your answer.

3. To what extent do you believe that the coach and athlete are "in each other's power?" One more than the other?

4. Explain why this is generally considered to be a situation that when carried beyond accepted norms is wrong ethically.

5. If this is a problem, where in our programs of professional preparation for coaching do we help the prospective coach to learn what is acceptable and right?

CHAPTER 20
DEVELOPING A JURISPRUDENTIAL ARGUMENT TO EXPLAIN THE POSSIBLE MISUSE OF INTERPERSONAL POWER BY COACH OR ATHLETE

Note: This paper represents an expanded version of the basic
        layout as explained in Chapter 7.

For various reasons, quite possible beyond the control of any one individual or group, the situation in intercollegiate athletics is regarded as disgraceful by many intelligent people in the United States.* In 1929 the Carnegie Report entitled American College Athletics stated that recruiting and subsidizing was "the darkest blot upon American college sport."[1] In 1974, almost fifty years later, the American Council on Education discovered that "there's a moral problem in college athletics."[2] Now in the 1980's Canada finds itself moving inexorably toward its own brand of recruitment, subsidization, and proselyting. Still further, alas, feminists struggling valiantly for equal rights for women in intercollegiate sport will inevitably construct, or be "caught up" in, a "Catch-22" situation for women athletes unless somehow wisdom prevails.

If indeed there is a moral problem in so-called big-time athletics in the United States, it would seem to revolve around the use of interpersonal power that a coach may exert over a recruited, subsidized athlete, or such power that an athlete could conceivably bring to bear on a coach, or the fact that universities as pattern-maintenance organizations (Parsons) are typically unwilling or unable to curb undue use of such power.

Discussions relating to this perplexing topic almost invariably result in the arousal of emotions and this, coupled with the ensuing amorphous argument, usually leaves the debaters in either a state of frustration or dejection. In an effort

---

* A paper presented at the Annual Meeting of the Philosophic Society for the Study of Sport, Trinity College, Hartford, Conn., Oct. 16, 1981.

to come to grips with this problem, I will seek to present a formally valid argument in proper form, an approach to argument akin to jurisprudence and mathematics as developed by Toulmin, that is "laid out in a tidy and simple <u>geometrical</u> form."[3] It should be kept in mind, however, that I am not speaking to <u>prove</u> that such-and-such is the case in one or more instances. I am merely attempting to show how one might go about developing such an argument to demonstrate that such interpersonal power had been, or could be, exercised by one person over another.

Flemming has asked the questio6, "Are we morally forbidden to treat a man entirely as a means to some other end?"[4] There have been several attempts in recent philosophical literature to seek appropriate and just answers to questions of this nature, but no previous application of this type of analysis has been based on the problems of this type that arise daily in highly competitive sport. For example, may we use a person to some extent for the good of the whole if the person's welfare is viewed as a "side constraint?"[5] In 1978 Wilson clarified such terms as "entrapment" and "exploitation" in discussing a love relationship.[6] Thus, it becomes obvious that there are general questions of a moral nature that arise when any form of unofficial power is used either for selfish <u>or</u> benevolent ends.

The basic concern in this present analysis, then, will be the step-by-step development of a sound argument that explains (1) how the coach in a U. S. university setting can exercise power over an athlete, and vice versa; (2) why it is generally considered wrong in a democratic society to use another person as a means to an end entirely or largely through the employment of deception, exploitation, and/or treachery; (3) why certain mitigating arguments endorsing the use of such power are either weak or illogical; (4) what additional arguments or backing may be employed to strengthen the general morality of society; and (5) why it is that many colleges and universities, as agents of society, have acted in such a way that they are negating their traditional responsibility.

II. SOME DEFINITIONS AND DISTINCTIONS

Granting the strength of an argument that "for one class of goods, the teleologist may use men entirely as means without fear that he will ever have to sacrifice someone to promote those goods."[7]   I will proceed on the assumption that in this society "the exercise of power over another for his own good is justified only if the path of reason is blocked, and then only if the person with power has a legitimate concern with the other's good. "8

I am using the term "power" here in the sense of an ability or capacity to exert control or influence over another. Official power often emanates from one's position in a hierarchical organization, but along with this position (or in personal life, generally speaking) moral questions can indeed arise when an individual attempts to exercise unofficial power. In our present situation, therefore, the coach has both official and unofficial power, but the athlete's power would typically be completely unofficial (unless he or she were a duly elected captain of a team).

It is important further to keep in mind the substantive difference possible when one uses power for either distributive or nondistributive goods. With distributive common goods, where each person must forego something to obtain these goods, there is an ever-present temptation in such contractual exchange to procure the benefits without any sacrifice. In the case of nondistributive goods, however, we can dismiss the idea of a contractual agreement because both parties automatically get what they want (Rawls' idea of social union).9 An example of this in competitive sport arises when eight men or women band together to form a crew to seek a trophy in a race against other crews. As Wilson explains (in describing a similar situation), "neither stands to gain by depriving the other of what he wants. No question of injury arises, because the good they seek cannot be partitioned."10 The situation would become distributive immediately, however, if and when eight rowers entered a singles rowing or sculling event.

Just before beginning my argument that many colleges and universities have been neglectful in regulating or controlling the use of interpersonal power by the coach and/or athlete, it seems appropriate to reiterate how serious the current situation in competitive sport is. Many people still argue that "sports build character," but a growing group of observers now argue that present-day sport simply reflects a decline in morality in the world. Perhaps the most recent truly devastating indictment of the sham and hypocrisy of much of what passes for intercollegiate sport was expressed by Judge Phillip Baiamonte when Norm Ellenberger, the former basketball coach of the University of New Mexico, was found guilty on twenty-one of twenty-two counts of fraud and the filing of false public vouchers. Instead of sentencing him to a term of from twenty-one to 105 years, he imposed a term of one year of unsupervised probation. As the judge stated, "What's going

through my mind at this point is the question, really, of how
fair it is to incarcerate a coach who is basically doing what almost everybody in this community wanted him to do--win basketball games at any cost and by whatever means might be necessary to do that."[11] However, as John Swinton said shortly
thereafter, " . . . as welcome as Judge Baiamonte's remarks
may be, one should realize that they don't do much to bring
justice to bear on the situation he deplores . . . Moreover, in
the often-sleazy profession of big-time college coaching, the
willingness to cut corners to land a blue-chip recruit or win a
game can be an attractive asset."[12] Further, as I am arguing
in this present analysis, the present pattern of recruiting and
subsidizing college athletes creates a source of interpersonal
power for the athlete himself ("herself" now too!) as explained
by Bob Cousy, former great basketball player and coach:

> You get a kid to come to your school nowadays by
> licking his boots. It's an unhealthy situation.
> Once you have committed yourself to begging him
> to come, there can never be a player-coach rela-
> tionship. The kid is the boss. There are plenty
> of rules that govern recruiting, yet there are no
> rules because there is no one really to enforce
> them.[13]

III. STEP I

In discussing the layout of arguments, Toulmin explains
that "an argument is like an organism," and then he proceeds
to designate the "chief anatomical units of the argument--its
'organs', so to speak."[14] I decided that his conception of the
logical form of a valid argument--as one in which there was a
combination of a formal, procedural argument in proper form
with a straightforward, elementary geometrical form--would suit
the present investigation admirably. As stated above briefly,
therefore, the main problem of this study is to examine the
various ways in which a head coach (especially) is in a position to employ or exercise undue power over an athlete, and
vice versa to a lesser degree. Secondly, I will seek to demonstrate the gradual development of an argument that should lead
one to a conclusion that society through its pattern-maintenance organizations (in this case, the college or university)
would normally be expected to control the use of such interpersonal power by coaches (or athletes).[15]

Keeping in mind Wilson's conclusion about when the exercise of power over another for his own good might be justified

(see above), I readily agree that in our society it can indeed be wrong to use a person "even when the person used is not hurt or made unhappy by being used."[16] In developing the pattern of argument here, I am simply stating that a head coach is in a position to exercise undue power over a recruited, subsidized athlete. I believe that there are at least nine ways in which this might be so--in either direction (with the coach exerting power or vice versa). Accordingly, I will then begin gradually with the building of my argument that will ultimately lead me to the conclusion that our society should step in where colleges and universities seem unwilling or unable to control undue use of such power. It should be kept in mind that this is not being presented as formal logic in which D (Data) by definition leads us to C (Conclusion). This is not a Modus Ponens situation; it is simply the beginning of a rational argument that one might expect in a court of law. (Note the similarity with the time-honored minor premise of Aristotelean tradition.) I simply wish to move forward gradually, steadily, and reasonably from D to C as is being explained in the present example from intercollegiate athletics as follows:

A head coach in the U.S. is in a position to exercise undue interpersonal power over recruited, subsidized athletes.	⟶ So	Universities should control undue use of such power in this society

The following, then, represent nine samples, elements, or sources of interpersonal power that a head coach could conceivably bring to bear on a recruited, subsidized athlete in the United States--elements that must be employed very carefully and with great foresight because of the major impact that they may have on young athletes striving for achievement and success. First, Wilson introduces the concept of 'love' as perhaps the major one of a number of such feelings that one person might have for another. Other terms to describe such a feeling are affection, friendship, sympathy, trust, respect, awe, and admiration. If an athlete has any or all of these feelings for his/her coach, then the coach is continually faced with an assessment of what constitutes a reasonable request that might be made of the athlete, and what might actually be an imposition. If the coach were to make too great a demand of the athlete based on the amount of love or similar emotion felt, the reaping of excess benefit from such an excessive demand could well constitute exploitation to a greater or lesser extent. Also, in the case of the athlete, other feelings that might accompany those indicated above would be gratitude, indebtedness, obligation, and desire for approval.[17]

Secondly, a frequent source of power over another that is held by the coach is that of fear--fear that can be overt, subtle, and is often irrational. A coach has a lever here that can be used if and when he deems it necessary to employ it in dealing with the athlete. The athlete may be afraid of losing his/her scholarship, education, place on the team, status as an athlete (and possible future employment), and even status as a person.

A third source of interpersonal power that could well place the coach in too strong a position vis à vis the athlete is that the athlete may have too strong a desire, or too pressing a need, to make the grade athletically. If this were to be the case, the coach could well realize this and be tempted occasionally to use such a desire or need for his/her own end--even if such use were against the best interests of the athlete concerned. Many athletes come from the lower-middle and lower economic classes, and there may well be an urgent need, and therefore a stronger desire, to "make it" both financially and socially in our society.

A fourth way that is open to an unscrupulous or selfish person in our society whereby s/he may take advantage of another person is through the exploitation of that individual's virtues or qualities of character. In the case of the athlete, such qualities as goodness of nature, tolerance, good manners, gentleness, unselfishness, and sense of responsibility can often be exploited by an ill-natured, greedy coach (who may indeed have become that way because of inordinate pressures exerted upon him or her).

Turning the "virtue coin" over, there is a fifth mechanism--that of character defects--that may be employed by person A to gain power over person B. The athlete may be gullible, susceptible to flattery, foolhardy, vain, or indeed may be subject to feelings of dislike or even hatred of a rival university or particular opponent (I'd die for dear old Yale if it meant we could beat those Harvard b-------!"). Such emotions are often very easily triggered by an unthinking or possible unethical coach.

Flipping the virtue-vice coin back on the other side again, it can be pointed out that down through the ages youth has been especially prone to idealistic, unselfish commitments to causes. Such willingness to pledge allegiance may take the form of love of, or pride in, or concern for another. This sixth mechanism that might be used by the coach appeals to such elements as loyalty, idealism, patriotism, etc. For the athlete this involves a commitment, often irrational, to someone or something outside of the individual.

A seventh mechanism often exercised to gain power over another person is that of knowledge. We are told that "knowledge is power," and therefore the ignorant, naive, and inexperienced person is practically powerless in this society in relation to those people who have the facts and know how to put them to work. In the case of the athlete, the head coach and his/her associates both individually and collectively know a great deal more than the young athlete. In fact, typically a disproportionate mystique is built up around such knowledge that is most often lacking in a scientific base. Nevertheless, the young athlete will usually put his or her trust in the coach and will typically follow the directions of the coach in just about all matters. Thus, the coach should ask himself/herself just what responsibilities go along with the holding of such knowledge and resultant power.

An eighth consideration for the coach, or any person in society relating to another for that matter, is the situation in which A finds B rendered relatively powerless because of some sort of temporary or permanent handicap or incapacity. Such a condition may be exploited by the coach who is presumably in possession of all of his/her faculties. (In fact, the coach could be more intelligent, more facile in thought and verbal capacity, and more self-confident.) Thus, the athlete could well be dominated in this regard by a coach who was either thoughtless or unscrupulous. This would be especially true if the athlete were injured, were worried about status as a student, or were lacking in confidence for one of a variety of reasons.

Finally, then, we can perhaps agree that there will always be opportunities to exert power over others in social settings, because in society as it can be envisioned we will always find greater or lesser dependency existing in human relationships. In the case of the athlete, we find typically a strong dependency on the coach and the establishment in the United States in the Western world because of the athletic scholarship system that has developed. This dependency is present until graduation, until eligibility is used up, or until a pro contract becomes available. (I should state parenthetically that I am in favor of the practice of striving for excellence in intercollegiate sport, and I see no problem--except for the question of how long we can afford it--in the granting of financial assistant to bonafide student-athletes where there is proven need.)

To show that this relationship has all of the qualities of a two-edged sword, I will now list briefly nine ways in which this situation could work in reverse--how a recruited, subsidized athlete could well exert interpersonal power on a coach in the United States:

1. Societal values and norms in big-time university sport--the idea that "winning is the only thing" --places the coach in a position where he/she can be directly influenced by the recruited, subsidized athlete.

2. Coach may have initially placed himself/herself in a position of undue dependency on the athlete by virtue of illegal and/or unethical recruiting tactics.

3. Coach may have made unrealistic commitments to athlete and has therefore limited his/her degrees of freedom in future decision-making.

4. Coach may have arranged for continuing illegal payments of one kind or another to athlete while he/she is at the university (or even later).

5. Coach may have a guilt complex for having brought an academically deficient person to the university--one who in all probability will not graduate.

6. Coach may have developed an unrealistic self-concept about the importance of his/her sport and his/her role as the coach of this activity; as a result, the coach may put up with poor and/or dishonest and/or illegal behavior on the part of the athlete by rationalizing that character is being developed.

7. Coach may have character defects that the athlete can exploit (e.g., vain, selfish, authoritarian, arrogant).

8. Coach may have character virtues that a clever athlete can exploit (e.g., fairness, honesty, true concern for fellow man or woman).

9. Coach may be placed in a position of weakness with one or more athletes (because of disabling injuries to other key athletes).

Thus, in this relationship between athlete and coach, it is important to keep the ideas of "entrapment" and "exploitation" in mind. Entrapment is defined as actions that lure another into difficulty, danger, or self-incrimination. Exploitation, which usually accompanies entrapment, is the utilization of another for selfish purposes. The latter, Wilson believes, can be active or passive in nature--passive when no deception is involved or necessary. He argues further that entrapment "is thus a form of treachery, an abuse of trust, very akin, as the metaphors suggest, to the treachery of the soldier who abuses the conventions for instituting a truce."[18] So if entrapment involves the acquisition of power through treachery, when exploitation is introduced the power is being used typically for selfish ends. Obviously, there are general questions of a moral nature that arise when any form of official or unofficial power is used either for selfish or benevolent ends. This is so because "any source of power provides a kind of lever with which one person can move another, a means of influencing the other to act or to refrain from acting in a certain way, a means neither rational nor straightforwardly coercive."[19] This makes clear to teachers and coaches what a tremendous responsibility they have in their everyday dealings with student-athletes. Conversely, as explained above, a sophisticated, unscrupulous athlete in big-time U.S. intercollegiate sport can entrap and exploit the coach in a similar manner.

IV. STEP II

Step II in the Toulmin argument lay-out involves the creation of "general hypothetical statements, which can act as bridges, and authorize the sort of step to which our particular argument commits us."[20] Such statements are called Warrants (W) so that they may be distinguished from both Data (D) and Conclusions (C). A warrant may be explained further as a sanction, justification, practical standard, canon of argument, value, or norm. So, on our way to the conclusion of argument started in Step I, I am now suggesting a warrant (a "How do you get there?" if you will) to the basic question mandated initially ("What have you got to go on?"), or the data. With the present argument, therefore, the warrant (W) can be a statement such as "In a democratic society it is considered morally wrong to use another person as a means to an end entirely or largely through the employment of deception, exploitation, and/or treachery." If I were now to symbolize the

relationship among the three elements (D, W, and C), it might
look as follows:

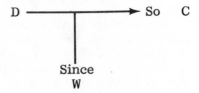

Or, to carry the present example through Step II:

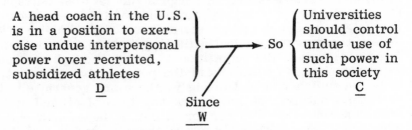

In a democratic society it
is considered wrong to use
another person as a means
to an end entirely or largely
through the employment of
deception, exploitation, and/
or treachery

The warrant here is designated as "incidental and explanatory,"
its function "being simply to register explicitly the legitimacy
of the steps involved and to refer it back to the larger class
of steps whose legitimacy is being presupposed."[21] Thus,
warrants are general, but data are specific. Warrants are
needed in all fields of endeavor, if we wish to judge any ideas
or arguments on a rational basis. Of course, there are categories of warrants, each of which could convey a different degree of intensity or force. Therefore, we might find it necessary to make use of a qualifying term (e.g., necessarily, presumably, probably, under "x" condition). All of this makes
the development of a valid argument more difficult and complex, because any such distinction or qualifier will affect the
conclusion (C) that may be drawn. For example, in the argument that has been developed so far, I might ask myself whether D necessarily (interpreted as needfully or essentially) leads
to C on the basis of the W that has been provided.

V. STEP III

In Step III, to help with the increasing complexity of
the argument a <u>Modal Qualifier</u> (Q) and a <u>Condition of Exception</u>
(R) are introduced. Q and R relate to W, but they are
distinct from it in that they speak about W's "ability" to speak
authoritatively about the relationship between D and C.   In
other words, in this example the modal qualifier (Q) speaks to
the strength that the warrant (W) confers in this argument.
Further, the condition of exception (R) can offer particular
circumstances of greater or lesser import that might negate or
refute the authority of the warrant (W).

In this example, I am bold enough to recommend that
the modal qualifier (D) should be interpreted to mean "necessarily" (thus regarded as needful or essential).   There has
developed over the years a truly substantive body of evidence
of all types indicating that both coaches and athletes have been
subjected to great pressures.   Accordingly, a great variety of
rules and regulations have been promulgated by the many athletic conferences.   And yet, as I explained above, conditions
were evidently no better in 1974 than they were in 1929.   This
confirms that in many instances the situation is truly out of
hand, and it is questionable whether any person, group of persons, or institution <u>can</u> do anything about what has been described by some as the "cancer" of higher education in the
United States.   (Witness the recent ruling by a judge that a
major university had to admit an athlete to a degree program
so that he could complete his fourth year of basketball eligibility.   Here the judge stated that the young man had indeed
been recruited to the university as an athlete, not as a student.)   For these reasons, therefore, I feel justified in the use
of the term "necessarily" as the modal qualifier (Q) when we
are considering the potential power that either the coach or the
athlete can bring to bear on the other.

Insofar as the other type of qualifier, called the condition of exception or rebuttal (R), affects the equation by negating the warrant in a somewhat different manner, I must be
careful to characterize the degree of force or intensity that
each condition of exception or rebuttal (R) can exert on the
conclusion being drawn.   In the present argument, a coach who
attempted to use excessive power over an athlete through deception, exploitation, and/or treachery could argue for complete freedom of action--such as the "survival of the fittest"
approach put forth by Plato in the Gorgias.[22]   One who assumes
such a position in our society today, however, would soon be

regarded as an outcast with psychopathic or megalomaniacal tendencies.

If I were to assume a more moderate position in searching for some conditions of exception (R), I can get some help from Wilson who offers three possibilities for consideration in such a circumstance--possibilities that I have adapted to the present argument as follows:

1.   That the athlete is not actually hurt by the exercise of such power over him/her.

2.   That the athlete doesn't believe that he or she is being used.

3.   That the athlete is not unhappy about being used in such a way (although there is indeed hurt).[23]

Or, as I believe, the situation has retrogressed to the point that:

4.   The society, for several reasons, doesn't feel strongly enough about these potential uses of power on the part of the coach (or athlete) to monitor and then control the situation when need be in a truly careful, conscientious, constructive, and ethical manner.

In Step III, therefore, I can now symbolize the relationship among a total of five elements (D, W, Q, R, and C) as follows:

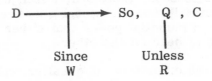

$$D \longrightarrow \text{So,} \quad Q \; , \; C$$

Since
W

Unless
R

Or, to carry the present argument symbolically through Step III:

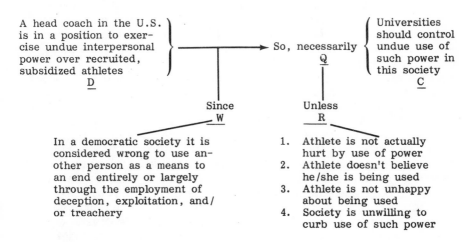

A head coach in the U.S. is in a position to exercise undue interpersonal power over recruited, subsidized athletes
D

So, necessarily
Q

Universities should control undue use of such power in this society
C

Since
W

Unless
R

In a democratic society it is considered wrong to use another person as a means to an end entirely or largely through the employment of deception, exploitation, and/or treachery

1. Athlete is not actually hurt by use of power
2. Athlete doesn't believe he/she is being used
3. Athlete is not unhappy about being used
4. Society is unwilling to curb use of such power

VI. STEP IV

In Step IV, which is the final step to be discussed in the "rounding out" of the argument that I have been developing, I return to a further consideration of the nature of a warrant. The warrant, as explained in Step II, is a general, hypothetical, bridge-like statement used to authorize or justify the conclusion being drawn on the basis of the data (evidence) provided. The warrant suggested here (see immediately above) explained that it is wrong to use a person in this society through some form of deception. To an extent, therefore, this warrant is being used to draw the conclusion that universities should monitor and control undue use of such power by any of its constituents (in this case, by coaches or athletes).

The above notwithstanding, I must inquire as to the applicability of the warrant as stated in all cases in a democratic society. This is why I raised some possible conditions of exception or rebuttal (R) in Step III. The first three possible exceptions offered (e.g., athlete is not actually hurt by use of power) can be argued from different viewpoints, but they do appear to be weak conditions of exception or rebuttal. In each instance the coach is being unfair to the athlete who presumably does not expect to be a victim of "deception, exploitation, and/or treachery." (Space does not permit a detailed discussion of these conditions of exception; such is available in a different context in Wilson, 1978, pp. 307-311, where the question of self-interested exercise of power over another is explained in some detail.) It is the fourth argument (condition of exception or rebuttal) that offers a challenge in regard to the applicability of the warrant offered. Why doesn't society exert more pressure on universities to carry out their presumed pattern-maintenance function, thereby showing much greater concern about coaches or athletes who either employ or are victims of deception, exploitation, and/or treachery? I suppose it could be argued that we, the people, views highly competitive sport and those involved with it as our "cultural maximizers" (i.e., sport serves communities and nations, its "function is to maintain or push further the culture's greatness and integration").[24] Arguing from this premise, I can therefore postulate that we "tend to look the other way" when our "cultural maximizers" commit infractions against our society's values and norms--unless the infraction is so heinous that it simply cannot be overlooked. (One recalls the situation in a community where a Big Ten university was located in the 1960's when the townspeople wanted to erect statues to three coaches who "deceived, exploited, and were treacherous" to twelve athletes--at least--nine of whom were Blacks struggling for equal opportunity in an "unequal" society.)

Or I might put this fourth argument in another context altogether--for the sake of argument in another society in culture. This warrant may be relevant and applicable in the United States, Canada, the United Kingdom, or the Federal Republic of Germany--in what is called the Western world. However, then I must ask to what extent it would be relevant and applicable in all countries in other cultures. Of course, I hope it is indeed relevant and applicable, but then I must ask myself if society "looks the other way" there too--as it seems to do all too often in the United States.

At any rate, in Step IV my aim is to present the idea of providing Backing (B) for any warrants I may choose to use in developing the pattern or layout of an argument. Thus, in the example I am developing, the backing (B) supplements or strengthens the warrant even further (keeping in mind that one might argue that he was using another person entirely or largely as a means to an end for his/her--the other person's --own good). How often have we all heard this type of argument offered as justification for a questionable act! The backing (B) I am offering to strengthen the warrant (W) in this example is that deception, exploitation, and/or treachery typically involve entrapment and manipulation as well. Rudinow distinguishes among manipulation, persuasion, and coercion by arguing that manipulation may be less open than the others in seeking to influence behavior. It often "seems delicate, sophisticated, even artful in comparison with the hammer-and-tongs

crudity of coercion...."[25] However, it may involve all three
and, therefore, I am able to add the following backing (B) to
warrant (W):   "The written and unwritten rules, regulations,
and laws of our society.   Manipulation of this type usually involves deception (or even coercion) to which there is a moral
reaction because of the effort to control or elicit behavior
through interference with another's operative goals and thereby to destroy or seriously damage his/her personal dignity."

Taking this final step (adding further backing B) ends
this present investigation.   Also, I recognize that there is a
"field-dependence" for backing (i.e., it matters a great deal
whether one is dealing with ethics, physics, or law, to name
three).   Here it might have been sufficient simply to state the
warrant (W) without adding the backing (B).   As Toulmin
argues, "the warrant itself is more than a repetition of these
facts; it is a general moral of a practical character, about the
ways in which we can safely argue in view of these facts."[26]
Finally, in this pattern of argument (that started as "D, so
C"), it ought to be possible to turn it around and move from
right to left (or "C, because D").

In Step IV, then, I have now introduced a sixth element
(B).   Thus, D, W, B, Q, R, and C are all worked into the
presentation of the complete argument and are symbolized as
follows:

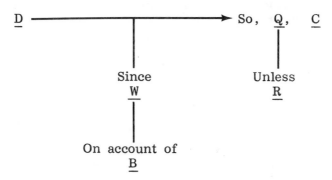

Or, to carry the present argument forward in detail through
the final Step IV:

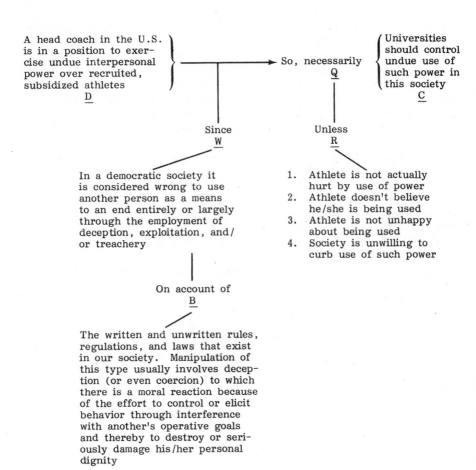

A head coach in the U.S. is in a position to exercise undue interpersonal power over recruited, subsidized athletes
D

So, necessarily
Q

Universities should control undue use of such power in this society
C

Since
W

Unless
R

In a democratic society it is considered wrong to use another person as a means to an end entirely or largely through the employment of deception, exploitation, and/or treachery

1. Athlete is not actually hurt by use of power
2. Athlete doesn't believe he/she is being used
3. Athlete is not unhappy about being used
4. Society is unwilling to curb use of such power

On account of
B

The written and unwritten rules, regulations, and laws that exist in our society. Manipulation of this type usually involves deception (or even coercion) to which there is a moral reaction because of the effort to control or elicit behavior through interference with another's operative goals and thereby to destroy or seriously damage his/her personal dignity

VII. DISCUSSION

Most of the time in this paper has been devoted to explaining the sources of interpersonal power that a head coach could conceivably bring to bear on a recruited, subsidized athlete in the U.S. (or vice versa to a considerable extent). Then I sought to demonstrate how Toulmin's layout for an argument of a jurisprudential nature could be developed in a simple geometrical form so as to be able to draw the conclusion that universities (and ultimately the society) should monitor and control undue use of such power. In this final section, a few opinions will be offered about the prevailing situation.

I believe that present-day education is not providing a sufficient quantity of humanness and concern for fellow man in the experiences that are offered. "If an experience expands awareness and intensifies personal significance, it is educational," argue Tesconi and Morris.[27] I may well agree with this statement, but I must inquire further as to the direction that this expansion of awareness and intensification of personal significance is taking. This is most certainly the plight of overly organized sport in many educational institutions--and the situation seems to be getting worse. As Etzioni stated recently, social scientists are beginning to re-examine their core assumption "that man can be taught almost anything and quite readily." As he laments, "We are now confronting the uncomfortable possibility that human beings are not very easily changed after all."[28]

Of course, this argument developed here can be made more easily against a coach because of the official power that he or she typically possesses. However, many athletes under the prevailing circumstances are also in a position to exert undue power over coaches who often appear to be victims of circumstances in the current environment. It is true that an argument of this type is not easily made and may never be settled finally. I do believe that a start has been made in sport philosophy using this layout for an argument, one that is neither strictly formal logic nor mathematical logic. Keeping in mind McPeck's recent argument that "even when the problem at issue is the rational assessment of some statement or argument, the major requirements for such assessments are epistmological in character, not logical,"[29] the present argument offered here is nevertheless a combination of a formal, procedural argument in proper form with a straightforward, elementary geometrical form.

Finally, then, it has become clearer to me through this study that both the coach and the athlete involved in highly competitive sport are continually faced with ethical decisions as to when it is right to exercise certain levels of power over the other. The disturbing fact is that many universities, and the states that ultimately control them, are typically unwilling to monitor these situations more carefully and to curb undue use of such power--even though established societal values and norms indicate that they should do so. This does seem to be a steadily disintegrating situation, and the universities are pattern-maintenance organizations charged with maintenance of the society's established values and norms. However, in a number of these instances, it has been social pressure from that same society that has silenced legitimate protest that might have otherwise prevailed.[30] This is assuredly a difficult and often embarrassing subject to bring up and to examine publicly, but who would argue that it is not an important one? As matters stand now, the coach receives little or no ethical training along these lines, nor does the athlete. It seems, therefore, that both of these parties will be subject to continuing manipulation and exploitation in ways that often destroy personal dignity. Unfortunately, the drift is in the wrong direction!

Footnotes

1. Carnegie Foundation for the Advancement of Teaching, The American College Athletics (Howard J. Savage et al., Eds.). New York: The Foundation, Bulletin 23, 1929.

2. New York Times, The. An article by F. Cady, March 10, 1974, Sec. 5.

3. S. Toulmin. The Uses of Argument. New York: Cambridge University Press, 1964, p. 95.

4. Arthur Flemming. "Using a Man as a Means," Ethics 88 (1978): p. 283.

5. Robert Nozick. Anarchy, State, and Utopia. (New York: Basic Books, 1974, p. 32.

6. John R. S. Wilson. "In One Another's Power," Ethics 88 (1978): pp. 299–315.

7. Flemming, p. 298.

8. Wilson, p. 315.

9. John Rawls. A Theory of Justice. Cambridge, Mass.: Harvard University Press, 1971, pp. 520–530.

10. Wilson, p. 291.

11. New York Times, The. "A Judgement on College Sports." A transcription from The Albuquerque Journal, July 12, 1981, Section 5.

12. New York Times, The. Letter to the Editor ("Flawed System Is No Defense"), July 26, 1981, Section. 5

13. New York Times, The. "N.I.T. Rings Down Curtain for Cousy." An article by Sam Goldaper, March 9, 1969, Section 5.

14. Toulmin, p. 94 et ff. Great stress is placed on Toulmin's logical apparatus here for possible future use by sport philosophers.

15. R. Jean Hills. Toward A Science of Organization. Eugene, Oregon: Center for Advanced Study of Administration, 1968, p. 74.

16. Wilson, p. 299.

17. Ibid., p. 303. It could be argued, of course, that these same elements apply in the professor/student relationship.

18. Ibid.

19. Ibid., p. 304.

20. Toulmin, p. 98.

21. Ibid., p. 100.

22. Plato. Gorgias. New York: Masterpieces of World Philosophy, Harper & Row, 1961, p. 73. (Frank N. Magill, Ed.).

23. Wilson, pp. 307-309. Here Wilson is reacting to an earlier article by L. Blum. My material represents an adaptation of these conditions of exception to the present argument.

24. Jules Henry. Culture Against Man. New York: Random House, 1963, p. 31.

25. J. Rudnow. "Manipulation," Ethics 88 (1978), p. 339.

26. Toulmin, p. 106.

27. Charles A. Tesconi, Jr. and Van Cleve Morris. The Anti-Man Culture. Urbana, Ill.: University of Illinois Press, 1972, p. 208.

28. Amitai Etzioni. "Human Beings Are Not Very Easy to Change After All," Saturday Review, June 3, 1972, p. 45.

29. John E. McPeck. "Critical Thinking Without Logic: Re-
     storing Dignity to Information," in Proceedings of the
     37th Annual Meeting of the Philosophy of Education Soci-
     ety, Houston, Texas, Aprol 26-29, 1981, 219-227.

30. Harry M. Johnson. "The Relevance of the Theory of Ac-
     tion to Historians." Social Science Quarterly, June 1969,
     pp. 46-58.

Questions for Discussion

1. What in essence is the investigator attempting to develop
    in Chapter 20? Is he actually attempting to prove that
    such a situation prevails in any one or more situations?

2. Explain some of the more basic ways in which a coach in a
    U. S. university setting can exercise power over an ath-
    lete? Do you agree that the reverse of such a situation is
    just as possible?

3. Explain what is meant by the terms "distributive goods"
    and "nondistributive goods."

4. To what extent do you agree that many colleges and uni-
    versities have been neglectful in regulating the use of in-
    terpersonal power by coaches over athletes?

5. If coaches and athletes are to be successful in highly com-
    petitive (elite) sport, what steps could we take now to im-
    prove the present situation and to work for a better "coach-
    ing environment" in the future?

CHAPTER 21
CAN THE PROFESSIONAL ATHLETE CLAIM TRUE PROFESSIONAL STATUS?

Note: This paper should be read in conjunction with Chapter 5, because it represents a practical application of what is discussed there.

No one can deny that highly competitive sport has become an important, perhaps vital phase of our North American way of life.* Further, this statement probably holds true for many of the world's developed nations. This development has taken place largely in the 20th century, and we presently find a situation where athletes may be classified roughly as either amateurs, semiprofessionals, or professionals. These designations have been related historically to the question of the material rewards to athletes depending upon their level of participation in sport. Typically we expect amateurs to receive no extrinsic rewards for their efforts, while semiprofessionals may receive some money or other emoluments because they presumably need or deserve such tangible reward to provide for their livelihood. Professionals have accepted the idea of playing a sport for a living. Today many of them offer a commodity for which the public seems willing to pay dearly. Thus, we now find the term "professional athlete" as part of our everyday vocabulary.

This professional athlete--whatever else we might think of him or her--has acquired a highly materialistic image. Granting that this person is a different breed than his predecessor in the earlier decades of the century, especially in such sports as football, basketball, tennis, and golf, we nevertheless tend to conclude that even here this individual is a "professional" in the limited sense of the word. He is usually after all the money that his physical talent can bring on the open market.[1] Sport is viewed as a means to an end--that person's security and ultimate happiness in life. There is nothing wrong

---

* A paper presented at the Annual Meeting of the Philosophic Society for the Study of Sport, SUNY at Buffalo, New York, Oct. 15, 1982.

with using a talent and working hard in this way, of course, if it is honest endeavor in a legitimate occupation. However, it can be argued that it could be so much more, in the sense that it might be possible for such a person to make himself a professional in the broader and finer sense of the term that society has come to recognize over the centuries. It is to this basic question that my argument will be addressed in this paper: Is the sport professional by the very nature of his/her task destined to be a member of a trade with extraordinarily high remuneration, or can those involved in this way ever aspire to full status as a member of a recognized profession?

To continue with these introductory remarks, may I state that it is not my avowed intention of becoming a sort of "moral Marine" at this point because of my interest in sport. I am not determined to establish a professional beachhead for what today often appears to be a somewhat venal trade. Everything considered, however, we must recognize that this person--the professional athlete--typically has an unusual talent which he has developed to a high degree in a cultural activity that has proved itself to be important in our society. This must be true, or else he wouldn't be making such a well-paid living of it!

Furthermore, it is probably true that a particular sport professional who has reached his peak of attainment is better qualified in this sphere of activity than he will ever be in any other phase of life. What could be more natural than to expect this person to become a true professional in the more recognized sense of the term and to devote the rest of his life to the promotion of his sport with the youth and adults of his country? There is typically no reason why the professional sportsperson in many sports--a person who usually avows love for that sport--cannot devote the rest of his life to a social ideal and become a really fine professional individual, one whose primary aim is to serve people through contributions to his own sport and to the highest ideals of sportsmanship. It could be argued that this represents a more lofty purpose than some of the occupations often pursued in later life where fame and/or notoriety in sport seems to represent a saleable commodity. Can we agree that such an approach could work because we know of selected instances of men and women who have made it work? This thought may not be as idealistic as it sounds. Further, it would do much to place the amateur/semiprofessional/professional controversy in a new light (Zeigler, 1975, pp. 227-228).

The Background of Professions

To place this topic in some historical perspective briefly, we recall that the idea of professions and rudimentary preparation for such work originated in the very early societies, yet the term "profession" was not used commonly until relatively recently (Brubacher, 1962, p. 47). However, centers for a type of professional instruction were developed in Greece and Rome as bodies of knowledge became available. In the Middle Ages universities were organized when the various professional groups banded together for convenience, power, and protection. The degree granted at that time was in itself a license to practice whatever it was that the graduate "professed." This practice continued in the Renaissance at which time instruction became increasingly secularized. In England especially, training for certain professions (e.g., law) gradually became disassociated from universities themselves (Ibid.).

But what is a profession today? There are many different meanings given, of course, but it is usually described as a vocation which requires specific knowledge of some aspect of learning in order to have the practitioner accepted as a professional person. The now legendary Abraham Flexner recommended six criteria as being characteristic of a profession as long ago as 1915 as follows: a professional person's activity was (1) fundamentally intellectual, and the individual bears significant personal responsibility; (2) undoubtedly learned, because it is based on a wealth of knowledge; (3) definitely practical, rather than theoretical; (4) grounded in technique that could be taught, and this is the basis of professional education; (5) strongly organized internally; and (6) largely motivated by altruism, since its goal is the improvement of society (Flexner, 1915, pp. 578-581). The crucial apsect of this analysis was, however, "the unselfish devotion of those who have chosen to give themselves to making the world a fitter place to live in" (Ibid., p. 590). In fact, it was Flexner's position that the presence or lack of this "unselfish devotion" will tend to elevate a doubtful activity to professional status, or lower an acknowledged profession to a venal trade.

Before I am brought to a screeching halt in my endeavor to consider the idea of possible professional status for the "pro athlete" by someone who argues that professional sport can be characterized by anything but "unselfish devotion," please allow me to move ahead from 1915 to some thoughts on the subject offered in the 1980s by Michael Bayles who has written extensively on the topic of professional ethics for the consulting professions. (We should keep in mind that there are categories

of professions recognized such as consulting, scholarly, performing, etc.)   He finds it impossible to offer a definition of the
term <u>profession</u> that would be generally accepted.   Arguing
that today there is too great a variety of professions to subsume
them all under one all-encompassing definition, he suggests an
approach whereby necessary features might be indicated along
with a number of other common features that would tend to elevate an occupation to professional status (Bayles, 1981, p. 7).

The three necessary aspects or components of a profession that are generally recognized are (1) the need for an extensive period of training, (2) a field where there is a significant intellectual component that must be mastered before the
profession is practiced, and (3) a recognition by society that
the trained person can provide a basic, important service to its
citizens (Ibid.).   Professions tend to have other features that
are common to most, but they don't seem to be absolutely necessary for such recognition.   For example, there may be some
sort of licensing by the state or province or certification by the
appropriate professional body.   Members of professions almost
invariably establish professional organizations or societies, but
membership may not be mandatory.   Further, a professional
typically has a good deal of autonomy in his or her work, and
yet those who work in large organizations characterized by a
considerable amount of bureaucracy often feel that they are constrained in their efforts by a superfluity of red tape.

We must keep in mind further that some professions are
immediately recognized as such (e.g., law); some groups are
striving for such status (e.g., management); and some groups
call themselves professionals (e.g., "pro" athletes).   In the
course of their development, groups such as this have gradually but increasingly become conscious of the need for a set of
professional ethics--that is, a set of professional obligations
that are established as norms for practitioners in good standing to follow.   These standard of virtue and vice, principles of
responsibility, and rules of duty have usually conformed to one
of two types or patterns that have been handed down over the
centuries.   As Hazard explains:

> One pattern is that of a creed or affirmation of
> professional belief.   The ethical principles of medi-
> cine or social work, for example, are stated this
> way.   The creed is short and obscure, but lofty,
> expressing the aims of the profession and adjuring
> personal commitment to them--a kind of oath of
> vocational office.   The other pattern is the legal
> code.   Not surprisingly, this is the ethical format

> in the legal profession; to an increasing extent it
> is being adopted in accountancy. It may be de-
> scribed as a set of detailed administrative regula-
> tions . . .

Hazard explains further that in some cases the regulations are
spelled out by the profession itself, whereas in others it is the
governmental agency that takes the lead. In the final analysis,
however, the creed seems to have been accepted as the better
approach than the code, perhaps because it is general and less
confining to the professionals concerned. Unfortunately, neither the creed nor the code have spoken too "intelligibly to the
fundamental ethical problems arising in the professions in question" (Hazard, 1978, p. 50).

Whatever interest sport philosophers may have in this
subject at present, there is no doubt but that "the ethics of
professional conduct is being questioned as never before in
history" (Bayles, 1981, p. ix). Bayles laments the fact that
when he first was called upon to teach professional ethics to
undergraduates in 1978 he could find very little if any materials from which to proceed. Recently, however, there has been
an extensive study treating the teaching of ethics in higher
education carried out by the Hastings Center, and it was discovered that there has been a considerable upsurge in the past
decade toward the development of resource material treating
ethical issues in many professional fields (Report by the Has-
ting Center, 1980). In the field of sport and physical education, there has been some interest in ethical conduct over the
years. However, this interest has been centered primarily on
the subject of ethical conduct by athletes and coaches, but
somehow it hasn't focused on the professional athlete and the
professional coach as such. The rise of sport as a social phenomenon has nevertheless been gathering momentum steadily
and increasingly throughout the world during this century.
Many people are now involved (and this number is increasing)
professionally or semiprofessionally with sport as coaches,
teachers, administrators, performers, and researchers. Believ-
ing that these people are generally ill-prepared to confront the
variety of professional problems and concerns that are confronting them daily, I decided that the time was ripe to begin serious consideration of this topic.

Development of the Argument

Because this is such a broad topic involving such a variety of people as explained above, the basic question that will

be addressed here is whether or to what extent the professional athlete can now or in the near future hope to claim true professional status.   First, then, we must consider briefly again
the type of profession with which we are dealing. Bayles (1981,
p. 9) distinguished between the consulting professions (e.g.,
medicine) and the scholarly professions (e.g., teaching).   However, it would seem logical to include also a category of performing (e.g., musician).   Careful examination of such distinctions
would demonstrate the difficulty of establishing a dividing line
with the result that a blurring occurs.   We often hear the
phrase "service" profession as well.   Thus, we might ask the
question as to just how much service should be given before a
profession becomes a vocation--a calling (from the Latin vōcātiō).
This brings us in full circle back to the "unselfish devotion"
characteristic referred to above by Flexner, the presence or
absence of which would do so much to change or establish the
full meaning of the term profession.

Proceeding then from the premise that a professional athlete would necessarily have to seek status as a member of a
performing profession, as opposed to the other two named (all
three of which should have a strong service component to qualify for such a designation), I will not attempt to lay out the
argument in a formal, procedural manner combined with a
straightforward, elementary geometrical form (Toulmin, 1964,
p. 94 et ff.).   I will seek to move forward gradually, steadily,
and reasonably from the statement that "As presently practiced,
professional athletes cannot qualify for acceptance as a true
performing profession" (D=Data) to a conclusion that "If such
status is desired, it will be necessary to alter many present
practices of the occupation" (C=Conclusion).

In proceeding with the argument, then, the next step is
to present some warrants (W=Warrants) that will serve as justifications or norms to lend authorization to the statement that
professional athletes must change their present practices significantly to achieve true professional status.   Thus, I will argue
in the strongest possible way that certain revised practices
must necessarily occur before such recognition can be attained.

First, the reader will recall that there are three necessary components of a profession that are generally recognized.
It is immediately obvious that the professional athlete has a
"need for an extensive period of training," although it must be
admitted right away that in Western culture (i.e., non-commu-
nist) the scholarly nature of such training has not been fully
established or recognized by society.   A second criterion for
an established profession was that it is "a field where there is

a significant intellectual component that must be mastered before the profession is mastered." On this point I would argue
that there should be a significant intellectual component that
should be mastered but, once again, society simply has no conception of what the ideal should be in this regard. By this I
mean that the finest type of professional athlete should understand his or her sport fully from a bio-scientific, social scientific, and humanities standpoint to meet this criterion. No
doubt a very few have this understanding in a limited way,
but such knowledge and understanding has been achieved implicitly through experience and not explicitly through scholarly
training.

The third necessary criterion was that there should be
"a recognition by society that the trained person can provide a
basic, important service to its citizens." This is an interesting
criterion to consider in relation to the presumably professional
endeavors of the athlete, because Western culture, for example,
has now granted such recognition implicitly, if not explicitly,
to professional sport. In fact, the ubiquitous nature of professional sport and athletics has reached a point where even I,
as a "self-proclaimed, lifetime jock" find myself flipping the dial
for some diversity with some regularity. However, there is no
escaping the fact that professional athletes are indeed providing a basic, important service for a great many of the citizens
of North American culture (be it through professional football,
baseball, hockey, basketball, tennis, or what have you?). To
conclude this section treating necessary criteria, therefore, I
believe that professional sport cannot yet qualify as a true
profession according to the presumably necessary criteria, but
I would also conclude that the case is there to be made for all
three of these criteria--if and when those involved ever see the
need for such development.

There are also three other warrants that can be offered
to strengthen the argument that professional athletes will have
to alter many of their present practices if they ever hope to
achieve true professional status. Bayles has argued above that
these "features are common to most professions, although they
are not necessary for professional status," however (1981, p. 8).
First, many professions have established, or have encouraged
state or provincial legislatures to establish for them, an ap-
proved scheme of certification or licensing. However, this practice is not universal, and I have often remarked ruefully--with
no disrespect to the trade of barber--"you can't cut hair in the
Province without a license, but you can prescribe exercise of
all types with no check on your qualifications to do so." Obviously, it will be a long time before certification or licensing is

required for participation as a professional in sport, or in any of the performing arts for that matter (as desirable as such a requirement might be on specific occasions). Nevertheless, it is interesting to note that a coaching certification scheme has been established in Ontario and other provinces in Canada. Although it is not yet mandatory at all levels, there is definite pressure upon organizations to engage only coaches with the requisite level of certification for the type of position available.

Second, many professions have established a variety of organizations and societies with some obviously more powerful than others, thereby resulting in competition for members within professions. These organizations are established to promote the aims and objectives of their members, but they have not until recently paid a great deal of attention to their members' economic interests to the same degree and extent as trade unions. Now, however, the idea of strikes or "working to rule" is becoming part of the marketing strategy of many professions, often to the extent that Flexner's earlier statement that true professionals are "largely motivated by altruism" may be seriously questioned. Where professional athletes stand on this point barely needs discussion. If we can believe much of what we read, professional athletes (along with many others in society) are doing their best to keep the proverbial seven deadly sins alive today. The sins of pride, avarice, anger, and envy come to mind first, but in notable cases sloth, gluttony, and lust are not far behind. Here I am not arguing that professional athletes should be any better or worse than the rest of us; the point is simply that true professionals who have banded together in professional societies have traditionally established creeds or codes urging their members to live up to high personal and professional standards of conduct. The players association or trade union of the National Football League doesn't appear to have been placing much stress recently on its creed or code of professional conduct (The New York Times, August 15, 1982, p. 27).

Third, members of professions (depending on the type of profession under consideration to a degree) have been permitted considerable freedom or autonomy in the execution of their work. The opportunity to be autonomous while working has been difficult for the professional athlete often because of the nature of his employment. The achievement of such autonomy has been even more difficult for the professional athlete in team sports than it has in the so-called individual or dual sports. As has been the case with certain other professions (e.g., the medical doctor within socialized medicine), autonomy becomes limited almost in direct proportion to the size of the bureaucratic organization with which the professional person is involved. This has certainly been true in specific team sports in the past (e.g., professional baseball), and it is only recently that a condition of servitude has been lessened by continual appeal to the legislative and law-making bodies of the land.

The Role of Professional Ethics. Much of what has been said to this point to justify the position that the respected professions have traditionally been characterized by generally recognized components (e.g., a significant intellectual component) and other important, but optional, components (e.g., certification and professional societies) leads to the conclusion that professional athletics could by its nature strive for true professional status. However, the situation at present is such that such status will be difficult to achieve unless many present practices are altered. The six warrants or justifications described above each to a greater or lesser extent have been traditionally related to the creed or code that a particular profession has established for itself. It is therefore from this creed or code that the implicit or explicit canons of practice or ethical obligations have developed. Thus, whereas attention has been focused recently on many professional problems related to ethics and values, there is little if any evidence to indicate that professional ethics has been of any immediate concern to professional athletes.

Granting that Bayles' treatment of professional ethics was limited largely to what he identifies as the consulting and scholarly professions, I have followed some of his leads in my attempt to relate this topic to the professional athlete as a member of what I have designated as a performing profession. The basic concern here in any profession of whatever type is to ascertain to what extent a specific profession's norms are related to the values and norms of the society within which the profession is functioning. For example, reasonable governance by law is fundamental to a democratic society; hence, members of a profession in a democratic society would be hard pressed by the society if they sought to deviate in their professional practice from established rule of law. Thus, the professional person is entitled to work individually or collectively to change societal norms if they clash in any way with his or her professional practice; nevertheless, the professional person is obligated to abide by the rule of law until such time as a possibly changing value or norm effects a legitimate change in the law (norm) in question. Proceeeding from the position that "professional norms express either obligations or permissions," Bayles summarizes his categorization as follows:

. . . Obligations may be of any three kinds. Standards present desirable or undesirable character traits to be sought or avoided. Principles state responsibilities that allow for discretion in the fulfillment of standards and may be balanced or weighed against one another. Rules state duties that prescribe rather specific conduct and do not allow for much discretion. Principles can explicate standards, justify rules, and provide guidance in their absence (Bayles, 1981, pp. 24-25).

Transferring our thought here to the professional athlete, one's initial reaction would be that professional athletes in most visible team sports on this continent are treated like irresponsible children (not professional practitioners), and some tend to behave accordingly.

Taking this discussion one step further in consideration of the types of ethical questions that arise for the responsible practitioner in any recognized profession--keeping in mind, of course, that all professionals are facing serious problems along these lines today--it is appropriate to raise questions of this type for professional athletes and their representatives to consider as follows:

1. Upon what bases are their services as performing professionals made available (to whom? and by whom?)?

2. What is the ethical nature of the athlete-client relationship in professional sport? What obligations does a professional athlete have to the professional organization, the spectators, the society?

3. When conflicts arise between the athlete's (individual and collective) obligations to the paying customers and to third parties (the owners, for example), how should they be resolved?

4. If a member of a profession has a responsibility to society, what professional obligations do professional athletes have to their chosen profession (if indeed they regard it as a profession)?

5. Finally, if sport as a profession were indeed to accept many of the professional obligations that

have been outlined, what must be done to ensure
compliance with those obligations and responsibilities that have been established in any creed or
code that may evolve?

(Space does not permit a detailed discussion of these questions
at this point, but their importance cannot be denied if the professional athlete ever wishes to claim implied or explicit status
as a recognized profession in society.)

Contemporary Facets of the Argument

To this point in the argument, I have simply proceeded
from Data (D) to Conclusion (C), the initial statement being
that as presently practiced, professional athletes cannot qualify
for acceptance as a true performing profession, and the concluding statement to the effect that, if such status is desired,
it will be necessary to alter many present practices of the
occupation. Then I enumerated a number of warrants (six to
be exact) to justify the argument being presented, and I argued
that a modal qualifier that could be employed (Q=Modal Qualifier) in this instance should be necessarily (as opposed to presumably, probably, under "x" condition. etc.).

In carrying out Toulmin's layout for an argument, there
are two other steps that should be introduced--a condition of
exception (R=Condition of Exception) that could be a type of
rebuttal and also further backing (B=Backing) that would supplement or strengthen the warrant(s) even further. Treating
the idea of further backing (B) first, the six warrants (W),
including the presentation of the many questions about professional ethics that must necessarily be considered by any recognized profession, have indicated conclusively that as a group
professional athletes have not met their professional problems
satisfactorily. For further backing it can be said that there
are many forces at work in our society that will prevent any
marked change in the status quo (e.g., the inordinate pressure
to win at almost any cost). Yet, I would agree with Mihalich
when he states "People who state that winning is more important than decency and honor and integrity are a disgrace to
sports and athletics and a disgrace to the human race" (1982,
p. 135). Conversely, to give some consideration to any possible rebuttal or conditions of exception (R), there are also
forces at work that may tend to bring about improved ethical
practices (or conceivably even worse practice on the way toward the mythical "Rollerball of 1984"). At any rate, let's be
somewhat optimistic by stating that with the development of
sport as a multinational business (e.g., soccer, hockey) that

there will be increasing international pressures that will serve
to bring about the establishment of larger, more integrated
units of operation. Although we may see the development of
new types of nationalism, we can hope that satellite communica-
tion and increased public suspicion of government will force
much greater public attention to all sorts of operations of this
type (business, athletics, or whatever). Further, if the goals
of democracy and socialism tend to merge and somewhat more
consensus is achieved in the 21st century, it is possible that
the somewhat artificial distinction between professions and trades
will continue to be blurred. After all, we all should be making
worthy contributions to societal and world progress, and presumably all should be following high standards of ethical conduct.

Finally, then, the evidence marshalled in this paper sup-
ports the argument that, as presently practiced, professional
athletes cannot lay claim to true professional status in this society.

Note

1. Mention must be made to indicate awareness of the fact
    that there are male and female professional athletes. The
    words he/she and his/her are used on key occasions, but
    then the writer retreats to what one old-line publisher
    calls the "impersonal he" for writing convenience.

References

Bayles, M. D. Professional ethics. Belmont, CA: Wadsworth,
    1981.

Brubacher, J. S. The evolution of professional education. In
    Proceedings (Part II) of the National Society for the
    Study of Education (N. B. Henry, Ed.). Chicago, IL:
    The NSSE, 1962.

Flexner, A. Is social work a profession? In Proceedings of
    the National Conference on Charities and Correction.
    Chicago, IL: Hildmann, 1915.

Hazard, G. C., Jr. Capitalist ethics. Yale Alumni Magazine
    and Journal, XLI (8), April, 1978, pp. 50-51.

Mihalich, J. C. Sport and athletics: philosophy in action.
Totowa, N. J.: Littlefield, Adams & Co., 1982.

New York Times, The. Players' union gestures defy N.F.L.
management, August 15, 1982, p. 27.

Report of the Hastings Center. The teaching of ethics in
higher education. Hastings-on-Hudson, N. Y.: The
Hastings Center, 1980.

Toulmin, S. The uses of argument. New York: Cambridge,
1964.

Zeigler, E. F. Personalizing physical education and sport
philosophy. Champaign, IL: Stipes, 1975.

Questions for Discussion

1. Does it make any difference whether a young person today takes up a trade or a profession?

2. How would you define the term "trade" and the term "profession?" Has the same distinction held historically?

3. Granting the author's argument that professions have certain recognizable characteristics which society evidently approves, in what ways do you believe that professional athletes live up to such a standard? In what ways do they fall short?

4. How important do you think professional ethics are for someone like yourself who is planning to enter a profession?

5. Where does the teaching/coaching profession fall short at present in regard to recognized, high-level professional status? Explain your position, indicating what we must improve upon and in what order of priority.

PART VI
CONCLUDING SECTION

CHAPTER 22
CONCEPTS OF PROGRESS

As we look ahead to where the field of sport and physical education and sport might be by 1990, or perhaps by the turn of the century, it is important to understand that it is impossible for us to have true historical perspective on our state of progress.* We need to recognize that our bias arises from the mood of the times in which we live. Our task is, therefore, to analyze the several meanings of the term "progress," and then to make our individual and professional determinations with the full understanding that our non-statistical types of measurement are subject to errors of observation. To make matters even more difficult, we are not certain about the element to be measured, the motive force, the process of change, the route of change, the goals toward which the elements are moving, and how any goals can be measured. Outside of that, we are in good shape.

Eugene Schwartz, in his insightful work entitled Overskill, states that:

> The twentiety-century version of progress turns out to be a blindly hurtling technology that has carried man to the moon, split the atom, created a cornucopia of commodites for a privileged few of the earth, and holds out a promise to carry with it the remainder of mankind. Whereas flaws and dangers inherent in progress were becoming more apparent, in the twentieth century the "laws" of progress were becoming ever more elusive . . . In the past two hundred years many attempts have been made to complete the edifice of the theory of progress, and on numerous occasions claims have been made that the elusive, universal law of progress is still undiscovered. Nor is it likely to be discovered, for in fact progress is a state of mind based upon faith rather than an element of nature (Schwartz, 1971, pp. 31-32).

---

* A paper presented to the American Academy of Physical Education, New Orleans, Louisiana, March 15, 1979.

I don't know about you, but I find it disturbing and discouraging to be told that progress in fact "is a state of mind based upon faith rather than an element of nature." It is not that I am opposed to acting on the basis of faith, although I recognize that we would have difficulty in resolving that question itself. For example, I have faith in scientific method, and I have faith that there will be eternal change--at least for the next few million years in our universe. However, I feel that there are several levels of progress that should be understood by us, and it is this question that I will explore briefly at this time.

Definitions of Progress

Keeping in mind that a concept is a general notion or idea, we realize at once that we use the word "progress" typically to explain two different concepts--that of 'forward movement' and that of 'proceeding to a higher stage.' Thus, when we turn our attention to the human's progress in evolution, it is immediately obvious that human development on this earth has exhibited progress when it is defined as forward movement or progression. But George Gaylord Simpson stated over a generation ago that he had rejected "the over-simple and metaphysical concept of a pervasive perfection principle" (1949, pp. 240-262). We cannot assume that change is progress, unless we are prepared to recommend a criterion by which our progress may be judged.

Next we are faced with the question whether we--that is, men and women--can dare to set our own criteria for human progress. Would we be exhibiting too much temerity to establish ourselves as both "judge and jury" in this regard? This question must be answered affirmatively, because to establish our own human criterion is to automatically assume that such is "the only criterion of progress and that it has a general validity in evolution. . . ." (Ibid.). Throughout history (and pre-history, we must presume) there have been examples of progress and examples of retrogression. Presumably also, if it is a materialistic world, a particular species can progress and retrogress and, fortunately for us, human beings give every evidence of being that organism which is progressing most rapidly on earth at present.

Today many of us take the notion of humans making progress for granted. The "idea of progress" is of relatively recent origin, however, dating back to the late seventeenth and early eighteenth centuries. It was Darwin's evolutionary theory that added a scientific base to the concept of 'progress' for humankind. Subsequently, we would need to make a careful analysis of each main period of history to understand whether the dominant social values and norms of a society were moving humans toward a better understanding of the "idea of progress." Bury, in his definitive work on this topic, explains how it wasn't until the late Renaissance that men realized their own capacity to structure their own world as skillfully as the citizens of the Classical World had controlled their destiny earlier (1932; reissued in 1955).

Durant, in one of his earliest works, asked the question "Is Progress a Delusion?" Seeking to encompass the problem of progress in a total view, Durant reviews history as follows:

> It is unnecessary to refute the pessimist; it is only necessary to enclose his truth, if we can, in ours. When we look at history in the large we see it as a graph of rising and falling states--nations and cultures disappearing as on some gigantic film. But in that irregular movement of countries and that chaos of men, certain great moments stand out as the peaks and essence of human history, certain advances which, once made, were never lost. Step by step man has climbed from the savage to the scientist. . . . (1928; reissued in 1953).

Then he delineates the stages of the human's growth as follows: (1) the invention of speech; (2) the discovery of fire; (3) the conquest of the animals; (4) the gradual development of agriculture; (5) the gradual introduction of social organization; (6) a perhaps dubious rise in the level of morality; (7) the development of tools (machines) to assist us: (8) the victory of man over matter that has not yet been matched with any kindred victory of man over himself; (9) the growth of education--"the development of the potential capacity for the comprehension, control, and appreciation of the world"; and (10) the power of writing to unite generations and of print to bind civilizations together (pp. 249-257).

Progress in Education

Durant's quite optimistic assessment of human progress was written in the mid-1920s. Considering the events of the intervening fifty years, it was revealing to read his analysis of the situation in his summarizing volume entitled The Lessons of History published more than four decades later. You may not wish to accept his definition of education as "the transmission of civilization" (1968, p. 101), but keeping this phrase in mind, he asserted that "we are unquestionably progressing." And then he continued with the following ideas:

> . . . Civilization is not inherited; it has to be learned and earned by each generation anew; if the transmission should be interrupted for one century, civilization would die, and we should be savages again. So our finest contemporary achievement is our unprecedented expenditure of wealth and toil in the provision of higher education for all. . . . Consider education not as the painful accumulation of facts and dates and reigns, nor merely the necessary preparation of the individual to earn his keep in the world, but as the transmission of our mental, moral, technical, and aesthetic heritage as fully as possible to as many as possible, for the enlargement of man's understanding, control, embellishment, and enjoyment of life (p. 101).

Despite Durant's cautious optimism, we are confronted with the fact that by the year 2000 the United States will in all probability have a population of more than 300 million. The threat of greater strain and stress looms large in all of life's many aspects. We will undoubtedly have to devise better uses of leisure. Where does education fit into this picture?

At present there are upwards of sixty million people enrolled at some level of our vast educational system, and more than $50 billion a year is being spent to finance this gigantic enterprise. The perennial questions remain: what is a good education--that is, what criteria shall we employ; how should the current situation modify educational practice; what type of environment should be provided to guarantee the best educational outcome; and, specifically, what is the function of the school?

Durant's ideas stated above must have answered this question for most people, because we really can't find many who would argue (along with educators like Counts and Dewey) that the schools should serve a more creative function--to provide young people with the knowledge, understanding, and attitudes whereby they could more effectively lead the way. Thus, even though there has been advancement, if not progress, the public is not willing to support education in keeping with the annual inflation factor. Operating funds are made available grudgingly; capital funding is really difficult to obtain; and there is evident discontent with education--a most disconcerting fact to those who have devoted their lives to the field of education. And so the struggle continues for us all as we seek to determine the ideal hierarchy of educational values in a pluralistic, evolving society. (Now the lethargic critics of fitness through jogging are even decrying the masochistic runners by asserting that they might get run over in those gutters at night; that they will probably be asphyxiated by automobiles' noxious fumes during the day; and that they might as well watch their orchids grow as run---after that first heart attack!)

The Need for Consensus

If we hope to influence progress in our society and in our profession, we must work for a greater amount of agreement about our professional goals--goals that are consonant with the norms and values in our United States society. Any evaluation of qualitative as opposed to quantitative progress would depend upon the extent to which our physical educational practice approximates an agreed-upon hierarchy of educational values. In my opinion, therefore, it is vitally important now that we speak out intelligently, honestly, and forthrightly regarding the many recurring problems that our profession faces between now and 1990. I believe it would be a tragic mistake at this time to become more honorary and to allow ourselves to slide into senility gracefully. We should be concerned about the results of scholarly work that are accumulating; we should be figuring out ways that we can aid and abet high-level scholarly work; and we should be sponsoring meetings where we and our younger colleagues can draw the all-important, ordered generalizations that will strengthen the theoretical underpinning of sport and developmental physical activity.

This means, of course, that we will have to assist in the establishment of criteria for the measurement of the goals we set (obviously a precarious enterprise). Then we will have to state what elements of our work should show progress; what the causal factors are that will produce the desired result; what the route of change may be; how the elements of progress may change with time; and toward which objectives and long range goals the elements we typically promote are moving--all in all, a prodigious task.

Why can't we agree on the following at least: (1) what a desired level of physical vigor and fitness is; (2) whether we believe that regular physical education and sport should be required--and to what level of education; (3) what attitudes toward health and ecological problems are needed for survival;

(4) what developmental physical activity is desirable in relation to other leisure activities; (5) who is responsible for therapeutic exercise for remediable physical defects; (6) what type of competitive sport experience is desirable for both sexes; and to what extent sport and developmental physical activity can contribute to character and personality development. It is urgent that we agree on these professional concerns soon (Zeigler, 1977, p. 235).

We are still being downgraded and shortchanged by our professional colleagues from many directions and from the public at large to a considerable extent. Why is this so, and what can we do to bring about progress in this direction? A large segment of the population has become sedentary with what Herbert Spencer more than a hundred years ago called "seared physical consciences." Scientists tell us that rapid behavioral evolution--that is, significant emotional, physical, and intellectual trait alteration--is at least possible with humans. Obviously, our unique field has a significant role to play in such future development.

Undoubtedly there is a tidal wave of change threatening to engulf the field of physical education at this very moment. Much of our tradition, our cherished orthodoxy, and ancient assumptions and myths will be challenged in the years immediately ahead. How we confront this opportunity for progress--the alternatives that are open to us--is explained in the anecdote that described how Destiny came to an island many centuries ago and confronted three people--a cynic, a mystic, and a physic(al educator). Destiny asked, "What would you do if I told you that in exactly thirty days this island will be submerged because of the after-effects of a shifting of polar ice? The first man, the cynic, said, "Why I would eat, drink, and make love for the whole month." The second man, the mystic, said, "I will go to our sacred grove with my loved ones, make sacrifices to the gods, and then pray without ceasing for the entire thirty-day period." But the third person, the physic(al educator) thought for a while in a confused and troubled state, and then he/she stated, "Why I might eat, drink, make love, and pray when the occasion presented itself, but my immediate plan of action would be to assemble our wisest scholars, researchers, and practitioners, along with aquatics specialists and experts in wilderness survival techniques, and begin to plan, organize, and work like mad to figure out how to live under water!" Well, I am not suggesting that you take this story literally, and that we are indeed going to have to learn how to live under water. But I do believe that we are going to be inundated during the 1980s by all sorts of people from other trades, professions, and disciplines who will seek increasingly to "get into the act" that might be called" sport and developmental physical activity." I want us to be recognized as professionals who are leading the way in the research, analysis, teaching, coaching, and promotion of human motor performance in sport, dance, exercise, and play. Is this too much to ask?

If we wish to continue our progress, we will have to redouble our efforts to provide our profession with a sound body-of-knowledge at the same time as we sharpen our "conceptual lenses" as to exactly what our purpose is. Simultaneously, we will need to improve our efforts in both undergraduate and graduate professional preparation. Finally, as a profession we will need to borrow marketing techniques with a psychological orientation. We will have to increase public awareness of their need for our product. While we improve the motivation techniques that we employ, we will need to strengthen our educational base and our instructional techniques. We should provide opportunities for sport and physical activity on an "easy entry" basis; encourage continuation of vigorous activity regularly; and arrange for reinforcement reminders that carry a positive message with humor (Kisby).

Concluding Statement

Finally, then, in the words of Durant,

> The heritage that we can now more fully transmit is richer than ever before. It is richer than that of Pericles, for it includes all the Greek flowering that followed him; richer than Leonardo's, for it includes him and the Italian Renaissance; richer than Voltaire's, for it embraces all the French Enlightenment and its ecumenical dissemination. If progress is real despite our whining, it is not because we are born any healthier, better, or wiser than infants were in the past, but because we are born to a richer heritage, born on a higher level of that pedestal which the accumulation of knowledge and art raises as the ground and support of our being. The heritage rises, and man rises in proportion as he receives it (1968, pp. 101-102).

Obviously, our duty and responsibility in physical education and sport is to improve upon the heritage that developmental physical activity can provide for all people everywhere; to transmit this knowledge and accompanying attitudes to as many people as possible in an effective manner; and to work unremittingly toward the professional preparation of leadership that will allow our field to achieve its unique potential. This represents a concept of 'progress' that is very difficult to refute.

Bibliography

Bury, J. B. The Idea of Progress. New York: Dover Publications, Inc., 1955. (First published in 1932.)

Durant, Will. The Pleasure of Philosophy. New York: Simon and Schuster, Inc., 1928. (Reissued in 1953.)

Durant, Will and Ariel. The Lessons of History. New York: Simon and Schuster, 1968.

Kisby, Russ. Conversation with Director, SPORT PARTICIPACTION, Canada.

Schwartz, Eugene S. Overskill. Chicago: Quadrangle Books, 1971.

Simpson, George G. The Meaning of Evolution. New Haven and London: Yale University Press, 1949.

Zeigler, Earle F. Physical Education and Sport Philosophy. Englewood Cliffs, N. J.: Prentice-Hall, Inc., 1977.

CHAPTER 23
CONCLUDING STATEMENT

In this final chapter of a volume devoted to introducing you to the study of ethics and morality as it might apply to sport and physical education, I will shift primarily into the first person to personalize this material even further. With this experiential approach I have sought to divide the information fairly evenly between ethics and morality from a personal standpoint and that which might be employed from a professional point of vantage.

This effort was made at this time knowing that there is still no single, non-controversial foundation upon which the structure of ethics can be built--and perhaps there never will be. Nevertheless, I felt that it was necessary at this time to design an approach to this subject that might meet the needs of a new generation of professional practitioners no matter which aspect of our work they may undertake.

In light of the pluralistic philosophies prevalent in our complex culture at present, I believed that it was only fair to present you with a series of six alternative approaches to ethical decision-making that are extant. In this chapter no effort was made to indoctrinate you toward any of these approaches that are often so controversial. Thus, you were provided with an overview in the hope that some experimentation might be carried out through their employment to a greater or lesser degree in the several teaching methods presented that stressed as much personal involvement as possible.

Although I did indicate at one point (Chapter 18) that I was inclined theoretically toward a scientific approach to the making of ethical decisions with a strong pragmatic orientation, nevertheless I made a decision to orient you initially to one plan of attack in Part II, the first part of which was recommended to me as eminently practical in this culture--i.e., it is in keeping largely with the values and norms of our North American society. This I called the triple-play approach, because I thought such a term would be catchy and therefore remembered more easily by people in sport and physical education. As you will recall, to this I added Toulmin's layout for an argument because it too seemed reasonable and related more readily to the types of arguments we encounter daily (e.g., courts of law). I realize full well that this may be considered to be imperfect by some specialists in philosophy; however, by now you may have found it to be most helpful nevertheless.

In addition to the overall teaching/learning sequence that was recommended in the course outline (Appendix A), you were invited to carry out a type of philosophic self-examination through the employment of an evaluative checklist. This was made possible in a way through which no personal embarrassment would result. Upon completion of this checklist, you were in a position to categorize yourself roughly for guidance purposes--keeping in mind that typically most of us seem to arrive at a "patterned eclecticism" stance because of our unique backgrounds as individuals. There is considerable subjectivity to an approach such as this, yet I can counter by stating that we should all seek to be as logical and consistent as possible as we search for the best way to conduct our lives.

After the orientation sections (Part I and II), the regular experiential course pattern emerged with lectures, debates, and case discussion each week during the term. I developed this text both from the standpoint of the participating athlete and from that of the professional teacher, coach, or administrator. My goal was to make as strong as case as I possibly could to encourage you to approach your chosen profession with high ethical standards--whichever of the alternative approaches to ethical decision-making you eventually choose for your own. There seems to be no doubt but that all professions need greater ethical sensitivity in these difficult times. Our need in sport and physical education is at least as great as the rest. At the very least I hope that this series of experiences has provided you with opportunities to think these often difficult and highly controversial issues through in a more explicit manner than you might have done otherwise.

Penultimately, may I offer the thought that excellence is vital in all aspects of our society if we hope to preserve our democratic way of life. I believe fervently that such excellence will be vital for us in the immediate future so that we may have a fighting chance of preserving our tradition of freedom on this continent. I am continually reminded (and impressed) by the words of Brubacher when he states, "Yet, somehow we must get, not just fired up, but incandescent about freedom. . . ." (1961, p. 3). This means that we simply can't forget that the freedom enjoyed by us as a matter of course "can only be won by being constantly rewon" (Ibid.).

Finally, I feel certain that we all recognize and appreciate that values, ethics, and morality are all part of our heritage, our present, and our future.   As a profession we in sport and physical education have a duty and responsibility to develop and promulgate <u>our own</u> creed and code of ethics and morality. In this way we <u>can make</u> our own unique contribution to the future of the great tradition that has been developed in this profession in the past, often with great difficulty and sacrifice by our colleagues of previous generations.   If we truly believe in what we are doing, there is no other choice for us to make.

Reference

Brubacher, J. S.   Higher education and the pursuit of excellence.   An address delivered at Marshall University, Huntington, West Virginia, April 25, 1961.

APPENDICES

APPENDIX A

PROPOSED COURSE OUTLINE

Ethics and Morality in Sport and Physical Education

Course Description

An inquiry into ethics and morality as these apply to sport and physical education. Competition, violence, rules, intersonal power, drugs, and athletic scholarships are some of the concepts examined. Various ethical approaches extant are considered. Opportunities to debate and for discussion are provided through debates and case discussions.

Approximately one half of the course is given over to the consideration of professional ethics for the person who is taking up this field as a career specialization. This will include the bases upon which professional services are made available; the ethical nature of the coach/teacher-athlete relationship; how to resolve conflicts between the professional person's obligations to clients and third parties; obligations to one's chosen profession; and the question of insuring compliance to one's professional obligations.

Note: This course outline is so arranged that it may be employed for a 10-week course experience or a 13-week course. However, under a semester arrangement of 15 weeks, it would be a simple matter to add a few extra debates and case discussions.

Prerequisite: Completion of second-year requirements in Physical Education. This course experience is suitable for upperclassmen at the undergraduate level or for fifth-year students.

It is not required or necessary that students wishing to elect this course have prior course experience with philosophy at the undergraduate level. However, the election of an introductory course in sport and physical education philosophy would be desirable and helpful. Examples of other desirable course experiences that might be elected prior to this course are an introductory course in philosophy, philosophy of religion, or philosophy of education.

1 lecture hour; 2 hours of other teaching/ learning techniques; one semester or term.

Class Organization

Basic class lectures for orientation purposes, formal debates on controversial issues, and case discussions of problems and issues involving ethical behavior will form the typical pattern of class organization. Students are invited to make recommendation (formally and/or informally) regarding the teaching/learning process employed.

Students are invited also to schedule appointments with the instructor in regard to the carrying-out of course assignments and any other related matters. Every effort will be made to "personalize" the course experience, so students should not hesitate to bring out their individual needs and/or interests in regard to the course content during the term. At the end of the course, an anonymous course evaluation will be conducted.

Tentative Schedule of Classes

Note: A class session represents 50 minutes typically--in some form of lecture, formal debate, case discussion, etc. After a series of orientation lectures, the typical pattern until the closing sessions will be as follows: (1) lectures on Mondays; (2) debates on Wednesdays; (3) case discussions on Fridays. This could also be arranged as 10, 13, or 15 three-hour blocks of time using the above format with a 20-minute break between sessions #1 and #2 and a 10-minute break between sessions #2 and #3.

Week No. 1   Lecture: "Introduction and Discussion of Course Outline" (including plan for debate assignments)

                Lecture: "Philosophical Self-Evaluation Checklist"

                Lecture: "Introduction to Ethical Problems Today"

Week No. 2   Lecture: "Development of an Ethical Outlook"

                Discussion: "Analysis of Self-Evaluation Checklist Results"

                Lecture &
Discussion: "Major Ethical Routes Available"

<u>Week No. 3</u>	Lecture: "One Plan of Attack: The Triple-Play Approach plus Toulmin's Layout for an Argument"
	Debate #1: "Resolved that an unacceptable level of violence is an inevitable concomitant of contact/collisions sports"
	Case (A)
	Discussion: "Discipline at Compton High"

<u>Week No. 4</u> Lecture: "Authoritatianism and Relativism"
Debate #2: "Resolved that living up to the 'spirit' of the rules is outmoded and incongruent in today's highly competitive sport"
Case (B)
Discussion: "Stealing at Chickamauga Township High School"

<u>Week No. 5</u> Lecture: "Situationism and Scientific Ethics"
Debate #3: "Resolved that coaches have too much interpersonal power over athletes in today's competitive sport"
Case (C)
Discussion: "Breaking Training Rules at Slocom High"

<u>Week No. 6</u> Lecture: " 'Good Reasons' Approach and Emotivism"
Debate #4: "Resolved that the use of all stimulants, pain-killers, and body-builders and developers should be banned and carefully monitored by officials administering sports competitions"
Case (D)
Discussion: "A Coach's Dilemma at Midwestern University"

<u>Week No. 7</u> Lecture: "Professional Ethics: Problems and Structure"
Debate #5: "Resolved that highly competitive sport develops desirable personality traits"
Case (E)
Discussion: "Athletic Recruiting at Midwestern University"

<u>Week No. 8</u>	Lecture: "Obligations to Clients and to Third Parties"
	Debate #6: "Resolved that a teacher/coach should never go out on strike"
	Case (F)
	Discussion: "Sportsmanship at Midwestern University"
<u>Week No. 9</u>	Lecture: "Professional Obligations and Ensuring Compliance"
	Debate #7: "Resolved that a high standard of coaching ethics should be developed and enforced by the profession"
	Case (G)
	Discussion: "Grading Practices for Athletes at Midwestern University"
<u>Week No. 10</u>	Lecture: "Developing a Creed and/or Code of Ethics for the Profession"
	Debate #8: "Resolved that athletic scholarships should be banned in colleges and universities"
	Case (H)
	Discussion: "Breaking a Contract at Central High"
<u>Week No. 11</u>	Lecture: "Developing a Coaching Philosophy with Special Reference to Ethics"
	Debate #9: "Resolved that the physical education profession should take a strong stand against elite sport at all levels of education"
	Case (I)
	Discussion: "Poison-Pen Letters at Midwestern University"
<u>Week No. 12</u>	Lecture: "Summary and Review" (for knowledge phase of final examination)
	Debate #10: "Resolved that a student's scholastic average should have a bearing on his/her athletic eligibility"
	Case (J)
	Discussion: "Special Physical Education at Baker High School"

Week No. 13   Lecture: "Summary & Review" (for teaching/
coaching ethical code on final examin-
ation)
Laboratory
Final: --a write-up of a case problem
Lecture: "Concluding Statement--Where Do We
Go From Here?"
(plus Course Evaluation)

Note: If this course is to be carried out on a semester
or 15-week basis, extra debates and case discussions may be inserted before Week No. 15's sessions.

If this course is to be conducted on a 10-week
or quarter basis, several debates and case discussions may be deleted with no essential problems. Adaptations may also be made for 6-week
or 8-week summer sessions--or even for a two-
week intensive plan meeting 3 hours a day.

Further, note that the laboratory final examination is scheduled for the final day (or week) of
classes, but the actual final examination itself
should be scheduled for 2-3 hours separately.

Textbook:

Zeigler, Earle F. Ethics and Morality in Sport and Physical
Education. Champaign, IL: Stipes Publishing Co., 1984.

Reading Assignments:

No extended bibliography is offered here. Instructors
and students may wish to gain further knowledge from the
many references at the end of the various chapters throughout
the book.

However, basic reading assignments are necessary to
cover the material offered in the course text. Instructors may
wish to make use of the "Questions for Discussion" included at
the end of each chapter beginning with Chapter 12 and ending
with Chapter 23. The following, then, are the recommended
required reading assignments on a week-by-week basis:

Week #1 - Course outline; Preface; Self-Evaluation Checklist;
Chapters 1, 2, & 8.

Week #2 – Chapters 3, 4, 5, & 10.

Week #3 – Chapters 6 & 7.

Week #4 – Chapter 12.

Week #5 – Chapter 13.

Week #6 – Chapter 14.

Week #7 – Chapter 15.

Week #8 – Chapter 16.

Week #9 – Chapter 17.

Week #10 – Chapter 18.

Week #11 – Chapters 19 and 20.

Week #12 – Chapter 21.

Week #13 – Chapters 22 and 23.

Evaluation

Evaluation of student performance will be based on the following:

1. Case discussion notes (10 sets of either or alternately the argument layout itself with triple-play approach included or the argument layout and a more detailed case analysis--see p. 96). This is to be handed in at the class session immediately after the case discussion is held.
   10 x 3 = 30 pts.

2. Formal debate(s) (i.e., one or two involvements depending upon size of class)
   1 x 15 = 15 pts.

3. Laboratory final (a case analysis during class in the next-to-last session)
   1 x 15 = 15 pts.

4. Final examination (including two parts with equal weighting: knowledge test and ethical creed/ code

   $$\underline{1 \times 30 = 30 \text{ pts.}}$$

5. Class participation (based on involvement, interest shown, improvement, status in various aspects, instructor's subjective opinion)

   $$\underline{1 \times 10 = 10 \text{ pts.}}$$

   $$\underline{\text{Total}} = 100 \text{ pts.}$$

APPENDIX B

WHAT DO I BELIEVE?

(A Professional, Self-Evaluation Checklist)*

Earle P. Zeigler, Ph.D.
The University of Western Ontario
London, Canada

---

* This professional, self-evaluation checklist is designed for practitioners in the field of (1) sport and physical education, (2) health and safety education, and (3) recreation and park administration. It has been developed by the author over a period of several decades. This 1982 version has been preceded by several earlier version dating back to the early 1960's. The author is appreciative of advice received from associates, students, and other publications.

The concept of 'freedom'--"the condition of being able to choose and to carry out purposes" (Herbert Muller, 1961) is basic to an understanding of the freedom spectrum at the end.

309

Instructions: Read the statements below carefully--section by section--and then indicate by an (X) that statement in each section that seems closest to your own personal belief. Keep in mind that you will quite probably not agree completely with any one paragraph!

Check your answers only after all six sections have been completed. Then complete the summarizing tally on the "answer sheet" prior to checking your position on the Freedom Spectrum at the end.

Note: Many of the words, terms, phrases, etc. have been obtained from the works of philosophers, educational philosophers, and sport and physical educational philosophers, living or deceased. We are grateful for this assistance, but we have thought it best to leave them unidentified so as not to prejudice the person taking the test.

I. The Nature of Reality (Metaphysics)

a. _____ Experience and nature constitute both the form and also the content of the entire universe (multiverse?) There is no such thing as a pre-established order of affairs in the world. Reality is evolving, and humanity appears to be a most important manifestation of the natural process. The impact of cultural forces upon man is fundamental, and every effort should be made to understand them as we strive to build the best type of a group-centered culture. In other words, the structure of cultural reality should be our foremost concern. Cultural determinants have shaped the history of man, and he has now reached a crucial stage in the development of life on this planet. Our efforts must now be focused on the building of a world culture.

b. _____ I believe that the older types of philosophizing have lost their basis of justification in the twentieth century. Their presumed wisdom has not been able to withstand the rigors of careful analysis. Sound theory is available to humankind through the application of scientific method to problem-solving. What is the exact nature of philosophy? Who is in a position to answer the ultimate questions about the nature of reality? The scientist is, of course, and the philosopher must become the servant of science as he helps the rational reconstruction of language. The philosopher must accordingly resign himself to dealing with lesser questions than the origin of the universe and the nature of man.

c. _____ Man's world is a human one, and it is from
the context of this human world that all the abstractions of
science derive their meaning ultimately. There is the world of
material objects, of course, that extends in mathematical space
with only quantitative and measurable properties, but we humans are first and foremost "concrete involvements" within the
world. Existence precedes essence, and it is up to men and
women to decide their own fate. This makes man different
from all other creatures on earth. It appears true that people
can actually transform life's present condition, and thus the
future may well stand open to these unusual beings.

d. _____ Nature is an emergent evolution, and man's
frame of reality is limited to nature as it functions. The world
is characterized by activity and change. Rational man has developed through organic evolution, and the world is yet incom-
plete--a reality that is constantly undergoing change because
of a theory of emergent novelty that appears to be operating
within the universe. People enjoy true freedom of will. This
freedom is achieved through continuous and developmental
learning from experience.

e. _____ Mind as experienced by all people is basic and
real. The entire universe is mind essentially. Man is more
than just a body; he possesses a soul, and such possession
makes him of a higher order than all other creatures on earth.
The order of the world is due to the manifestation in space
and time of an eternal and spiritual reality. The individual is
part of the whole. It is therefore people's duty to learn as
much about the Absolute as possible. There is divided opinion
within this position regarding the problem of monism or plural-
ism. The individual person has freedom to determine which
may he/she shall go in life. Man can relate to the moral law
in the universe, or else he can turn against it.

f. _____ The world exists in itself, apart from our de-
sires and knowledges. There is only one reality; that which
we perceive is it. The universe is made up of real substantial
entities, existing in themselves and ordered to one another by
extra-mental relations. Some feel that there is a basic unity
present, while others believe in a non-unified cosmos with two
or more substances or processes at work. Things don't just
happen; they happen because many interrelated forces make
them occur in a particular way. People live within this world
of cause and effect. They simply cannot make things happen
independent of it.

II.   Ethics and Morality (Axiology/Values)

a. _____   The source of all human experience lies in the
regularities of the universe.   Things don't just happen; they
happen because many interrelated forces make them occur in a
particular way.   Humans in this environment are confronted by
one reality only--that which we perceive is it!   The "life of reason" is extremely important, a position that emanates originally
from Aristotle who placed intellectual virtues above moral virtues in his hierarchy.   Many holding this stance believe that
all elements of nature, including people, are inextricably linked together in an endless chain of causes and effects.   Thus,
they accept a sort of ethical determinism--i.e., what people are
morally is determined by response patterns imprinted in their
being by both heredity and environment.   A large number in
the world carry this fundamental position still further by adding a theological component; for them the highest good is ultimate union with God, the Creator, who is responsible for teleological and supernatural reality.   As a creature of God, human
goodness is reached by the spirituality of the form attained as
the individual achieves emancipation from the material (or the
corporeal).   The belief is that a person's being contains potential energy that may be guided or directed toward God or away
from Him; thus, what the individual does in the final analysis
determines whether such action will be regarded as right or
wrong.

b. _____   There should be no distinction between moral
goods and natural goods.   There has been a facts/values dualism in existence, and this should be eradicated as soon as possible by the use of scientific method applied to ethical situations.
Thus, we should employ reflective thinking to obtain the ideas
that will function as tentative solutions for the solving of life's
concrete problems.   Those ideas can serve as hypotheses to be
tested in life experimentally.   If the ideas work in solving
problematic situations, they become true.   In this way we have
empirical verification of hypotheses tending to bring theory
and practice into a closer union.   When we achieve agreement
in factual belief, agreement in attitudes should soon result.   In
this way science can ultimately bring about complete agreement
on factual belief or knowledge about human behavior.   Thus,
there will be a continuous adaptation of values to the culture's
changing needs that will in turn effect the directed reconstruction of all social institutions.

c. _____   The problems of ethics should be resolved
quite differently than they have been throughout most of history.   Ethics cannot be resolved completely through scientific

method, although an ethical dispute must be on a factual level
--i.e., factual statements must be distinguished from value
statements. Ethics should be normative in the sense that we
have moral standards. However, this is a difficult task because the term "good" appears to be indefinable. The terms
used to define or explain ethical standards or norms should be
carefully analyzed logically. Social scientists should be enlist-
ed to help in the determination of the validity of factual statements, as well as in the analysis of conflicting attitudes as
progress is determined. Ethical dilemmas in modern life can be
resolved through the combined efforts of the philosophical moralist and the scientist. The resultant beliefs may in time change
people's attitudes. Basically, the task is to establish a hierarchy of reasons with a moral basis.

d. _____ Good and bad, and rightness and wrongness,
are relative and vary according to the situation or culture involved (i.e., the needs of a situation are there and then in
that society or culture). Each ethical decision is highly individual, initially at least, since every situation has its particularity. The free, authentic individual decides to accept responsibility when he/she responds to a human situation and seeks
to answer the need of an animal, person, or group. How does
the "witness react to the world?" Guidance in the making of
an ethical decision may come either from "outside," from intuition, from one's own conscience, from reason, from empirical
investigation, etc. Thus, it can be argued that there are no
absolutely valid ethical principles or universal laws.

e. _____ Ethics and morality are based on cosmic laws,
and we are good if we figure out how to share actively in them.
If we have problems of moral conduct, we have merely to turn
to the Lord's commandments for solutions to all moral problems.
Yet there is nothing deterministic here, because the individual
himself/herself has an active role to play in determining which
ethical actions will bring him or her into closer unity with the
supreme Self. However, the fact of the matter is that God is
both the source and the goal of the values for which we strive
in our everyday lives. In this approach the presence of evil
in the world is recognized as a real human experience to be
met and conquered. The additional emphasis here is on logical
argument to counter the ever-present threat of the philosophy
of science. This is countered by the argument that there is
unassailable moral law inherent in the Universe that presents
people with obligations to duty (e.g., honesty is a good that is
universal).

f. _____ Our social environment is inextricably related to the many struggles of peoples for improvement of the quality of life--how to place more good in our lives than bad, so to speak. We must be opposed to any theory that delineates values as absolute and separates them from everyday striving within a social milieu. The truth of values can be determined by established principles of evidence. In an effort to achieve worldwide consensus on any and all values, stated positions must be criticized in public forums. Cultural realities that affect values should be reoriented through the achievement of agreed-upon purposes (i.e., through social consensus and social-self-realization on a worldwide basis). The goal, then, is to move toward a comprehensive pattern of values that provides both flexibility and variety. This must be accompanied by sufficient freedom to allow the individual to achieve individual and social values. However, majority does rule in evolving democracies, and at times wrong decisions are made. The concept of 'democracy' will prevail to the extent that "enlightened" decisions are made, and we must guarantee the ever-present role of the critical minority as it seeks to alter the established consensus. A myth of utopian vision should guide our efforts toward the achievement of truly humane ethical values.

III.   Educational Aims and Objectives

a. _____ Socialization of the child has become equally as important as his intellectual development as a key educational aim in this century. There should be concern, however, because many educational philosophers seem to assume the position that children are to be fashioned so that they will conform to a prior notion of what they should be. Even the progressivists seem to have failed in their effort to help the learner "posture himself." If it does become possible to get general agreement on a set of fundamental dispositions to be formed, should the criterion employed for such evaluation be a public one (rather than personal and private)? Education should seek to "awaken awareness" in the learner--awareness of himself/herself as a single subjectivity in the world. Increased emphasis is needed on the arts and social sciences, and the student should freely and creatively choose his/her own pattern of education.

b. _____ Social-self-realization is the supreme value in education. The realization of this ideal is most important for the individual in the social setting--a world culture. Positive ideals should be molded toward the evolving democratic ideal by a general education which is group-centered and in which the majority determines the acceptable goals. However, once that majority opinion is determined, all are obligated to conform until such majority opinion can be reversed (the doctrine of "defensible partiality"). Nevertheless, education by means of "hidden coercion" is to be scrupulously avoided. Learning itself is explained by the organismic principle of functional psychology. Social intelligence acquired teaches people to control and direct their urges as they concur with or attempt to modify cultural purposes.

c. _____ The concept of 'education' has become much more complex than was ever realized before. Because of the various meanings of the term "education," talking about educational aims and objectives is almost a hopeless task unless a myriad of qualifications is employed for clarification. The term ("education") has now become what is called a "family-resemblance" one in philosophy. Thus, we need to qualify our meaning to explain to the listener whether we mean (1) the subject-matter; (2) the activity of education carried on by teachers; (3) the process of being educated (or learning) that is occurring; (4) the result, actual or intended, or (2) and (3) above taking place through the employment of that which comprises (1) above; (5) the discipline, or field of enquiry and investigation; and (6) the profession whose members are involved professionally with all of the aspects of education described above. With this understanding, it is then possible to make some determination about which specific objectives the profession of education should strive for (as it moves in the direction of the achievement of long range aims).

d. _____ The general aim of education is more education. Education in the broadest sense can be nothing else than the changes made in human beings by their experience. Participation by students in the formation of aims and objectives is absolutely essential to generate the all-important desired interest. Social efficiency can well be considered the general aim of education. Pupil growth is a paramount goal, as the individual is placed at the center of the educational experience.

e. _____ A philosophy holding that the aim of education is the acquisition of verified knowledge of the environment; recognizes the value of content as well as the activities involved in learning, and takes into account the external determinants of human behavior. Education is the acquisition of the art of the utilization of knowledge. The primary task of education is to transmit knowledge, without which civilization cannot continue to flourish. Whatever man has discovered to be true because it conforms to reality must be handed down to future generations as the social or cultural tradition. Some holding this philosophy believe that the good life emanates from cooperation with God's grace, and that development of the Christian virtues is obviously of greater worth than learning or anything else.

f. _____ Through education the developing organism be becomes what it latently is. All education may be said to have a religious significance, which means that there is a "moral imperative" on education. As man's mind strives to realize itself, there is the possibility of realization of the Absolute within the individual mind. Education should aid the child to adjust to the basic realities (the spiritual ideals of truth, beauty, and goodness) that the history of the race has furnished us. The basic values of human living are health, character, social justice, skill, art, love, knowledge, philosophy, and religion.

IV. The Educative Process (Epistemology)

a. _____ Understanding the nature of knowledge will clarify the nature of reality. Nature is the medium by which the Absolute communicates to us. Basically, knowledge comes only from the mind--a mind which must offer and receive ideas. Mind and matter are qualitatively different. A finite mind emanates through heredity from another finite mind. Thought is the standard by which all else in the world is judged. An individual attains truth for himself by examining the wisdom of the past through his own mind. Reality, viewed in this way, is a system of logic and order that has been established by the Universal Mind. Experimental testing helps to determine what the truth really is.

b. _____ The child experiences an "awareness of being" in his/her subjective life about the time of puberty--and is never the same thereafter. The young person becomes truly aware of his/her own existence, and of the fact that he/she has become responsible for his/her own conduct. After this point in life, education must be an "act of discovery" to be truly effective. Somehow the teacher should help the young person to become involved personally with his/her education, and with the world situation in which such an education is taking place. Objective or subjective knowledge must be personally selected and "appropriated" by the youth unto himself/herself, or else it will be relatively meaningless in that particular life. Thus, it matters not whether logic, scientific evidence, sense perception, intuition, or revelation is claimed as the basis of knowledge acquisition, no learning will take place for that individual self until the child decides that such learning is "true" for him/her in his/her life. Therefore the young person knows when he/she knows.

c. _____ Knowledge is the result of a process of thought with a useful purpose. Truth is not only to be tested by its correspondence with reality, but also by its practical results. Knowledge is earned through experience and is an instrument of verification. Mind has evolved in the natural order as a more flexible means whereby people adapt themselves to their world. Learning takes place when interest and effort unite to produce the desired result. A psychological order (problem-solving as explained through scientific method) is more useful than a logical arrangement (proceeding from the simple fact to the complex conclusion). There is always a social context to learning, and the curriculum must be adapted to the particular society for which it is intended.

d. _____ Concern with the educative process must begin with an understanding of the terms that are typically employed within any educational program. The basic assumption is that these terms are usually employed loosely and often improperly. For example, we should be explaining that a student is offered educational experiences in a classroom and/or laboratory setting. Through the employment of various types of instructional methodology (e.g., lectures, etc.), he/she hears facts, increases the scope of information (knowledge), and learns to comprehend and interpret the material (understanding). Possessing various amounts of ability or aptitude, students gradually develop competencies and a certain degree or level of skill. It is hoped that certain appreciations about the worth of the individual student's experiences will be developed, and that he/she will form certain attitudes about familial, societal, and professional life ahead. This type of ordinary language analysis can be broadened, and conceptual analysis is needed as well. Finally, societal values and norms, along with other social influences, will help educators determine the best methods (with accompanying experimentation), of course, of achieving socially acceptable educational goals.

e. _____ An organismic approach to the learning process is basic. Thought cannot be independent of certain aspects of the organism; it (thought) is related integrally with emotional and muscular functions. Man's mind enables him to cope with problems of human life in a social environment. Social intelligence is closely related to scientific method. Certain operational concepts, inseparable from metaphysics and axiology (beliefs about reality and values), focus on the reflective thought, problem-solving, and social consensus necessary for the transformation of the culture.

f. _____ There are two major epistemological theories of knowledge in this philosophical stance. One states that the aim of knowledge is to bring into awareness the object as it really is. The other emphasizes that objects are "represented" in man's consciousness, not "presented." Students should develop habits and skills involved with acquiring knowledge, with using knowledge practically to meet life's problems, and with realizing the enjoyment that life offers. A second variation of epistemological belief here indicates that the child develops his/her intellect by employing reason to learn a subject. The principal educational aims here must be the same for all people at all times in all places. Others holding this position basically add to this stance that education is the process by which people seek to link themselves ultimately with the Creator.

V. Values in Specialized Field (Sport & Physical Education)

a. _____ I believe in the concept of 'total fitness' which implies an educational design pointed toward the individual's self-realization as a social being. In our field there should be an opportunity for selection of a wide variety of useful activities. Instruction in motor skills is necessary to provide a sufficient amount of "physical" fitness activity. The introduction of dance and art into physical education can contribute to man's creative expression. Intramural sports and voluntary physical recreational activities should be stressed. This applies especially to team competitions with particular stress on cooperation and promotion of friendly competition. Extramural sport competition should be introduced when there is a need. Striving for excellence is important, but it is vital that materialistic influence be kept out of the educational program. Relaxation techniques should have a place too, as should the concept of 'education for leisure.'

b. _____ I believe that the field of sport and physical education should strive to fulfill a role in the general educational pattern of arts and sciences. The goal is total fitness, not only physical fitness, with a balance between activities emphasizing competition and cooperation. The concept of 'universal man' is paramount, but we must allow the individual to

choose his/her sport, dance, and exercise activities for him-
self/herself based on knowledge of self and what knowledge
and skills he/she would like to possess. We should help the
child who is "authentically eccentric" feel at home in the physical education program, and also find ways for youth to commit themselves to values and people. A person should be able
to select developmental physical activity according to the values
which he/she wishes to derive from it. This is often difficult
because of the extreme overemphasis on winning in this culture. Creative physical activities such as modern dance should
be stressed, also.

     c. _____ I believe that education "of the physical"
should have primary emphasis in our field. I am concerned
with the development of physical vigor, and such development
should have priority over the recreational aspects of physical
education. Many people, who hold about the same educational
philosophy as I do, recommend that all students in public
schools should have a daily period designed to strengthen their
muscles and develop their bodily coordination and circulo-re-
spiratory endurance. Physical education must, of course, yield
precedence to intellectual education. I give qualified approval
to interscholastic athletics, since they do help with the learning of sportsmanship and desirable social conduct if properly
carried out. But all these things, with the possible exception
of physical training, are definitely extracurricular and not part
of the regular educational curriculum.

     d. _____ I am much more interested in promoting the
concept of 'total fitness' rather than physical fitness alone. I
believe that physical education should be an integral subject in
the curriculum. Students should have the opportunity to select a wide variety of useful activities, many of which should
help to develop "social intelligence." The activities offered
should bring natural impulses into play. To me, physical education classes and intramural sports are more important to the
large majority of students than interscholastic or intercollegiate
sports and deserve priority if conflict arises over budgetary
allotment, staff availability and facility use. I can give full
support to team activities, however, because such competitive
sport experiences can be vital from an educational standpoint
if properly conducted.

     e. _____ I believe that there is a radical, logically
fundamental difference between statements of what is the case
and statements of what ought to be the case. When people express their beliefs about physical education and sport, their
disagreements can be resolved in principle. However, it is

logical also that there can be sharing of beliefs (facts, knowledge) with radical disagreement in attitudes. In a democracy,
for example, we can conceivably agree on the fact that jogging
(bicycling, swimming, walking, etc.) brings about certain cir-
culo-respiratory changes, but we can't force people to get actively involved or to hold a favorable attitude toward personal
involvement. We can prove the correctness of a belief, therefore, but we cannot prove the correctness of an attitude.
Thus, I may accept the evidence that sport, dance, and exercise bring about certain effects or changes in the organism,
but my attitude toward personal involvement--the values in it
for me--is the result of a commitment rather than a prediction.

     f. _____ I am extremely interested in individual per-
sonality development. I believe in educational "of the physical," and yet I believe in edcuation""through the physical" as
well. Accordingly, I see physical education as important., but
also occupying a lower rung on the educational ladder. I believe that desirable objectives for physical education and sport
would include the development of responsible citizenship and
group participation. In competitive sport, I believe that the
transfer of training theory is in operation in connection with
the development of desirable personality traits, but sports
participation should always be a means, not an end.

VI. Values in Specialized Field (School Health Education)

     a. _____ I believe that health is a basic value of hu-
man living. The truly educated individual should be physically fit, should live near the maximum of his/her efficiency, and
should have a body which is the ready servant of his/her will.
But even though I believe health is a basic value for all the
others, I would have to place it at the bottom of the hierarchy
of educational values. Worship must be placed at the top, because through it man is brought into conscious relation with
the infinite spirit of the universe. Thus, health education
would not be included in a listing of the essential studies of
the curriculum except where it might be included incidentally
under biology. Nevertheless, I am interested in building
wholeness of mind and body, the development of strong, healthy
bodies, the formation of good habits of mental and physical
health, and the right start in the teaching of health, safety,
and physical education to children. There is no question in
my mind but that educators should work for a larger measure
of integration in the individual by promoting more intensive
study of the body that will lead to scientific knowledge: anatomy, body chemistry, hygiene, physiology, etc. Further,

they should give attention to sex characteristics and habits that lead to a greater understanding of the place of sex in human life with implications for hygiene. But such knowledge is made available to students as a "service" program in the schools --a service that is provided to humans, and through this contribution to health they are enabled to pursue higher educational goals.

b. _____ I believe strongly that the child must develop an awareness of the need for self-education about the various aspects of personal and community health. Such educational experiences will not take place, of course, unless the educational process itself is a natural one--a give-and-take situation in which the student is allowed to observe and inquire freely. Obviously, controversial issues should never be avoided with such an approach. Typically, the search for truth is an individual matter, but it is most important to test majority opinion when action is needed in a group situation. The debating of issues relating to health knowledge and practices will help the student decide what is most important fo him/her in this society and culture at this time. In this way he/she will be able to commit himself/herself to personal and community health values.

c. _____ I believe in the development of physical vigor and health. There is no question in my mind but that the school should provide an atmosphere conducive to both emotional and physical health. Furthermore, knowledge about the principles of physical and emotional health is a proper ingredient of the curriculum. I believe that the community does have a responsibility to provide clinical facilities for therapy, but this does not mean that they are part of the school program or curriculum any more than are boilers in heating systems. I assert that the home must have the complete responsibility for assisting youth to acquire desirable health habits--that is, unless we wish to establish some form of community youth organizations to accomplish this end. Frankly, the health of adolescents is for the most part too good and their sources of energy are too great to make health problems real to them. In similar vein, sex education is certainly not a proper function of the school. Look at it this way: is it logical that teaching of the means for securing the health values would be incomplete anyhow until the perspective from which they are viewed is also taught? This perspective is found only in the humanities--in literature, art, religion, and philosophy. In summary, therefore, every person needs a basic core of knowledge in order to lead a human life--and this includes the learning of health knowledge. This argument is consistent with the central purpose of the school--the development of the individual's rational powers.

d. _____ As I see it, there can be no such thing as a fixed or universal curriculum in either of these three fields. Men and women should be strong and possess vigorous health. Positive health should be a primary educational aim. Such a program would necessitate the cooperative involvement of many agencies. Health knowledge and attitudes should be realized through the provision of experiences involving problem-solving. Direct health instruction should be offered, but such learning can and should be supplemented indirectly in the science curriculum as well. Sex education and family relations are very important. Instruction in mental hygiene also needs serious attention in our increasingly complex society.

e. _____ I believe that man should be a strong yet agile creature, and that this standard should apply to girls as well as to boys. Health, as I see it, is a primary objective of education, and the child definitely needs health instruction. The success of the school health education program depends upon the degree of cooperation among home, school, and community agencies. An educated person must understand the difference between health and disease, and he/she must know how to protect and improve his/her own health, that of dependents, and that of members of the community. As I see it, the program of school health, physical education and sport, and recreation may be administered as a unified program within a school system. All aspects of the total program may be coordinated because they are related in so many ways. Through unity, these subdivisions, which are basically related even though they are developing as separate professions, could probably serve the needs of school children and youth much more effectively than is the case so often at present. To be truly effective, school health children should be concerned with helping the individual to lead a rich, full life. This means more than providing a health service so that students can maintain minimum health needed to pursue intellectual work with the least amount of strain. Health should be defined positively--as that quality which enables us to live most and serve best.

f. _____ I have certain beliefs about the need for sound health and the importance of health education. These beliefs are based on cumulative evidence that has been gathered by health scientists. However, daily life is typically such that these beliefs based on facts are not translated into practice in my own life pattern. This is so because I do not always hold strong enough attitudes regarding their implementation.

We need to form the questions we ask--and the answers we then give--in the same clear fashion in which scientists seek to describe the purposes, methodological techniques, findings, and conclusions of their funded research investigations. Our language used in health education is as "disease-ridden" as that which we use in all other phases of life. So we actually need language therapy in our health education classes to help us purvey scientific health knowledge more effectively.

VII. Values in Recreation (Education)

a. _____ I find much confusion prevalent when I attempt to figure out what recreation, leisure, and play are all about. Definitions of these various terms have been inadequate to say the least. Much of the confusion and disagreement has undoubtedly emanated from our misuse of language in several ways. For example, some leaders in the field call professional preparation for recreational leadership "recreation education," whereas correct language usage would seem to indicate that recreation education is that phase of education that teaches people to take part in different aspects of recreation as a part of general education. Our task is, therefore, to find clear, acceptable meanings for these terms given above, and then educate people so that they will use these terms properly so that all may understand. This would go a long way toward the establishment of consensus about recreational values. Further, as the field of recreation gradually develops an undergirding body-of-knowledge to support practice, we will need to improve also the ordinary language employed in the professional preparation phase of the field. How can anyone make a decision about recreational values, for example, unless he/she develops beliefs based on facts, and then cultivates attitudes about what is truly important?

b. _____ As I see it, work and play are typically sharply differentiated in life. Play serves a most useful purpose at recess or after school, but it should not be part of the regular curriculum. I believe that the use of leisure is significant to the development of our culture, but I realize also today that "winning the Cold War" is going to take a lot more hard work and somewhat less leisure. I see leisure pursuits or experiences as an opportunity to get relief from work while it serves a recreative purpose in the life of man. The surplus energy theory of play and recreation makes sense to me. So does the more recent bio-social theory of play--the idea that play helps the organism to achieve balance. I feel that the "play attitude" is missing almost completely in many organized sports. Play and recreation are, therefore, very important to me. I believe these experiences should be liberating to the individual. People can develop their potentialities for wholesome hobbies through recreation. Furthermore, recreation can serve as a "safety valve" by the reduction of psychic tensions which are evidently caused by so many of life's typical stresses. Even though play should not be considered as a basic part of the curriculum, we should never forget that play does indeed provide an "indispensable seasoning" to the good life. Extracurricular play and recreational activities and a sound general education should suffice to equip the student for leisure activities in our society.

c. _____ I believe that all types of recreational needs and interests should be met through recreation education. The individual should have the opportunity to choose from among social, aesthetic and creative, communicative, learning, and physical recreational activities within the offerings of what might be called "a community school" in the broadest sense of the term. It is absolutely imperative, of course, that these choices be made according to the person's sense of personal values and in accord with his desire to relate to people. All are striving for self-realization, and the recreation education program can provide opportunities for both individual expression and group recreational undertakings. Play seems necessary for people of all ages, and it assumes many different forms. We should not forget that one of its functions is simply personal liberation and release.

d. _____ I believe it is difficult to separate the objectives of recreation education from physical education when physical activities are being considered. Within the schools I recommend a unified approach for physical, health, and recreation education. In this discussion I am only including those recreational activities which are "physical" in nature. All these leisure activities should be available to all on a year-round basis. I see recreation education as a legitimate phase of the core curriculum, but would include further recreational opportunities, as well as opportunity for relaxation, later in the day. My core curriculum is adapted from what has been called educational progressivism, and the extracurricular activities are quite as integral as "spoke and hub activities." In fact, the word "extra" is now most misleading.

e. _____ I am inclined to favor the adoption of the name "recreation education" for the field. I see advantages in a unified approach whereby the three specialized areas of health, physical education, and recreation in schools would provide a variety of experiences that will enable the individual to live a richer, fuller life through superior adjustment to his/her environment. I believe that education for the worthy use of leisure is basic to the curriculum of the school--a curriculum in which pupil growth, as defined broadly, is all-important. Secondly, play shall be conducted in such a way that desirable moral growth will be fostered. Thirdly, over-organized sport competition is not true recreation, since the welfare of the individual is often submerged in the extreme emphasis that is so frequently placed on winning. I believe it is is a mistake to confuse the psychological distinction between work and play with the traditional economic distinction that is generally recognized. All citizens should have ample opportunity to use their free time in a creative and fruitful manner. I do not condemn a person who often watches others perform with a high level of skill in any of our cultural recreational activities, including sport, so long as the individual kept such viewing in a balanced role in his/her life.

f. _____ I believe that the role of play and recreation in the development of personality and the "perfectly integrated individual" is looming larger with each passing year--and that this role has not been fully understood or appreciated in the past. For this reason it seems quite logical that education should reassess the contributions that recreation and play do make in the total education of people. That there is a need for research along these lines is self-evident. I believe further that we should examine very closely any theories of play and recreation which grant educational possibilities to these activities. The self-expression theory of play suggests that the human's chief need in life is to achieve the satisfaction and accomplishment of self-expression of one's own personality. Here is an explanation that seems to consider quite fully the conception of the human as an organic unity--a total organism. I believe that human beings are purposeful creatures striving to achieve those values which are imbedded in reality itself. To the extent that we can realize the eternal values through the choice of the right kinds of play and recreation without flouting the moral order in the world, we should be progressive or liberal enough to disregard a dualistic theory of work and play. Another difficulty that confronts us is differentiating between physical education and recreation. Recreation has developed to the point where it is now clearly one of our major social institutions. I believe that recreation can make a contribution to the development of an integrated individual in an integrated society growing in the image of the integrated universe. Today we are actually faced with a recreational imperative!

Note: Appreciation should be expressed at this point to the following people: John S. Brubacher, Abraham Kaplan, Morton White, William Barrett, E. A. Burtt, Van Cleve Morris, Ralph Harper, Herbert Spencer, J. Donald Butler, George R. Geiger, Theodore Brameld, John Wild, Harry S. Broudy, James Feibleman, Roy W, Sellars, Isaac L. Kandel, Alfred N. Whitehead, Mortimer J. Adler, Wm. McGucken, Pope Pius XII, Herman H. Horne, Theodore M. Greene, and William E. Hocking--and, of course, Paul Weiss.

Answers: Read only after all <u>seven</u> questions are completed. Record your answer to each part of the checklist on the summarizing tally form below.

The Nature of Reality (Metaphysics)

a. Somewhat Liberal (Reconstructionism)

b. Analytic (Analytic Philosophy)

c. Existentialistic (atheistic, agnostic, or theistic)

d. Liberal (Pragmatic Naturalism)

e. Traditional (Idealism)

f. Traditional (basically Realism, with elements of so-called Naturalistic Realism, Rational Humanism, and positions within Catholic educational philosophy)

II. Ethics (Axiology)

a. Traditional (including elements of Strongly Traditional; Realism, plus theology)

b. Liberal (Pragmatic Naturalism; Ethical Naturalism)

c. Analytic (Emotive Theory; "Good Reasons" approach)

d. Existential (atheistic, agnostic and some Christians)

e. Traditional (Idealism; Christian)

f. Somewhat Liberal (Reconstructionism; Ethical Naturalism)

III. Educational Aims and Objectives

a. Existentialistic

b. Somewhat Liberal

c. Analytic

d. Liberal

e. Traditional (including elements of Strongly Traditional)

f. Traditional

VI. The Educative Process (Epistemology)

a. Traditional

b. Existentialistic

c. Liberal

d. Analytic

e. Somewhat Liberal

f. Traditional (including elements of Strongly Traditional)

V. Physical Education and Sport

a. Somewhat Liberal

b. Existentialistic

c. Traditional (including elements of Strongly Traditional)

d. Liberal

e. Analytic

f. Traditional

VI. School Health Education

a. Traditional

b. Existentialistic

c. Traditional (including elements of Strongly Traditional)

d. Somewhat Liberal

    e. Liberal

    f. Analytic

VII. <u>Recreation (Education)</u>

    a. Analytic

    b. Traditional (including elements of Strongly Traditional)

    c. Existentialistic

    d. Somewhat Liberal

    e. Liberal

    f. Traditional

(<u>Proceed to next page!</u>)

SUMMARIZING TALLY FORM

	LIBERAL	Somewhat LIBERAL	TRADITIONAL	Strongly TRADITIONAL	EXISTENTIALISTIC	ANALYTIC	
Category I							Metaphysics
Category II							Ethics & Morality
Category III							Educational Objectives
Category IV							Epistemology
Category V							Physical Education & Sport
Category VI							School Health Education
Category VII							Recreation (Education)

(Continued on next page)

Further Instructions: It should now be possible--keeping in mind, of course, the subjectivity of an instrument such as this-- to determine your position approximately based on the answers that you have given and then tallied on the previous page.

At the very least you should be able to tell if you are liberal, traditional, existentialistic, or analytic in your philosophis approach.

If you discover considerable eclecticism in your overall position or stance--that is, checks in three (3) or more positions on opposite sides of the spectrum, or some vacillation with a check or two in the existentialistic or analytic categories--closer analysis may be necessary to determine if your beliefs are philosophically defensible.

Keep in mind that your choice under Category I (Metaphysics or Nature of Reality) and Category II (Axiology/Values) are basic and in all probability have a strong influence on your subsequent selections.

Now please examine the Freedom-Constraint Spectrum on the next page again. Keep in mind that "Existentialistic is not considered a position or stances as the others are (e.g., Idealism). Also, if you tend to be "Analytic," this means that your pre-occupation is with analysis as opposed to any philosophical system-building.

Finally, then, after tallying the answers on the previous page, and keeping in mind here that the goal is not to "pigeonhole you forever more," did this self-evaluation show you to be:

(   )   Strongly Liberal--5 to 7 checks to the left of center?

(   )   Liberal--4 to 5 checks left of center?

(   )   Somewhat Liberal--3 to 4 checks left of center?

(   )   Eclectic--check in 3 or 4 positions on opposite sides of the spectrum's center?

(   )   Somewhat Traditional--3 to 4 checks right of center?

(   )   Traditional--4 to 5 checks right of center?

(   )   Strongly Traditional--5 to 7 checks to the right of center?

( ) <u>EXISTENTIALISTIC</u>--3 to 6 checks (including Category 1) relating to this stance.

( ) <u>ANALYTIC</u>--3 to 6 checks (including Category 1) relating to this approach.

THE FREEDOM-CONSTRAINT SPECTRUM

Note: The reader may wish to examine himself/herself--his/her personal <u>philosophical</u> stance--based on this spectrum analysis. Keep in mind that the <u>primary</u> criterion on which this is based is the concept of 'personal freedom' in contrast to 'personal constraint.' Muller's definition of freedom calls it "the condition of being able to choose and to carry out purposes" in one's personal living pattern. Within a social environment, the words "liberal" and "traditional" have historically related to policies favoring individual freedom and policies favoring adherence to tradition, respectively. (Traditional positions in educational philosophy are indicated in parentheses on the figure below.)

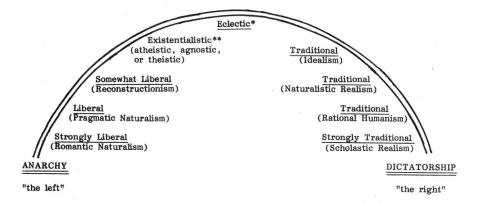

Analytic--philosophy "in a new key"--subscribes to a philosophical outlook with ancient origins, but which has moved ahead strongly in the 20th century. The assumption here is that man's ordinary language has many defects that need to be corrected. Another objective is "the rational reconstruction of the language of science" (Abraham Kaplan). Preoccupation with analysis as opposed to philosophical system-building.

---

* The <u>eclectic</u> approach is placed in the center because it assumes that Xs have been placed in several positions on opposite sides of the spectrum. Most would argue that eclecticism is philosophically indefensible, while some believe that "patterned eclecticism" (or "reasoned incoherence") represents a stance which most of us hold.

** Existentialistic--a permeating influence rather than a full-blown philosophical position; keep in mind that there are those with either an atheistic, agnostic, or theistic orientation. Has been placed to the left of center because of emphasis on individual freedom of choice.

E. F. Zeigler

APPENDIX C

THE UNIVERSITY OF WESTERN ONTARIO
London   Canada

Winter Term, 1983   Final Examination
Time: 3 hours   PE 393b
Instructor: Zeigler   Ethics and Morality in Sport
                                      and Physical Education

Name:_____   Student Number:_____

Instructions: This final examination for PE 393b has two parts
to it as follows: (1) knowledge test based on lectures and readings (short answer typically), and (2) description of ethical
creed and code. Equal weighting will be applied to each section
in the grading of the examination (i.e., 50 points out of a 100
for each part; see page 5 of outline for weighting in the course).
So divide your time quite equally--that is, approximately 1½ hours
for each part of the examination.

Part One (Knowledge Test)

1. What are the three tests in the "triple-play approach" call-
    ed?

    a. _____   b. _____

    c. _____   (½ pt. each)

2. The test of the "reward for the agent" (not part of the ans-
    wer in #1 above) refers to the various forms of

              _____ _____   (½ each)

3. Explain the logic (modus ponens) of utilitarian ethics in the
    following:

    a. The act that (etc.)   ($\frac{1}{2}$)

    b. This act will (etc.)   ($\frac{1}{2}$)

    c. Therefore, (etc.)   ($\frac{1}{2}$)

334

4. Explain act utilitarianism briefly. _____

    _____ ($\frac{1}{2}$)

5. Explain rule utilitarianism briefly. _____

    _____ ($\frac{1}{2}$)

6. What is the doctrine called that states that the "moral right-
    ness and wrongness of actions varies from society to socie-
    ty and that there are no absolute universal moral standards
    binding on all men at all times." (Ladd)

                    _____ _____ ($\frac{1}{2}$)

    How does this differ from so-called cultural relativism?

    _____ ($\frac{1}{2}$)

7. Theories of conduct based on consequences, such as utili-
    tarianism, are often described by another name implying
    purpose:

                    _____theories   ($\frac{1}{2}$)

    However, there are also theories of conduct not based on
    consequences only. In some of these we consider probable
    consequences (future orientation), and also often certain of
    the condition in which an act was carried out that lie in the
    past (e.g., duties of gratitude). These are known as

                    _____theories. ($\frac{1}{2}$)

8. Utilitarian theory of punishment is _____
    (offender deserves to be punished), whereas John Rawls'
    conception of "justice as fairness" is one "rescue attempt"
    (according to Kaufmann) for

                    _____justice.   ($\frac{1}{2}$)

    Kaufmann takes this one step further by arguing that "dis-
    tributions can never be

                    _____."   ($\frac{1}{2}$)

9. Aristotle defined virtue as being "concerned with emotion and action," and actions thus may be "objects for praise or blame." However, they may also be "objects for pardon and sometimes for pity." Thus, he concludes, "we must in a study of virtue distinguish the _____ from the ($\frac{1}{2}$)

    _____." ($\frac{1}{2}$)

10. There are statements of fact; however, ethics is concerned mainly with statements of _____. ($\frac{1}{2}$)

    The main moral words used in ethics are _____, ($\frac{1}{2}$)

    _____, _____, and _____. ($\frac{1}{2}$)   ($\frac{1}{2}$)   ($\frac{1}{2}$)

11. If we were to divide ethics into two main categories, they can be identified as _____ and ($\frac{1}{2}$)

    _____ _____. ($\frac{1}{2}$)

    In this course we have been primarily concerned with one of the above; what has the other category (field of inquiry) concerned itself with typically? _____ ($\frac{1}{2}$)

    _____.

12. Rand describes "a person's <u>implicit</u> sense of life" based on a "preconceptual, emotional, subconsciously integrated appraisal of existence, man, and that person's emotional responses and character essence." Take it from this point and explain what she thinks should happen thereafter--the goal.

    _____

    _____. (1)

13. The instructor distributed a table to explain five "Major
    Philosophical Approaches to Ethical Decisions" extant in the
    Western world. Name these approaches:

    a.   b.

    c.   d.

    e.

    Briefly contrast any two of them. _____ ($\frac{1}{2}$)

    _____ ($\frac{1}{2}$)

14. Name the <u>six</u> terms included in Toulmin's layout of an argu-
    ment.

    a.   b.   c.

    d.   e.   f.

                                        ($\frac{1}{2}$ each)

    Now match up the three terms selected from the above six
    with the appropriate terms used in the "triple-play ap-
    proach."

    _____ and _____ ($\frac{1}{2}$ each)

    _____ and _____

    _____ and _____

15. The underlying presupposition is so-called scientific ethics
    is that there is no distinction between _____ _____ ($\frac{1}{2}$)

    and ($\frac{1}{2}$) _____ _____. (ethical naturalism)

    Explain what characterizes this method of determination for
    ethical decision-making.

    _____

    _____. ($\frac{1}{2}$)

16. Some ethical non-naturalists, while agreeing that ethical sentences cannot be reduced to or translated into any other kind of sentence, believe that some can be accepted and others rejected. This group of prescriptivists (e.g., Baier) employ what has popularly been termed as a _____ (½) approach. Disputants search for a viewpoint from which they can determine fairly and effectively the superiority of one kind of argument over another. Baier feels that such a viewpoint is best and may be called

____ _____ _____ ____ _____. (½)

17. A third approach to ethical-decision-making is known as a definist approach or theory. The ethics of Christian idealism can be characterized in this way. It implies that all ethical statements are disguised theological statements and that accordingly we should conform to or do what is fitting in any ethical dilemma with which we are confronted. Of the five "major approaches" distributed in the table, which two relate to this approach?

a. _____ (½) b. _____ (½)

18. Emotive theory in ethical decision-making explained in the table is known as non-cognitivist, metaethical theory. (Both naturalism and nonnaturalism are regarded as cognitive theories--that is, they view moral utterances in the declarative form as statement-making utterances that claim the existence of certain moral facts either right or---i.e., wrong.) The argument here is that the main function of ethical sentences is not to express propositions at all, but simply to express the speaker's feelings and attitudes--or perhaps to evoke feelings in the listeners. Thus, a person with a strong existentialistic orientation might approach ethical decision-making employing a non-cognitivist, metaethical theory. Explain briefly on what basis they can be placed under what has been termed non-cognitivism.

_____

_____. (1)

19. There has been a consistent approach within ethical decision-making that has argued that we may know whether actions are right or wrong in a way other than by consideration of the value of their consequences. It has been argued
that ethical insight is non-rational and even unique. This
approach has been classified under deontological nonnaturalism. The argument is that moral obligation cannot be
reduced to acts which ought to be done so that more good
will result than in any other way, but that in a particular
situation we are either directly aware of what we ought to
do ethically, or we are not (Pritchard). This position has
been known as

_____ . (1)

Note: The following questions in Part One are based on the reading assignments in the course manual or text.

20. Describe briefly one ethical problem that you have been involved with, or have heard of, in connection with sport and
physical education. What makes it an ethical problem?

_____

_____

_____ . (2 pts.)

21. In what sense might we argue ethically that "women's emancipation" is needed in Canadian sport and physical education.
What ethical principles are involved?

_____

_____ . (2)

22. When Schwartz argues in his "unstated axioms of science"
listing that "man is not naturally depraved," what approach
to ethics is he contradicting?

_____ . (2)

23. If a euphemism is "telling it like it ain't," could an ethical
    argument be mounted against those who want to change the
    name of a physical education unit to that of human kinetics
    or kinanthropology? Explain your position pro or con.

    _____

    _____. (2)

24. How might it be argued ethically that certain abuses preva-
    lent in overly commercialized U.S. intercollegiate athletics
    (only) should be condemned (i.e., on the basis of what
    ethical principles)?

    a. _____ b. _____ c. _____ ($\frac{1}{2}$ each)

25. Why is it argued that Canada is at the "crossroads" in
    international sport? Explain how ethical considerations can
    be a factor in such a discussion.

    _____

    _____. (2)

26. With those people who expressed values found in "the Olym-
    pic experience," name the type of value rated more highly
    and give an example or two.

    _____ _____ (2)

    _____.

27. If the universities, and society indirectly, permit a similar
    situation to develop for women in commercialized competitive
    sport at universities as has occurred for men, what ethical
    dilemma will occur?

    _____(2)

    _____.

28. In this society it can be argued that "the exercise of power over another for his own good is justified only if the path of reason is blocked, and then only if the person with power has a legitimate concern with the other's good." (Wilson, 1978). Give two examples explaining how a recruited, subsidizes athlete could well exert unethical interpersonal power on a university coach.

a. _____ . (1)

b. _____ . (1)

29. If it is indeed true that North America's "resultant optimism was very shortsighted and unrealistic because the historic model being created could not be transposed into a theory of historical development with general applicability," what can we in the field of sport and physical education do as we seek to help in the renewal of ideas and ideals that will have to take place?

a. _____ . (1)

b. _____ . (1)

30. In the field of physical education is indeed "undergoing modification" as explained, explain briefly what ethical obligations we should keep in mind as we work together with our colleagues to help our field attain its "rightful place" in education and within society.

_____

_____

_____ . (2)

Part Two (Teaching/Coaching Ethical Code)

Introductory Note: An ethical code can be described as a systematic collection of rules and regulations about the teaching/coaching function in physical education and sport. An ethical creed might be defined as a system of beliefs and opinions about the teaching/coaching function in the field. Medicine has its Hippocratic Oath that seems to fit the definition of a creed given above, whereas the legal code of the law profession is much more extensive and detailed (as we might expect). (Hazard)

"Professional ethics may be viewed as a system of norms
. . . . The concern here is with what the behavior of professionals should be rather than with what it is, and with the
criteria that should be used to evaluate professional conduct
and professions . . ." (Bayles). Here we are not concerned
with "all the norms that apply to professionals, only those that
pertain to them in their professional conduct and activities"
(Ibid.).

Proceeding from the premise that an ethical code for this
field would represent a fairly complete statement of our professional obligations (i.e., the requirements of professional norms),
an obligation is "the prescription or proscription of a norm:
what it is right or wrong to do (or not do) or be" (Ibid.).
(Keep in mind that a norm may also state a permission--that is,
refusal to follow a certain course of professional action considered immoral.)

Here, therefore, we are to concern ourselves primarily
with the following:

1. Standards--presenting desirable or undesirable character
                traits to be sought or avoided.

2. Principles--stating responsibilities that allow for discretion
                in the fulfillment of standards and may be bal-
                anced or weighed against one another.

3. Rules--explaining duties that prescribe rather specific con-
                duct and do not allow for much discretion.

    Note: "Principles can explicate standards, justify rules,
            and provide guidance in their absence" (Ibid.).

            For example, a coach should demonstrate great con-
            cern for the individual welfare of his players (stan-
            dard); should ensure that safety practices are
            scrupulously followed (principle); and should never
            leave the practice field unless some responsible per-
            son is left in charge (rule).

Finally, based upon your advance preparation, develop
your outline of the ethical code that you believe should be invoked by the coaching profession of Canada at this time. Keep
in mind the distinction (standards, principles, and rules) being
made as aspects of obligations or norms. Topics that might be
considered are as follows:

1. Upon what bases are professional services made available
    (to whom and by whom?)? (10 pts.

2. What is the ethical nature of the coach-athlete relationship?
    (10 pts.)

2. When conflicts arise between the coach's (individual and
    collective) obligations to athletes and to third parties (his/
    her employer), how should they be resolved? (10 pts.)

4. Granting that a member of the coaching profession has a
    responsibility to society, what professional obligations do
    coaches have to their chosen profession? (10 pts.)

5. What should be done to ensure compliance with the obliga-
    tions and responsibilities that have been established in the
    development of any creed/code of professional ethics for
    coaches? (10 pts.)

Finis

APPENDIX D

THE UNIVERSITY OF WESTERN ONTARIO
London   Canada

LABORATORY FINAL EXAMINATION

P.E. 393b

Winter Term, 1983
Time: 1½ hours
Instructor: E. F. Zeigler

Instructions:

     Keeping in mind the format revision distributed in class
for ethical decision-making (as <u>one</u> recommended approach),
and also the weekly analyses that you prepared, please carry
out the following steps in the one and one-half hours provided:

1. Make an outline on approximately two pages of the various
    headings suggested for use in the weekly analyses you
    carried out.

2. Read the case carefully and make brief notes at appropriate
    points in your outline as to how you will analyze this case
    ethically.

3. Finally, for approximately the final hour of this 1½ hour
    exam, write up your analysis of the case as clearly, suc-
    cinctly, and <u>legibly</u> as possible.

"Teacher-Student Relations at Morgan
High School"

Morgan High School, with an enrollment of approximately 1000 students, was one of two high schools in an upstate community in the Midwest. A great majority of the students travelled to school by bus. Mr. Curtis, the high school principal, was congenial, kind, and easy-going. He was trustworthy and assumed that everyone else had this quality. He seemed to believe that if you closed your eyes to problems, they would not exist. He was lax in disciplining students in various ways. If, for example, a student skipped shool, the principal might pat him on the head and tell that he wanted a promise that this wouldn't happen again. The student might agree, and then exit laughing to himself. Many students were evidently lacking in respect for him, because they would talk back to him and get away with it. As a result some members of the faculty had lost their respect for him too.

Karen Gibbs, aged 24 and married, was in charge of health and physical education for the girls. A most enthusiastic and conscientious person, she also had a manner which encouraged a number of the students to confide in her about their personal problems. In one of her classes this year, there was a new 19-year-old, third-year student by the name of Lisa Keras.

Lisa was a straightforward individual, who spoke quite sharply to the principal when he asked her for her home address. When the English teacher mispronounced her name, she was told that an English teacher ought to be able to pronounce her name. The information soon got around that Lisa's family had evidently moved around a lot. Her father was a transitory construction worker, so the family lived in a trailer. Presumably Lisa was "going steady" with an older man who lived with the family about seven miles out of town.

Lisa was in Mrs. Gibbs' physical education class, which met twice a week, as well as in a health education class. Lisa soon found a friend in Karen Gibbs, although her abrupt manner continued with most others, students and teachers alike. When she asked to be excused from class for the second time, Mrs. Gibbs became somewhat concerned and advised Lisa to see the school nurse. Upon checking with the nurse later, Karen learned that Lisa had not reported to her. One of the other students said that Lisa had gone downtown after she left class.

The relationship between Mrs. Gibbs and Lisa continued to develop most favorably. It became evident that Lisa needed a friend close to her age. One day she told Mrs. Gibbs that she would like to have "deeper roots" in some community, because all of this "flitting around" from place to place wasn't much fun. She indicated also that maybe then she wouldn't have so "damned many problems" in her life. She didn't say any more than that, however, so Mrs. Gibbs didn't want to pry into her personal affairs and changed the topic of conversation.

At the beginning of class a short time later, Lisa complained that she had a toothache and asked Mrs. Gibbs to give her a pass to leave the building. Karen explained that only the principal and the school nurse were permitted to issue such passes. Later Mrs. Gibbs learned that Flora did actually obtain a pass from the nurse to go to her family dentist in a nearby town. The nurse had made a record of the request and had listed the name of the dentist. Mrs. Gibbs thought to herself that it was unusual that a family dentist would be established already, since Flora's family had just recently moved to town.

In the locker room shortly thereafter, Karen heard some of her students giggling over the type of cigarettes Flora was smoking. Trying to act unconcerned, Mrs. Gibbs edged into the conversation, but no further information could be learned. Then she learned that Flora was missing from school quite often, evidently on days other than she had either her physical education or health classes. When Mrs. Gibbs saw Lisa next, she asked her how things were going. Lisa said that she hadn't been feeling so well, and added further that they ought to have a "good talk" sometime soon.

Karen began to wonder what was going on with this new student. As a result of some "general inquiries," she learned that Lisa spent a great deal of time in the local "teen-shop." Evidently she had several prescriptions and had purchased a variety of pills. The word was that she had a lot of money with her typically, and that she had cash to fill these prescriptions. One of the students volunteered to Mrs. Gibbs that Lisa has teased her saying, "When you grow up, you'll be able to take pills like I do." All of this began to worry Karen, so she asked Lisa about her health the following day and also inquired whether she was taking any medication. Lisa said that she was feeling much better and seemed quite evasive about the whole matter.

Now Mrs. Gibbs became really concerned. She realized that she shouldn't jump to conclusions, but she thought it best to talk to the nurse again. They decided to place a call to Lisa's family dentist, and were not too surprised to discover that he had never heard of Lisa or any other member of her family. Karen and the nurse decided to take their suspicions to Mr. Curtis, the principal. They all felt that there was a great deal of circumstantial evidence against Lisa, but that somehow they ought to follow up on the matter. Curtis felt that the burden of the investigation ought to fall on Karen's shoulders because the two of them evidently had such a good relationship. This began to worry Mrs. Gibbs. She wanted to be helpful, of course, but she didn't want to betray a student's trust in any way. If a teacher is disloyal to any student, her relationship with any and all others could be jeopardized.

The next morning Mr. Curtis decided to contact the state police. He felt that he could explain the situation and ask for advice. An Officer Ford came to the school immediately to talk to Karen, the nurse, and Mr. Curtis. The officer said that an effort had to be made to obtain some evidence--if there was any to be discovered. Mrs. Gibbs was asked to cooperate by taking Lisa's purse from her locker during a gym period. The combination to her locker was easily obtainable. Then the police could check out the purse's contents, especially the composition of her prescription pills. Now Karen was really worried. She wanted to help, but she wondered about the ethics of what she was being asked to do. It just didn't seem right to "borrow" someone's personal property without that person's knowledge.

INDEX